Praise for *Rubber Bullets: Power and Conscience in Modern Israel:*

". . . *Rubber Bullets* provides the best insight into the epic shifts now taking place in Israeli politics."
— Thomas L. Friedman, *The New York Times*

"This excellent book will serve as a means for the non-Israeli to understand the contemporary reality of Israeli society well beyond the fog of myth and conventional wisdom. For Israelis, it is an intriguing and sometimes provocative and troubling journey into our national soul."
— Shimon Peres

". . . this is one of the most original and stimulating books about Israel and Zionism for a long time. . . . Mr. Ezrahi describes brilliantly how Zionism came to devalue the Western ideals of individual happiness and self-realization . . . (his) underlying message is vitally important, and one that only an Israeli could have given. Not only can an Israeli criticize his own society with a candor almost impossible for outsiders, Jewish or gentile, but only an Israeli—and by his own lights a patriotic one—could cut through the Zionist rhetoric that perplexes not only Anti-Zionists but those who claim to revere Israel."
— Geoffrey Wheatcroft, *New York Times Book Review*

"Fascinating. . . . a work of political and moral analysis in which the author's humanity and intelligence are abundantly evident on every page. . . . His early chapters, in which he defines a kind of Israeli exceptionalism—the ways in which Jewish history made Israel different—are fascinating and moving. . . . Readers coming from an American society in which private life is dominant might yearn for some 'epic-historical time' to erode their absorption with themselves. Mr. Ezrahi is coming from the other direction, and his vision of his own trajectory provides fresh and even startling insight into the trajectory of Israel itself."

—Richard Bernstein, *The New York Times*

"Ezrahi, an Israeli academic and peace activist, combines remarkable imagination and insight with a graceful, evocative style. His superb book offers perhaps the wisest exploration thus far of the deep emotional factors underlying the continual dispute within Israel over national boundaries."

—Leonard Bushkoff, *The Christian Science Monitor*

". . . (a) powerful, clear-eyed treatise on Israel's inner turmoils. . . . (Ezrahi) is an intellectual detective who systematically uncovers clues to explain a nation's coming of age. . . . his prose sparkles with good sense and shrewd insights. He writes analysis in the best sense: taking small moments or decisions and weaving them into a convincing tapestry of social and ideological change."

—Glenn Frankel, *Washington Post Book World*

"Yaron is one of the intellectual leaders of Israel and *Rubber Bullets* is his glowing personal testament. I know of no other book in English that conveys so brilliantly and heartbreakingly the struggle of Israel's democratic secular forces to uphold the freedom and dignity of the individual in a fear-racked society prone to think collectively. This wonderful book will delight and encourage everyone who cherishes Zionism's founding vision of the Jew as a person as well as a citizen."

—Alfred Kazin

"At a time when many Americans are urging a return to communitarian values, this [book] is a revealing affirmation of the virtues of individualism from one who has seen the darker side of communal norms. . . . [*RUBBER BULLETS* is] thought-provoking from beginning to end."

—William B. Quandt, *Foreign Affairs*

ALSO BY YARON EZRAHI

The Descent of Icarus: Science and the Transformation of Contemporary Democracy (1990)

Rubber Bullets

Rubber Bullets

Power and Conscience in Modern Israel

>   > > > >

>   > > > >

by YARON EZRAHI

University of California Press

Berkeley   Los Angeles   London

University of California Press
Berkeley and Los Angeles, California

University of California Press, Ltd.
London, England

First Paperback Printing 1998

Library of Congress Cataloging-in-Publication Data

Ezrahi, Yaron.
    Rubber bullets : power and conscience in modern Israel / by Yaron
Ezrahi.
      p.   cm.
    Previously published: 1st ed. New York : Farrar, Straus, and
Giroux, 1997.
    Includes bibliographical references and index.
    ISBN 0-520-21416-1 (pbk. : alk. paper)
    1. National characteristics, Israeli.   2. Political culture—
Israel.   3. Political ethics—Israel.   4. Political violence—
Israel.   5. Arab-Israeli conflict—1993- —Public opinion.
6.   Public opinion—Israel.   7. Israel—Politics and
government—1993-   I. Title.
DS113.3.E98   1998
956.9405—dc21   97-37529
                                                                       CIP
                                                                       r97

10 9 8 7 6 5 4 3 2 1

To Sidra, Talya, Ariel, and Tehila

Contents

Rubber Bullets

Introduction

One Saturday night in January 1988, about four weeks into the Intifada, I was sitting in our family room in Jerusalem watching the evening news on television. My eighty-four-year-old father, Yariv, was sitting behind me and my sixteen-year-old son, Ariel, sat at my feet. The pictures on the screen were switching rapidly from one encounter between Palestinians and Israelis to another. Suddenly the camera settled, almost inadvertently, on a single Israeli soldier who was crouching while pointing his gun at a group of shouting, stone-throwing Palestinian youth. I felt cold sweat crawl down my back and I was seized by the impulse to cover my father's eyes with my right hand while somehow keeping my son's eyes wide open with my left.

Later I realized how torn I was between the desire to spare my father, a child of the Zionist dream, the pain of recognizing what has been happening to that dream and the determination not to spare my son that pain, so that he might still partly distance himself from the dream—which was going sour shortly before he would be called to risk his own life as an Israeli soldier.

That Saturday night I felt more sharply than ever before the deep cracks that have begun to form in the epic story of our return to and liberation in this land; I felt a profound sense of loss, of the diminished power of the narrative that has bonded five generations of my family. At the end of the nineteenth century, my grandfather Mordechai, a pioneering Hebrew scholar, educator, and socialist Zionist, came to Palestine from the Ukraine and changed his family name from Krichevsky to Ezrahi ("citizen"). Just a few years later his father, my great-grandfather Yaakov Krichevsky, a Hasidic Jew, came to join his son in one of the earliest Jewish settlements at Sejera. My father, Yariv, who would become a musician, was Mordechai's youngest son, and the only child born to him in Palestine. He was born in Jerusalem in 1904. I was born in Tel Aviv in 1940. My own place in this story was imprinted on my mind on May 15, 1948, when, as an eight-year-old child, I stood in the crowd gathered outside the Tel Aviv Museum as David Ben-Gurion declared the establishment of the State of Israel. This is the story into which my son Ariel was born in Jerusalem in December 1972.

This book is largely an account of what led up to, and what followed, the moment that Saturday night when I suddenly felt a break in the story. We Israelis have grown up believing that our individual lives are meaningful only insofar as we partake in the unfolding historical drama of Israel's return and liberation. Israel is one place where the mood and the spirit of ordinary lives are affected by politics, where biography has come to be above all a reflection of a moment in history, where people like us wait for the news reports as if they were daily verdicts on our personal lives. This is why seeing the Israeli soldier pointing his gun at the violent, yet unarmed, Palestinian youths on TV that night felt like such a turning point. Can we, I asked myself, envision an album of images of our extended family which includes that picture? Can we go on binding our children to a narrative whose latest chapters seem to lose the thread of the story? And how does the Palestinian revolt and Israel's violent response bear on our understanding of the earlier chapters of the story?

A few months later, as if to answer my questions (or avoid the necessary choices they forced upon us) the Israeli army adopted "rubber bullets"—steel bullets coated with rubber—for its soldiers to use in confronting the demonstrators. No official stated explicitly the objective of this change. Were the rubber bullets meant to spare those shot at or, rather, to protect the tender souls of Israeli soldiers, who were expected to use their guns to control the uprising? Did the rubber covering represent Israel's genuine intention to restrain the use of physical force or rather the elasticity of the liberal Israeli's conscience? Might the rubber bullet merely have represented a compromise between our recent recognition of the need to use force to secure our independence and our traditional moral critique of power, our own moral identity as Jews?

Because of the questions it has raised, and their implications, the rubber bullet might be the most revealing icon of contemporary Israeli civilization, inverting and then superseding the *sabra*—the omnipresent local prickly pear, emblem of the relation between inner sweetness and hardened façade—as the embodiment of the dilemmas of power and conscience in modern Israel. But could rubber bullets—rubber gloves on our iron fists—still save us, allow us to hold on to the narrative of our liberation? Will our children grow up to cherish what we are doing now, or are we imposing on them a burden of unbearable collective memories?

These were some of the questions I asked myself as the Israeli army was trying to cope with the Palestinian uprising. While rubber bullets (and later plastic bullets as well) proved lethal, killing or maiming demonstrators and bystanders when shot at close range, still the Israeli army's decision to temper the use of arms in this way was historic. At that moment, Israel began to take the first small steps on the long and arduous path to a peace agreement with the Palestinians.

While the Intifada forced us to see the Palestinians in a new light—no longer as just refugees, religious fanatics, and terrorists; not just as "Arabs" (who after all, the thinking went, already have so many states in the region), but as a nation living in our midst—the Intifada by itself would not have caused such a dramatic change. The shift in our perceptions of the Palestinians and the decision to blunt our own swords (if not yet to bury them) would have been impossible if there had not been profound internal changes in Israeli culture, society, and politics. The rubber bullet was the culmination of at least two decades of internal transformations in attitudes toward the role of force in our history.

The most important factor in these transformations has been the emergence of Israeli individualism. Despite, and partly in defiance of, Israeli collectivism, the Israeli individual as a cultural, moral, political, and economic actor has come of age. As a private person, not just a reflection of the group, this individual, joining the increasingly articulate, cacophonous chorus of Israeli voices, has begun to challenge the hold of Israeli collectivistic orientations at all levels. As a narrative of the return, repatriation, and liberation of a people, which from the very beginning emerged from a contest of opposing ideologies, the Zionist epic has increasingly had to face the internal challenge of the potentially subversive narrative of the individual, subjective self. With the gradual spread of liberal-democratic values and the incipience of an Israeli culture of the self, entrenched collective notions about power and war began to be questioned.

The notion of war as a historic conflict between the Jewish people and its enemies confronts the perspective on war as a scenario in which individuals kill and are killed. While peoples can fight for many years, survive defeats and fight again, individuals die only once. Collectivist historical perspectives allow us to regard such losses as worthy of long-term gains for the group. But from the perspective of the individual self, what becomes mercilessly compelling is the finality of death, and the enormous difficulties of justifying death or fixing its meaning over time. Since 1967, if not earlier, the romantic idea of the Israeli army—of armed Jews fighting to secure historic, religious, or metaphysical justice for the Jewish people—has become demystified by individual Jews' experiences of killing and being killed in wars, as well as by the moral ambiguities and ideological contradictions inherent in the encounter between a vision of liberation and the realities of conquest. These changes have challenged the claim of the Zionist–Israeli epic of liberation as the only valid account of our experience, and turned the state into an arena for the fiercely competing voices of self and community. As a result, our national story has had to accommodate not only the Palestinians' narrative from without but also the alternative narratives of Israeli individuals from within.

By their very nature, these narratives express a considerable diversity of Israeli identities composed of a rich variety of ethnic, familial, religious, cultural, and personal orientations. Among the most pertinent to the changing Israeli attitudes toward military force are the voices of sons who have been sent to the battlefield and the voices of women, most of whom have stayed behind. My discussion will focus therefore on the role of power in the formation of male and female identities, the relations between sons and fathers, and the relative places of public and private lives in modern Israel.

What makes the establishment of the State of Israel so revolutionary is that it succeeded in transforming at least a part of the Jewish people from a powerless minority into an armed majority, putting the issue of power and its uses at the very center of the modern Jewish experience. For the first time since antiquity there are now armed Jews who can and do use force, who must justify the exercise of force to other Jews and to their neighbors, and who are shaped by the experience of using military force and living with the consequences. For the first time in many centuries, Jewish religious and secular texts, Jewish fantasies, dreams, memories, and aspirations, must engage the choice of whether to fight our enemies or to negotiate from a position of power. Jewish history, politics, and culture must once again be interpreted in light of the experience of power and the use of arms. Nevertheless, the establishment of Israel not only as a "Jewish state" but also as a democracy has implied a commitment to subordinate both the internal and the external uses of force to democratic constitutional strictures and accountabilities. The assassination of Yitzhak Rabin, at a crucial juncture in the peace process, linked the foreign and domestic fronts of Israeli democracy. The opposition to the peace process, which is the effort to check the use of force against the Palestinians, converged with the attack on the domestic constitutional process.

With the emergence of Yitzhak Rabin as a major Israeli

leader, history conspired with personality to create a mythical biography that converged with the key stations of the odyssey of an entire nation. As a native of this country, and a young Israeli warrior in the 1948 War of Independence, Rabin embodied the "new Jew" born out of the dreams of our pioneering fathers, the blue-eyed soldier boy with the shock of golden hair who would restore independence and honor after generations of massacres and humiliations. In June 1967, as Israel's commander-in-chief during the Six-Day War, he became a symbol of our glory; as the man who turned a war of survival into a spectacular victory, he represented our final transformation from victims into invincible warriors. After the debacle of the Yom Kippur War in 1973, Rabin was again called upon to lead the nation, which had lost trust in its leadership. But at the end of his troubled term of office as Prime Minister, he had yielded to the nationalist, religious Gush Emunim's determination to settle in territories occupied in 1967. Their appeal in welding pioneering Zionist rhetoric with messianic religious fervor proved almost irresistible.

At the end of 1987, as Minister of Defense in Yitzhak Shamir's Unity Government during the Intifada, Rabin became involved once again with the tragedy and senselessness of the occupation; this time he was directly implicated in the initial harsh repression of the rebellious Palestinians, instructing his soldiers to "break their bones." Although beating was supposed to be less lethal than shooting, it proved just as brutal.

Rabin then presided over one of the darkest moments in Israel's history, the often bloody encounter between armed Israeli soldiers and stone-throwing Palestinian youth in 1987–88. This was perhaps the lowest, most corrupt moment in the history of the Israeli army, a fall from the heights that Rabin had come to personify in 1967. The darkest moment in Rabin's and our collective biography was ultimately to prove intolerable for him and for most of us. It signaled the beginning of a turn in history, the beginning of a process of self-transformation, the point at which we started the arduous climb toward peace. While the Intifada exposed the tragic consequences of the sin of occupation and its destructive influence on our soldiers, withdrawal from parts of the land of Israel appeared to most religious and secular nationalist Israelis as an act of betrayal.

When a self-appointed "soldier of God," a young Jew named Yigal ("he will redeem"), the son of Geula ("redemption"), fatally shot Yitzhak Rabin on November 4, 1995, the slain leader became a symbolic wound on our body politic, an emblem of the cost of carving ideas in human bodies, and an expression of the dangerous inner contradictions between religion and politics, the agonizing tensions between the Jewish and the democratic sources of modern Israeli identity. The Jewish fanatics who heard divine voices ordering them to kill both Palestinians and Jews exposed the links between external and internal violence in the Israeli experience.

Rubber Bullets is a personal reflection on the clash between nationalistic and liberal-democratic conceptions of power in Israel, on the attempts to reconcile the logic of military force in the pursuit of national liberation with the integrity of the original commitment to democracy. In Israel's first few decades, there was little evidence of the characteristic liberal-democratic public ambivalence toward state power or any appreciation of how the democratic order is vulnerable to domestic violence. In other liberal-democratic nations—England,

France, America—the suspicion of power is rooted in the traumas of domestic violence: in the authoritarian and arbitrary uses of such power against the people by the church, the monarch, and the aristocratic oligarchy, or the rebellious acts of citizens against their governors. On the face of it, the history of discrimination and persecution of Jewish minorities in authoritarian states (and even in liberal ones) should have created powerful political, cultural, and intellectual motives for a Jewish commitment to the separation of state and society, the defense of individual rights, and deep distrust of state power. But the establishment of the State of Israel seemed to encourage the opposite trends. The immediate need to fight a war of survival, to justify the ultimate sacrifice of lives, and later to cope with terror, coupled with a delayed reaction to the Holocaust, reinforced the tendency to idealize state power and weakened the force of liberal-democratic principles. For the first half century of its existence, the Israeli democracy was not sustained by a deeply rooted democratic ethos. Because the creation of Israel symbolized for Jews a revolutionary change from a condition of powerlessness and vulnerability to one of empowerment and armed force, the state and its army came to embody the idea of Jewish national freedom and independence. This condition discouraged the development of Israeli constitutionalism or internal ambivalence toward the uses of military or police force. Even so, the clash of diverse Jewish conceptions of the identity of the State of Israel which has found its expression in the Israeli multiparty system and coalition governments has served to strengthen a commitment to democracy. No single Jewish Zionist dream—not the idea of a Jewish socialist commonwealth, nor that of a Jewish theocracy, nor that of a secular nationalist "greater Israel" in all its historic lands—could be realized without all the others being excluded by force. Constantly constrained by national emergencies and waves of nationalism, the Israeli democracy has evolved from a pragmatic compromise among clashing Zionist visions of Israel's destiny, an eclectic assemblage of broken utopias. An increasingly open, pluralistic, and internally divided Israeli society finally began to impose greater strictures on the use of military force.

During the 1980s and 1990s, a bitter domestic controversy over the Israeli invasion of Lebanon and over the occupation of the West Bank and Gaza, the use of the Israel Defense Forces during the Intifada, and later the agreements with the Palestinians and the withdrawal of Israeli troops from the occupied territories, weakened the status of Israeli soldiers and policemen as uncontested symbols of "Jewish power" and as a focus of solidarity and support beyond political or ideological divisions. The fact that Rabin's assassin had served in Golani, an elite IDF unit, dramatizes this.

After decades of what came to be called a national consensus, the Zionist narrative of liberation dissolved into openly contesting versions: the one advanced by the right-wing camp sought to extend the narrative to the occupied territories, and the other, advanced by the liberal or social-democratic camp, sought to restrict its relevance to narrower boundaries. The democratic camp has been reinforced by the salience of individual Israeli selves who have begun to question the Zionist narrative in the most fundamental ways. The spread of liberal-democratic sensibilities has empowered the Israeli to distinguish his or her individual voice from the voice of the group, not least in regard to the issue of power. As individualistic, subjective views on the war experience and on the role of the

Israeli state, especially since the late 1980s, have taken root in
the broader Israeli society, Israelis have grown more divided
about the use of physical force in relation to both their Arab
neighbors and their own citizens (Jews and Arabs). This transformation undoubtedly prepared the way for the historic Israeli decision to abandon the pursuit of a decisive military
victory over the Palestinians and seek a peace settlement
through negotiation. The spread of the values of democratic
and economic individualism has also undermined the domestic Israeli tradition of state paternalism and spurred private
initiatives in areas formerly controlled by the Israeli bureaucracy. In reaction, some Israelis have steadily become more
anxious about losing parts of the "Land of Israel" as well as
Jewish cultural hegemony within Israel. This attitude has been
cultivated in particular among Jewish settlers in the occupied
territories and among Orthodox and ultra-Orthodox Israeli
Jews. By insisting that decisions affecting the territorial boundaries of Israel and its corporate identity can be sanctioned only
by a "Jewish majority," the proponents of such views have, in
fact, defined Israel as an ethnocracy, and have become increasingly antagonistic to the political and constitutional foundations of Israeli democracy.

The assassination of Prime Minister Rabin escalated the tensions between the chauvinistically Jewish and the democratic
perspectives on the issue, weakening the intermediate groups
that could hold these poles of Israel's identity together. It
dramatized the relations between the peace process, the readiness to concede territories under Israeli control, and the rising domestic conflict among Jews. While the shock of the
murder of the Prime Minister provoked an instant wave of
support for the cause of peace which he had come to symbol-

ize, in the longer run the trauma of domestic political violence reinforced those who were not prepared to risk further rifts in what they regarded as Jewish solidarity, even for the chance of ending the conflict with the Arabs. Approximately three months after the assassination, when Palestinian terrorists began a wave of suicide bombings on Jerusalem and Tel Aviv buses, the Israeli public was horrified and the sacrifices required by the peace process appeared to many to be even more untenable. On May 29, 1996, a slim majority returned the right wing to power—like the slim majority that had brought a Labor government to power four years earlier. This confirmed the country's persistent pattern of division between conflicting political blocs of almost equal strength, making the shift between right-wing nationalistic and left-wing social-democratic governments dependent on the swing of a few dozens of thousands of votes.

The two political blocs represent, however, mutually exclusive modern Jewish worldviews. The one, founded on a long memory of persecution, genocide, and a bitter struggle for survival, is pessimistic, distrustful of non-Jews, and believing only in Jewish power and solidarity. The other, nourished by secularized versions of messianism as well as the Enlightenment idea of progress, a deep sense of the limits of military force, and a commitment to liberal-democratic values, is cautiously optimistic, confident in the possibility of Arab-Israeli coexistence and a future Israel as an open and advanced society unthreatened by war. While this latter view has, for extended periods of time, been eclipsed by ethnocentric solidarity and group entrenchment, it has shown remarkable resilience, as indicated by its resurgence during the late 1970s (the peace with Egypt) and again in the 1990s (the agreements with Jordan and the Palestinians). At different times, each of these opposing views has been empowered to act, thus contributing to its own self-fulfillment. A defensive, distrustful military-oriented policy naturally reinforces similar orientations on the part of the adversary, just as a moderate and compromising posture by a state not eager to flex its muscles encourages prospects of peaceful accommodation. Even when Israeli leaders had few grounds to expect moderation on the part of their adversaries, statesmen like Rabin and Anwar el-Sadat of Egypt knew that the secret of peace depended on decisions that not only reflect but, in fact, change the basic attitudes of the adversaries; that, even in the Middle East, moderation, like belligerence, can be a self-fulfilling prophecy.

In some respects, these two Israeli views, like the hard and soft parts of the rubber bullet, are the two sides of the same corporate Israeli personality—two sides between which many Israelis can easily seesaw under the influence of current leaders, decisions, and events. A large section of the population can shift quickly between trust and distrust, future and past orientations, peace and war, democratic openness and tribal nationalism. Hence, Israeli leaders who seem to go too far, or too fast, in either of these directions, without taking the other into account, tend to pay dearly. Menachem Begin and Ariel Sharon were political casualties of the decision to invade Lebanon in 1982, having started a war which many Israelis regarded as frivolous and unnecessary for Israel's security. Yitzhak Rabin and Shimon Peres were, each in a different sense, casualties of the decision to yield territories to, and compromise with, the Palestinians, thus alienating many Israelis distrustful of this course. Because both hope and fear influence Israeli attitudes and policies toward the Arabs, the course of the future movement toward peace is not likely to be linear. But, in the longer run, I believe, hope may prove more resilient than fear.

Also on the domestic front, the coming years will continue to be formative, dangerous years of upheaval. New laws designed to temper Israeli parliamentarism and facilitate stronger personal leadership, and the massive political attacks on the status of the Supreme Court following the May 1996 elections, have exposed inherent weaknesses in the system. Deepening divisions between nationalists and liberals and the grave domestic conflict over the relations between religion and politics are likely to be the source of further instability. Still, the vision of a peaceful and democratic Israel is irrepressible. It is a vision, a prospect, of an Israel where power is held within clearer geographical, political, constitutional, and moral boundaries, an Israel where the emerging voices of the Israeli selves, and their diverse narratives, signify the beginning of a liberal post-epic era in Israeli democracy.

> > > *I*

From History to Autobiography

The Impoverished Language
of the Israeli Self

Many years ago, my father told me that when I was just three
or four years old my grandfather would follow me with a note-
book and a pencil and write down what I said. I remember
hoping that my father was telling me a story about adult appreciation of a precocious child, of my early signs of intellectual promise. But no. My grandfather, Mordechai Krichevsky
(later Ezrahi), a leading member of a circle of Hebrew scholars and intellectuals who had devoted decades to the revival
of Hebrew culture in Palestine, was engaged at the time in a
fierce polemic. While some of his peers insisted that the ancient Hebrew language should be modernized by scholars,
he argued that modern Hebrew would emerge as a living
language from the mouths of babes, from the spontaneous
utterances of the first generations of children born in a
Hebrew-speaking community. So my grandfather was not
really listening to me, not trying to save any gems of wisdom
falling from my lips. He was only using me as a source of data
with which to test and defend his faith. It was not what I said
that interested him, but the linguistic forms of my Hebrew
sentences.

Many years later, in the general reading room of the library

at the Hebrew University of Jerusalem, I found what I was looking for among the volumes of *Leshonenu La'am* (*Our Language
for the People*), which my grandfather had co-edited. In the volume published in 1944 was a section entitled "From the
Mouths of Babes." There I read the following: "The father of
four-year-old Yaron scolded him and Yaron cried. When he
stopped crying, he came to his father and said, 'Abba, you
made me cry.' " Not even the most sympathetic reader, I would
think, would see in this rather unexceptional communication
signs of a precocious child. Yet my grandfather had obviously
found what he was looking for. The grammatical form used
by his four-year-old grandchild to express the Hebrew equivalent of "You made me cry" ("*Ata hivketa oti*") was a rare form,
and this was important.

In retrospect I was pleased, of course, to have made, between playing and crying, even the tiniest contribution to the
revival of Hebrew as a spoken language in Zion. But the fact
that it was not my pain or insult that was important but the
grammatical form of its expression made me cherish this episode as a reflection of a deeper and more persistent experience: the difficulty of discovering or inventing one's private
voice in the midst of this chorus of pioneers, all singing the
epic of the return of the Jews from exile and the resurrection
of our ancient language in the Holy Land. The Hebrew language as the language of God, or as the revived language of
the Jewish people, was not a suitable medium for communi-
cating personal thoughts or feelings. An epic language that is
suitable for describing great deeds and events, or a fixed li-
turgical language that is suitable for communal prayers—these
are not congenial tools for self-expression. Such a language

resisted even the experiences of the children of the early pioneers, who grew up speaking it. "Who could have written in such a high language," asked a soldier in Israel's War of Independence of 1948, "what really happened on the battlefield?"[1]

To be born in Tel Aviv in 1940 and turn eight about four weeks before the Declaration of Israel's Independence was to grow up in the shadow of monumental history, to be dwarfed by a narrative stretching between catastrophe and redemption. It could dry up an early appreciation for anything personal, for private language, private space, private time, even private life. As the very first generation of children born as native Hebrew-speakers in this land, we were expected to realize the dream of our parents and grandparents: to speak the new Hebrew and embody the new kind of Jew. When I was born, the Jewish community in Palestine was already two or three decades into evolving a more colloquial vernacular Hebrew. But the conversational Hebrew I heard in my boyhood was still thick with layers of majestic, biblical, midrashic, or classical literary style. In retrospect, the spoken Hebrew of my home, or, more precisely, the Hebrew of my native-born father, Yariv, was a beautiful, mostly literary Hebrew, forged in the Ben-Yehuda circle my grandfather belonged to. It must have been difficult in this environment to have contact with forms of personal, subjective, idiosyncratic discourse.

While holding intimate conversations in Hebrew must have

---

[1]Netiva Ben-Yehuda, *When the State of Israel Broke Out* (Jerusalem: Maxwell-Macmillan-Keter, 1991) (in Hebrew).

been as difficult as carrying on small talk in Latin—and must have sounded as ridiculous—in our home in Tel Aviv, which was a conservatory of music, the medium for expressing the most delicate nuances of feelings and intimacy was the violin. Beyond interpreting such works as Beethoven's sonatas on his violin, my father composed and improvised, conveying to us his moods and emotions. His playing opened gates to the self which I could appreciate only years later. Any young person, of course, might have been impressed by such playing. But it may have struck me so forcefully because I was growing up in a society obsessed with collective liberation and cultural revival. The Zionist leaders and educators of the time, focused so intently on the monumental implications of our ancient tribe's return to its land, were not concerned with cultivating the solitary self, the lyrical personal voice of the individual. The modern Hebrew prose and poetry we read in our elementary and high schools were immersed, in both style and content, in the collective political and cultural agenda of the Israeli revolution; they offered few examples of personal expression. It is probably not a coincidence that David Fogel, a Hebrew poet and novelist who was one of the first to succeed, as Robert Alter puts it, in "forging a Hebrew self," was a non-Zionist Jew who lived outside Palestine and died in World War II. It is as if one had to stand apart from, or even to defy, the Zionist epic of return in order to carve out a Hebrew idiom that could express the inner self relatively free of the life of the tribe. In his poem "The Street Has Made Us Tired" [*Rav hel'anu ze harehov*], first published in 1938, Fogel wrote: "Into solitude we shall withdraw, for the crowd has made us tired." Historically, however, Israeli culture has identified such expressions of the self with abandonment or betrayal of a besieged community.[2]

This limitation certainly inhibited Israeli literary sensibilities and delayed the recognition and acceptance of such writers as Fogel and U. Z. Gnessin. It took much longer before Israelis could accommodate individualistic sensibilities and view the expressions of subjectivity not as negations or abandonments of the group but as intrinsically valuable in themselves. Only in the late 1950s did the first publications of a young generation of Hebrew poets who wrote in a very personal style begin audaciously to convert the emerging spoken Hebrew and the accumulating deposits of contemporary Israeli experience into a new poetics of the Israeli self. In 1966, one of those modern Israeli poets, Nathan Zach, stated explicitly the objections of a group of his contemporaries—Yehuda Amichai, Dalia Rabikovitch, and Dan Avidan among them—to the ideologically loaded, formulaic, stylized forms pervasive in the Hebrew poetry and literature of the times. He wrote against the reverence for ornamental, majestic, often pompous literary Hebrew and advocated the development of minimalistic, conversational, first-person language forms.

---

[2]See "David Fogel (1891–1944) and the Emergence of Hebrew Modernism," *Prooftexts: A Journal of Jewish Literary History*, Vol. 13, No. 1 (Johns Hopkins University Press, January 1993), especially the articles by Robert Alter, "Fogel and the Forging of a Hebrew Self" (pp. 3–13), and Michael Gluzman, "Unmasking the Politics of Simplicity in Modernist Hebrew Poetry: Rereading David Fogel" (pp. 21–43). Still, there are also alternative interpretations which discern significant early expressions of the lyrical voice of the self in the context of Hebrew Zionist culture, such as H. N. Bialik's poems "My Soul Has Sunk Down" (1908) and "A Twig Alighted" (1911).

For decades such shifts in literary sensibilities remained compartmentalized and confined; throughout most of the first five decades of Israel's existence whatever forms of subjective individual idioms of expression were created and refined by Israeli writers remained relevant and accessible mainly to a limited, highly educated elite. Even today, they have penetrated neither the sphere of public political speech nor the domain of educational practices. The rhetorical style of Israeli political leaders such as Ben-Gurion, Begin, Peres, and Netanyahu has been largely "prophetic," declamatory, impersonal, and sloganistic, although it has grown less pompous over time.

The resistance to personal, individualized styles of speech in Israeli public life, the sense that the public sphere as the cultural domain of collective group speech cannot accommodate public communication of individual or personal expressions, has been manifest also in the formal, often ceremonial, intonation of Israeli radio and television news broadcasters. Israeli anchorpersons have for a long time read the news in characteristically declamatory impersonal voices, as if they were acting out a Greek tragedy. The attempt to avoid figures of speech and use normative Hebrew vocabulary and accent, of course, only reinforced the sense of the news as an ongoing high historical narrative.

The extent to which Israeli broadcasters succeed in their attempts to forge a stiff, impersonal style and produce a kind of socially collective voice, free of individual vocal personality traits, can even be seen when they cross the lines with other forms of cultural mediation. Chayuta Dvir was hired to moderate a chamber music festival in northern Israel. Sitting in the hall listening with delight to the intimate chamber music pieces, in interpretations which brought out the special beauty of this conversational musical genre, I was jolted by Dvir's steely, distant, "official" voice, as she announced, in the familiar epic intonation with which she and others have for years brought us the news about the war: "The next piece is Schubert's Quartet Number 2." She sounded totally out of touch, almost like a divine commentator on simple human pleasures. It would be instructive to compare the vocal style of such Israeli broadcasters with that of some broadcasters of National Public Radio in America, for instance, who succeed in giving listeners the illusion that the person in the studio is talking directly to them. From time to time broadcasters such as Yitzhak Roeh have tried to break out of this style. Roeh's late-night television news program *Almost Midnight* was first aired in 1979; the title suggested his readiness to relax the tyranny of formal precision and introduce a less structured air of informality. Roeh's style was personal, intimate, ironic, laid back, and humorous. It was as if he were inviting his viewers to take a less anxious, more humane look at our collective life; it was a kind of momentary relief from the suffocating grimness and tension with which we have characteristically met the unfolding drama of modern Israel.

As expected, this approach was not welcomed by the incumbent nationalist guardians of our soul. The program was terminated a few months later, and even the protests of such Israelis as the poet Abba Kovner, who praised Roeh's personal style for helping Israelis survive the "shock of the news," were ignored. It was as if those in charge realized that Roeh's colloquial, ironic style could legitimate some skeptical distancing on the part of his viewers—that a conversational style does not properly prepare the public for heroic sacrifices, but might help us extricate ourselves from the state of mobilized, anxious attentiveness in which we lived. After the popular TV satire *Nikkui Rosh* (a product of the 1970s resembling America's *Saturday Night Live*) was removed from the screen by political pressure, such programs survived until recently only as fragments in the children's series *Zehu Zeh* on Friday afternoons.

Despite the cultural policy of maintaining the hegemony of the high epic style of public speech and communications, the spread of ordinary colloquial Hebrew style could not be stopped. Its gradual effects on public life chipped off the stiff, rocklike ceremonial pathos of the older pioneer generation. Seeing old newsreels easily provokes grins among younger audiences. The election in 1993 of one of the most radical embodiments of the informality and low colloquial Hebrew style of the Israeli-born generation, Ezer Weizman, to the ceremonial position of Israel's President is quite significant in this connection. Weizman had served as a pilot and commander in the Israeli air force and spent most of his life in the military—one of the principal sources of irreverent colloquial Hebrew in Israel. By contrast (to take one example), Israel's third President, Zalman Shazar, was a man of letters and a great Zionist orator. Many Israelis still remember how President Shazar invited the ridicule of young Israelis when he opened the annual football season with a passionate speech in formulaic Hebrew. It sounded as if the game and the players were crucial for the holy history and liberation of the Jewish people. Shazar's application of lofty literary Hebrew nevertheless gave a wonderfully instructive insight into the comic side of Israeli grimness and the limits of the cultural forms which have mediated our experience. In the same way, the distance between habits of speech of the pioneer and Israeli-born generations was for many years a subject of countless jokes. The most typical one is about the Hebrew teacher who drowned in the waters off Tel

Aviv because bystanders could not understand what he wanted when he cried out in classical Hebrew, "Redeem me! Redeem me!" ("*Hoshiuni! Hoshiuni!*"), instead of the colloquial Hebrew equivalent for "Save me! Save me!" ("*Hatzilu! Hatzilu!*").

I have come to the conclusion that the often irreverent language which has come to be widely used in nationally televised parliamentary debates does not simply undermine public respect for Israeli legislators, nor (as many commentators suggest) does it just give a bad name to the parliament and perhaps to politics as such. What worries many Israeli educators may actually have had some salutary effects. It may have punctured the epic conception of politics so often guarded by the political leadership and rendered it less invincible. Colloquial political speech (by which I do not mean verbal violence) makes leaders who were spoiled by decades of Israeli public docility more vulnerable and provides a real service to the pedagogy of democratic political participation. If a high rhetorical style creates distance and seems to imply accountability to principles or to history, a low style encourages interruptions and improvisations; it diminishes credulity and makes leaders more directly accountable to their live audience—participants of the political process. Israeli politics has not remained unaffected by the impulse of a growing number of Israelis born here to shake themselves free of heavy standard Hebrew, which, as Netiva Ben-Yehuda insists, has prevented us from expressing our real experiences and telling the truth about our lives. For too long we had neither the language nor the tone to challenge those who addressed us in the high, pompous language of politics as history.

Low styles of speech do not necessarily correspond, of course, to the development of individualized idioms of expression. The evolution of ordinary colloquial Hebrew, of informal conversational style, and even of modern Hebrew poetry has certainly been contributing to the growth of a resilient democratic individualism in Israel. As we shall see, however, the development of a culture of the self depends not only on self-expression but also upon such things as conceptions and practices of private space and private time. It took centuries for modern Western individualism to evolve from such cultural practices and traditions so that the voice of the individual could be distinguished from and opposed to the voice of the community—for the sonnets of Petrarch to transform medieval poetic formulas beyond very limited social circles or for the *Confessions* of Rousseau to offer language as an instrument for inquiring into, and expressing, the interior self. Petrarch is especially interesting for the Israeli situation because of the ways in which his poetry empowers the lyrical as against the epic voice. As Thomas Greene put it in his commentary on this poet: "The imperial imagination of Roman epic, whose vocation was the ordering of history and space, yields to a private intuition . . . [of] a speaker who is chief actor and a sufferer and a mythic center"; it yields to poetry which expresses the "raptures of a psyche [where] the very divisions of meaning are meaningful." Such exchange of "epic breadth for lyrical immediacy" is illustrated in Petrarch's sonnet 164: "I swim through a sea that has no floor or shore, I plow the waves and find my house on sand and write on the wind."[3]

---

[3]Thomas M. Greene, *The Light in Troy: Imitation and Discovery of Renaissance Poetry* (New Haven: Yale University Press, 1982), pp. 117–18. See also Philippe Ariès and Georges Duby, *A History of Private Life* (Cambridge, Mass.: Harvard University Press, 3 vols. 1988, 1989, 1990).

Petrarch's ability to transform Latin into a graceful poetic language with which to express the tenderness and the discontinuities found in an honest gazing at oneself, and his ability to use vernacular Italian to express the transient, often melancholy, unresolved feelings of solitude and loss, forged a lasting vocabulary for the individual self. The work of Petrarch and his successors gradually undermined the linguistic and stylistic conventions underlying Greek and Roman epics and didactic Christian literature. But it took centuries for the interior self to be articulated in a social context, for the modern individual to emerge as a political agent, a carrier of rights, and a voice able to make claims on and criticize society.

Such shifts as between Latin and the vernacular—between the presumed God's-eye view of the entire cosmos and the inherently partial, limited human view—the rise of perspective in Renaissance painting as a symbolic expression of the presence of the individual person in the world, and the rise of autobiography as a literary genre in the writings of Montaigne and Rousseau were all significant stations in the emergence of modern democratic individualism. Without such deep cultural undercurrents no society can evolve and ground a genuine liberal-democratic polity even if it has, like Israel, adopted democratic legal and institutional structures which for the most part were developed elsewhere.

Jews who were emancipated from the European ghettos, in which traditional, mostly Orthodox religious life persisted, were able to be transformed by the rich European culture of individualism. Some Jews—like Spinoza, for example—even made singular contributions to this culture. But the establishment of modern Israel was inspired more by religious, nationalist, and socialist variants of collectivism than by liberal-democratic individualism. Liberal-democratic values were not particularly influential in shaping Zionist ideology and political practice, nor was the birth of a Jewish state, so deeply embattled with its neighbors, going to encourage the spread of such liberal-democratic orientations toward politics. For those of us Jews who were born in Palestine, or born in Israel during the first few decades after Independence, the Western culture of the self became available only gradually, and what was not available had to be reborn, reinvented, or excavated in classical, even archaic linguistic and cultural forms of Hebrew. Now Israeli individuals seem increasingly to seek, *within* the inherited communal cultural forms, niches for expressing the personal voice.

Shlomit Barnea, the high school girl who chose David's lamentation over Saul and Jonathan as a vessel for the private eulogy of her brother Jonathan, killed in the suicide terrorist bombing of a Jerusalem bus on February 25, 1996, is a dramatic illustration:

I am distressed for thee, my brother Jonathan; . . . I grieve for your friends, for Mother, Father, Uri, and myself. . . . Very pleasant hast thou been unto me, wonderful was thy love to me . . . the love of an older brother. . . .

How the mighty are fallen . . . not by a bullet in an ambush attack . . . You died on the altar of the peace in which you had unyielding faith. . . .

The evolution of the deep structures of Israeli subjectivity, the lyricization of Jewish and Hebrew epic cultures—the creation of an Israeli self—have in fact only just begun.

2

The Limits of Private Space

In the summer of 1950, at the age of ten, I was sent by my parents to spend a month on a kibbutz with a friend of our family. I traveled to Gvat, a kibbutz in the Valley of Yisrael in the northern part of the country. My host was David, a Czechoslovak Jew, an exceptionally enthusiastic and dreamy person who came to be my personal idea of the pioneer, the *chalutz*. David would get up every morning around four-thirty and be at work in his apple orchard shortly after five "to beat the summer heat," which would become inescapable by noon. He spent the afternoons in a little workshop in his backyard, molding clay masks to be used in the kibbutz's puppet theater, which he had created. So in the mornings I would walk to the field to see David at work, where he shared with me his secret of how to increase the tree's yield by bending and tying thin branches in a certain way; in the afternoons I would sit in his workshop observing how every conceivable human expression could be frozen into a clay mask so as to travel with David's imagination to unknown destinations.

After a couple of weeks, David thought I should get to know some of the kids in the kibbutz. He introduced me to Rahel, the nine-year-old daughter of a neighbor. When we met I instantly liked her. Rahel was very cordial and suggested that I come for a swim with her and her group at the kibbutz children's home. We set out with a cheerful, noisy bunch of kids who were half walking, half jumping, screaming, or singing, like kids anywhere else in the world. When we arrived at the pool—in fact, a huge irrigation water reservoir—Rahel and the others, as if in response to an order from above, suddenly took off their clothes and jumped stark naked into the water. I stood frozen at the edge of the pool in my bathing suit, the naked children staring at me. I felt stunned and embarrassed, as if they were all dressed and I alone was naked. Rahel swam close to the edge where I was standing, practically begging me to jump into the water. After what felt like an eternity, I jumped in with my bathing suit on. Rahel swam away to merge with her group, and I was left with a sense of irrecoverable loss, painfully accepting my stigma as an outsider. I was clearly and irremediably a city boy, a native of that inferior place where money is paramount and fallen people live. I had declined the invitation to enter paradise.

For each of us, of course, our body is the place where we forge our own private self, and the ground of our most intimate exchanges with other selves. The innocently naked body, the body in paradise, is not a likely site for development of one's self. As a dwelling for the private self, the body must be a "fallen" body, a body rescued from innocence. It was only when their eyes were opened "and they knew that they were naked" that Adam and Eve "sewed fig leaves together and made themselves aprons." It is then that Adam told God, "I was afraid because I was naked and I hid myself." Knowledge of nakedness is probably the beginning of private space, and the space between the fig leaves and Adam's and Eve's bodies may have been the earliest space of subjectivity—the beginning of a culture of the self.

The importance of such private spaces, such hiding places, is not diminished when the gaze of God is replaced by the gaze of society. It is from that point that John Locke, a leading early spokesman of the liberal idea, expanded the definition of private space—the wall between the individual person and the community—beyond the individual body (protected by habeas corpus) to include also private property as the fruit of one's labor. By contrast, the collectivist socialist program criticized private property as a source of social inequality and the cause of the replacement of natural freedoms by relations of dominion and dependence.

On the kibbutz, the denial of private space and private property for a long time deprived members of vital resources for cultivating a sense of self and individual uniqueness. The powerful idealism of the collectivist socialist assault on private property and the equation of the development of private property with material egotism and class exploitation have obscured the idealistic dimension of Locke's focus on the other side of private property as a means for the creation and protection of the private living quarters of the self, of spaces resistant to the invasive social (or divine) gaze, the searing light which makes a person transparent, which extinguishes the opaque, dimmer, more gentle sanctuaries where the vulnerable, often fragile, individual soul can grow.

Jerome Bruner has noted that even in Enlightenment Europe the private domain was not as real or self-defining as the public world of work and power. He cites Keith Thomas's observation that the desire to seek shelter from the eye of the community was often regarded as shameful. Even Diderot "saw the proliferation of furniture containing secret compartments as a sign of the age's moral deterioration."[1] Gradually, however, the distinct claims of the individual were upheld by liberal-democratic politics and law. In our century, this development has been attacked by both socialist and nationalist collectivisms. In modern Israel, and especially in the kibbutz, these two traditions converged to impose formidable constraints on individualism.

While the kibbutz communities have never constituted more than a tiny minority of Israel's larger society—4.9 percent of the Jewish population in 1953 and 2.3 percent in 1994—their pivotal role in projecting ideals of altruism, camaraderie, self-sacrifice, voluntarism, patriotism, and a high work ethic has made the kibbutz experience much more relevant for our understanding of modern Israel than the size of the kibbutz communities would seem to warrant.

Most significant were the radical kibbutz experiments in child rearing: the attempts to create and shape the Israeli-born Jew as a new kind of Jew, and the preoccupation with what Bruno Bettelheim, with a mixture of fascination and irony, called "the children of the dream." In Israel's early years shared, "natural" nakedness was only one aspect of a much more pervasive social truth: the fact that the kibbutz child was almost never left alone and unobserved either by other children or by the adult in charge (usually the *metapelet*, which means literally the woman who "takes care"—the surrogate

---

[1] See Jerome Bruner, *Acts of Meaning* (Cambridge, Mass.: Harvard University Press, 1990), p. 136.

mother of the children in the children's home that the kibbutz created outside the family space). Observers like Bruno Bettelheim and Melford Spiro before him noted repeatedly the omnipresence of the child's peers, the social gaze at one's body when one was "naturally" having an erection, masturbating, menstruating, defecating, and the like. While in other Western cultures these behaviors tend to take place within private spaces and are associated with each child's formative dialogue with his or her own body, in the kibbutz the omnipresence of the social gaze turned potentially separate individuals into members of kinds of extended family communities. Although the omnipresent gaze of others subsided somewhat, just as many communal practices were relaxed in most kibbutz communities, the general attitude persisted: no private space, no solitary experience, no personal toys, books, or clothes. Rather, the kibbutz sponsored group singing, group dancing, group eating, group nature trips—indeed group everything.

Another key motive in raising children as a group of native siblings was, of course, largely to separate children and their parents and replace the moral authority of parents with the moral authority of the group. This policy was often explicitly aimed at invalidating the family as a unit within which separate individual selves could be cultivated. This condition both intrigued and disturbed many observers. As a student of the kibbutz culture, Bettelheim, for example, wondered where in such a system the moral voice of the individual could be nourished and reinforced enough to generate the strength to assert itself against the voice of the community. Where could a person raised in such conditions get the courage to speak his or her own mind (an act which Spinoza, for one, thought to be so essential for the formation of the modern person)? How could such conditions allow for the kind of inner strength that enabled a Martin Luther to insist, "Here I stand, I cannot do otherwise"—an act which (as Bettelheim aptly observes) heralded the Reformation, in which individual conscience was set against community mores?[2]

Students of kibbutz communities have pointed further to the connections between the pejorative labeling of individualism as selfishness and careerism and the development of such character traits as emotional flatness, lack of individual initiative, and difficulty in self-expression.

The primacy and the omnipresence of the community in the kibbutz and in the larger Israeli society seem to have inhibited the growth of individualism and the culture of the self, two aspects of democratic life that have been essential for the formation of assertive, competent, critical, and largely independent citizens in other Western societies.

While city children like me were part of the much larger, more individualistic middle-class culture, there were many channels through which weaker versions of kibbutz values penetrated and shaped our own. The left-wing youth movements, for example, often recruited city youth to kibbutz settlements

---

[2]Bruno Bettelheim, *Children of the Dream* (London: Thames & Hudson, 1969), p. 130. (Studies of second- and third-generation kibbutz-born members based on data collected and analyzed from twenty kibbutz communities recorded the resentments felt by many kibbutz-born persons against group sanctions directed at signs of individuality and difference, the equation of uniqueness with being arrogant or ridiculous. The early patterns changed in time as a result of many factors, including the opening of kibbutz schools to outside children and permitting children to sleep regularly with their families.)

and left others forever feeling guilty for not joining. Teachers, and entire schools, such as my own high school (Tikhon Hadash in Tel Aviv), were affiliated with various parts of the socialist-Zionist movement; they inculcated a concern for equality and discouraged social, material, and cultural differences. We wore uniforms through high school and our parents were told not to send us to school with expensive fruit or foodstuffs, which other families might not be able to afford. These practices were very appealing but they also implied that various forms of individualism were ways of showing off—violations of an important moral norm. The obvious association of austerity in clothes, food, and other matters with the pioneering ethics of hardship and sacrifice only reinforced these attitudes.

The socialization process and the solidarity it generates have been particularly powerful and consequential in the Israeli army. Here the suppression of individuality has been open and explicit—a practice rationalized, as in other armies, by the need for unit cohesiveness and discipline. The fact that for decades the Israeli army was enlisted to serve such key civilian functions as teaching Hebrew to immigrants, providing elementary education for underprivileged soldiers, and helping to rehabilitate ex-convicts generated among soldiers forms of solidarity which mitigated or diluted the drawbacks of military rank and obedience. Moreover, the perception of the Israeli army as a people's army blunted the edge of military hierarchy and discipline and made the army organization appear less remote and threatening. In turn, the army's role in generating and upholding Israeli national solidarity made civilian life more permeable to the army's values and mores. Thus, the civilian functions of the army have reinforced the connections between group discipline, solidarity, and military values and symbols. Service in the army has become perhaps the most critical defining component of Israeli identity, and this has reinforced the pull of collective communal values across Israeli society. The disproportionate representation of kibbutz members among the officer corps in the Israeli army indicates the high degree of convergence between the spartan values inculcated in the kibbutz and in the army alike, and has made the army the setting where the cherished values of kibbutz communities are indirectly transmitted to young people.

Anthropologists have noted that in Western societies traditions of individualism are manifest in patterns of social interaction. Edward T. Hall,[3] for one, argues that whereas Westerners behave in public spaces as if they assumed that an impermeable, invisible circle protected the private space of each individual, such a sacred individual space seems to be generally lacking in Middle Eastern societies, where bodies are in closer proximity to each other. In modern Israel, the absence of such invisible spatial boundaries around individuals has been widely evident. While there is apparently a progressive process of change in the direction of greater respect for private space, the behavior of Israelis in public spaces is still one of the most common irritants for visitors as well as Israelis returning from long periods in Western Europe and North America. I think it more accurate to suggest, however, that Eastern European immigrants have been just as oblivious to personal space as immigrants from the Levant. Such patterns are, of course, reinforced among low-income groups whose members (in all societies) cannot afford the living quarters

---

[3]Edward T. Hall, *The Hidden Dimension* (New York: Doubleday, 1966).

and opportunities that allow access to private space. While recent changes in Israeli culture seem dramatic in some respects,
the legacy of past practices is still powerful. Once I found myself telling my students at the Hebrew University of Jerusalem
that there is a very curious social phenomenon called a
"queue," in which people spontaneously line up, standing one
after another in a line without touching or shouting, for example in bus stations or banks; students who wanted to observe
or study such curious behavior, I said with only slight exag-
geration, would have to travel abroad.

The permeable private space in Israeli society is also manifest in the architectural design of residential neighborhoods
in Israeli cities. While in many cities elsewhere in the world,
especially in the poorer neighborhoods, apartments and apartment buildings are so physically close that neighbors are virtually present in each other's domestic spaces, in Israel the
scarcity of resources, including land, was only one, albeit important, factor. No less significant have been the patronizing
attitude of the state, a primary agent of mass housing projects
for new immigrants, and the weak resistance on the part of
these newcomers, many of whom had not internalized an appreciation for private space, nor did they feel sufficiently empowered to keep their private space from being invaded. David
Grossman's novel *The Book of Intimate Grammar* (1991; English
translation 1994) is full of powerful scenes of Israeli communal neighborhood life in the 1960s: the strong smells that
travel from the kitchens of these apartments, the sound of
telephones ringing and conversations in several European languages, the sights of intimate family life that appear in the
windows, and the intense interactions among the neighbors.

There is perhaps no more striking example of the assault

on the idea of private space than an Israeli cemetery. Israeli cemeteries are in fact an illuminating iconography of the poverty of Israeli individualism. Graves and headstones are crowded to the point of virtually touching one another, so that one's experience of mourning is almost inescapably social. Whenever I stand in front of my mother's grave at the cemetery in Holon, near Tel Aviv, I need to close my eyes in order to capture an intimate moment with my feelings and memories. But when I walk out, the sight of a forest of often identical-looking graves crowded together like a congregation sometimes gives me an eerie feeling of consolation, as if the dead are not left alone now, any more than they were when they were among the living. After all, I was raised in this society to believe that to be alone is to be lonely.

The difficulties of escaping the social gaze are compounded in Israel by the relatively small size of the country. Even in its largest city, Tel Aviv, when I was growing up, it was exceedingly difficult to locate a space for the precious experience of anonymity. Even in relatively remote parts of the city or in its outskirts, one would have a pretty good chance of being spotted by a relative, a friend, or a neighbor. Anonymity is so scarce in such circumstances that one can passionately crave an experience like walking alone totally unknown, say in the streets of New York City, as if it were a distant utopia. I suppose such feelings may be the counterimage of the communitarian fantasies of some of my American friends who dream of basking in the warmth of a familylike community in the kibbutz or elsewhere in Israel. Bruno Bettelheim, who actually lived in a kibbutz for the purpose of writing his book in the 1960s, reflected later on his experience. "My photographer companion could not accustom himself to how kibbutzniks felt free to walk in on him at any hour of the day or night no matter what he was occupied with. Eventually both of us, who initially liked the idea of living in a true community, felt a recurrent need to escape for a few hours to the ambiguity of city life, where we could for moments be ourselves; where we were not expected to want to be always with others. . . . What made it hard was that this longing for a bit of privacy which to us seemed so natural was felt by others to be a deliberate shunning of their company." While several decades later this description would probably appear exaggerated, it indicates a still deeply ingrained attitude not just in the kibbutz but in the wider society as well. Particularly in the presence of those who have known you from childhood, you are always compelled to relate to others in the context of your established past. In such a dense social milieu, anonymity—a resource so vital for experimenting with untried possibilities of selfhood, for breaking loose from confining identities—is scarcely possible. Can the class clown ever be taken seriously if even only a few of his classmates are still around throughout adulthood? Can one transcend one's own weaknesses where the people around one remember them? Can one afford to be weak in the presence of those who always held one to be a symbol of strength? It is nice, of course, that an occasional nickname like the one attached to my high school friend "Zebra" stuck to him through adulthood, and not only among our original classmates. But it also reveals the distressing constraints imposed by social intimacy.

The fact that we Israelis know each other all too well can also keep us from exercising detached, impersonal judgment in matters where such judgments are important. The sociologist Joseph Ben-David observed years ago that because of the difficulties in ensuring the anonymity of grant applicants to Israeli foundations, Israeli scientists often find it very difficult to depersonalize their professional evaluations of competing proposals. It is difficult, although by no means impossible, to develop a detached, "objective" review process in a small society, where a scientist may need only to know the research topic or the methodology of the applicant to know his or her identity. In the army—another institution which requires detached judgments—the celebrated informality and fraternity among Israeli soldiers is also linked with a very disturbing record of disrespect for rules and standards, as well as negligence which all too often ends up in fatal accidents. A culture of "buddies" is not congenial to rigorous individual discipline, independent judgment, and the detachment necessary for handling complicated technical tasks. Camaraderie discourages respect for standards of merit, and encourages patronage and inbreeding. Such patterns are, of course, well known in other countries as well. But in Israel these forms of behavior have been reinforced by deeply rooted religious, ethnic, and ideological attitudes which urge the individual to submit to the moral authority of the peer group, often privileging loyalty to friends over responsibility to tasks.

The vitality and the invasive expansionism of the collective and its spatial presence in modern Israel cannot be adequately understood without considering the long, painful history of the ways Jews were restricted from expressing themselves publicly and collectively in their host societies. The very establishment of a "Jewish" public space for the physical and symbolic articulation of Jewish collectivity was, of course, a major objective of the Zionist revolution. No doubt the value placed on Jewish public space derives in part from memories of the way

Jewish communal identity was confined in the ghettos of European cities, or of the demand that Jews enter public space
either as a visibly stigmatized, underprivileged group or as individuals who had been emancipated from their Jewish particularism—as persons who had effaced all external traces of
Jewish identity. For Zionists the establishment of the State of
Israel in 1948 meant, among other things, that a Jewish power
would protect a sphere in which Jews could unleash dormant
desires to appropriate and shape public space—to project, as
a group, their character and preferences in urban and rural
landscapes, public buildings, street life, communal festivals,
state rituals, and military parades. These processes have become the foci of a new kind of social and political discourse
about what is culturally or aesthetically appropriate and what
is not—for example, why the architecture of the Supreme
Court building in Jerusalem, in which the architects tried to
balance a templelike sacred and a mundane humanistic perspective on law and judicial authority, is so successful[4] and the
fortresslike structure and impersonal spaces of the Hebrew
University campus on Mount Scopus so problematic; or why
the space created before the Western Wall has undermined
the intimacy of religious experience there; or what city-
planning guidelines should be set for renovating the area of
the former port of Tel Aviv. It is this exuberant effusion of
new forms of Jewish group presence in public spaces that has
often made Israel so compellingly attractive to Diaspora Jews
and immigrants. "The largest group of Jews I had ever seen
in my life," a fellow graduate student at Harvard confided to

---

[4]See article by Ziva Sterenhell, *Ha'aretz*, December 4, 1992, p. B4.

me upon returning from his first visit to Israel, "was a thousand very well-dressed Jews in the Yom Kippur service in our synagogue. Imagine," he said almost breathlessly, "imagine my feelings at the sight of a thousand Jewish women in bikinis on the beach of Tel Aviv!" Other Jews have responded with similar enthusiasm to their first experience of billboards in Hebrew, Israeli street life, and, of course, Jewish soldiers and policemen in uniform.

It is partly because the Jewish drama of return and liberation has converged with the cultural appropriation of public space in Israel that the individual Israeli Jew has tended to identify public space more readily with freedom than with restriction. Moreover, inasmuch as throughout most of Jewish history collective practices were hidden in private spaces, the natural strains between public and private, corporate and individual space must have been much more muted for Jews in the past. In Western societies the divisions between public and private spaces have often corresponded with the guarded boundaries between the respective domains of the collective and the individual. When the corporate identity of the host society was defined in narrow, nationalist terms, Jews found it difficult to enter public space even as individual citizens who would deny or ignore their particular Jewish religious and ethnic affiliations. For such Jews the home was often a shelter for a suppressed Jewish identity and the place where the family transmitted and cultivated Jewish traditions. But even in the rare cases where the host society defined itself in sufficiently open terms to accommodate Jews as individual citizens, the Jewish home remained the repository of group memories and identities. So for Jews the home could not easily function as a place for the self, apart from the group, the way it did for members of the other societies.

In modern Israel, the creation of protected public space for the articulation of corporate Jewish life has freed the home as a resource for the individuation of the Israeli self. Where public institutions carry the principal burden of cultivating Jewish traditions, private space could serve the individual Jew as a person as it has served individual Italians, French, and English. During Israel's early years, to be sure, such a separation between the spaces of the home and the nation was unlikely because all too often in the home children were socialized into the political and social conditions of their pioneer parents. One's home, joined with one's school and youth movement, served as a vehicle of ideological messages. Today, although the poverty of Israeli individualism and the focus on collective identity still blur the lines between public and private spaces, the prospect for greater private space is rather promising. The emergence of such space is likely to indicate the deepening roots of Israeli liberal-democratic culture. For the citizen as a private person, private space is vital to counteract the invasiveness of public life and balance its political effects. Thus, the creation and development of private space could have significant long-term consequences for Israeli politics and culture alike. The restoration of public and private spaces as discrete yet interacting domains—domains of the collective and the individual—could instigate a new kind of internal dialogue, a new kind of negotiation, between Jews as a group and as individuals, as well as between Jews as citizens and their state.

If the uses of private space by individual Jews in the Diaspora depended upon the liberal or antiliberal tendencies of their host societies, in Israel the creation and deployment of private space within an evolving culture of individualism will reflect the extent of the liberal tendencies of a Jewish polity. A separation between group and individual identities and the delineation of distinct domains of public and private spaces not only would deepen the roots of liberal-democratic culture among Jews but also would make Israel more hospitable to its non-Jewish, especially its Arab, citizens. An Israel that can define at least some spaces as public in the inclusive civic sense, rather than in the particularistic, exclusive ethnic or religious sense, is a polity that can accommodate, along with its commitment to corporate Jewish identities, the democratic idea of the people as an association of free individuals. Currently, Israel's national cemetery on Mount Herzl in Jerusalem—the burial place of slain Prime Minister Rabin—and Rabin Square, next to the Tel Aviv Municipality, may be developing into such spaces.

3

Escape to Nature?

Rousseau consecrated nature not only as a temple for the individual soul, not just as a shelter from the oppressive social gaze, but as a sanctuary for democratic education. In his view, the social gaze makes each of us behave theatrically rather than sincerely. It encourages us to meet social expectations, to make ourselves loved and respected, to yield to the despotism of public opinion and fashion rather than following the inner voice of our own conscience. In his theory of education, therefore, Rousseau recommends that the child be taken out of society and placed in nature, where (under the guidance of a tutor) his character and independence can be sufficiently strengthened to allow him to reenter society without risking the loss of his individuality. This romantic view of nature as the ultimate retreat for the individual—as the purest form of private space—radiates not only from Rousseau's writings but from his grave, surrounded by trees on a tiny island in a small lake near Geneva.

The ideas of nature as a retreat from the burden of civilization; an escape from the noisy city crowds; an arena for the individual's encounter with the primordial, prehistorical, possibly divine, order; a place of self-reflection and self-reform; a haven for initiating a new beginning; a measure of the alienation of life in the domain of the artificial, of the distance from paradise; the repository of the nostalgia for lost innocence and lost harmonies, for life before the Fall—all these have been fundamental to the development of the culture of the self in the West. Such ideas have inspired and penetrated important traditions of painting, music, poetry, gardening, architecture, and city planning. In America, the creation of national parks and the protection of nature preserves were motivated largely by the value attached to protected spaces for the experience of solitude and privacy, for the intimate edifying dialogue between self and nature—a fact which is often forgotten in the age of mass camping grounds where seemingly all of society goes "on vacation."

For an Israeli, the idea of nature as a place where the self can escape from society is but a momentary dream doomed to a rude awakening. In this perhaps most contested of all lands—where the three religions have focused their prophecies of destruction and redemption; where mountains dripping with wine are a blessing and dry land a divine curse; where the heavens speak the glory of God; where temples have been built on the ruins of other temples—in this land, the escape into nature is invariably a political act which denies the existence of one category of human beings while affirming the existence of another, which places one people in nature and another in history.

In Israel, where nature, like a thin layer of dust covering ancient scrolls, is but the back side of human scriptures; where any hill can be a shrine covered by dirt and any valley hide a sunken city; where the earth is but a buffer between past and present; where nature is younger than history, no landscape is a retreat from society and any scenery is but politics in disguise.

Mark Twain, who toured Palestine in 1867, had no doubts that Presbyterian tourists would find evidence to support a Presbyterian Palestine, Baptists would find a Baptist Palestine, and Catholics a Catholic Palestine. Yeshayahu Nir, in his illuminating *History of Photography in the Holy Land between 1839 and 1899*, provides ample support for Twain's observation. Landscapes of the Holy Land can scarcely be treated as "natural." They are always used in attempts to preach, proselytize, justify, celebrate, criticize, or condemn. Most pervasive in nineteenth-century photography was, of course, the impulse to depict "biblical landscapes" as a means to validate some versions of the biblical narrative. Nir notes the different styles of British Protestant and French Catholic photographers, their distinct sensibilities and images of the place. Equally instructive are late-nineteenth-century Zionist photographers, who preferred the pastoral landscapes of Jewish farms and vineyards to traditional landscapes of Jerusalem in ruins or of landmark churches, synagogues, and cemeteries. The Zionist ideological commitment to the Jewish return to nature—the celebration of the physical muscular Jew, the farmer, the *chalutz,* as a reaction against the religious culture of ancient texts, their frail and pale past masters, and the interior landscapes of their schools—did not accommodate the idea of nature as a sanctuary for the individual Jew. The return to nature was a commitment to the naturalization of an entire people as an act of collective emancipation from the "culture of exile," a deliberate attempt to leap over two thousand years of Jewish history and somehow retrieve the primordial universe that existed before expulsion from the land.

Inspired by this orientation, some early pioneers attempted to empower the Jew as an observer of nature. In the introduction to *Lessons in Observation and Knowledge of Homeland (She'urai Histaklhut Veyedi'at Hamoledet)*,[1] the Hebrew book for elementary-school teachers, my grandfather and his colleagues—Yechieli and Ozrakowsky—describe their aim of adapting the Hebrew language to the task of an accurate discourse about nature. They note the shortage in modern Hebrew of suitable words for describing nature. In trying to close the gap, they criticize the insulation of Diaspora Jews from nature and their confined lives within the walls of the ghetto. "Now that we have broken out and have entered the open spaces of the field," they wrote, "we have to strengthen the capacity of our youth to free themselves from this sad legacy." Inspired by leading thinkers of the European Enlightenment, they were committed to the uses of nature not only as a means to reinforce their students' love of the "homeland" but also as a place to cultivate independent observations, judgments, and expressions. Following Bacon, Rousseau, and others, they stress, for example, the role of direct observation by the students themselves as a way to diminish the authority of teachers in mediating and interpreting experience.

In the decades that followed, the study of nature as a means for the cultivation of individual independence was eclipsed by the study of nature under the increasingly loaded rubric of *moledet* (homeland) as a component of collective national culture. Zionism generated a wide range of strategies for appropriating nature as a means of reinforcing the sacrifices and

---

[1]Jaffa: Kohelet Publisher, 1912.

attachment of the Jewish immigrants and their children to the land of Israel. One was based on the idea of conquering nature as a dangerous, uncultivated place—of drying out the swamps or making the desert bloom. Another was based on the romantic assimilation of nature into the dreams, nostalgia, and narratives of the pioneers. This inspired painters like Abel Pan to turn the silhouettes of native Bedouin girls with clay jars on their heads into portraits of Rachel and Rebecca, and encouraged Israeli philologists to discover ancient layers of biblical Hebrew behind the Arabic names of various places. Examining modern Hebrew literature, Sidra Ezrahi notes that "the ubiquitous Bedouin is the romantic embodiment of the self in a double sense: at the same time native, autochthonous man in an organic, pre-industrialized connection to the land and the aboriginal Semite, ancestral Jew. The Bedouin, like the Dead Sea Scrolls, becomes a relic of an authentic past, of the lost self. Of course, the Bedouin who is claimed as ancestral self then becomes altogether invisible as other, not because he is overlooked but because he is so totally co-opted."[2] They are just as indigenous to the place, to the sense one has of the picturesque and the beautiful and the authentic landscape, as I suppose a native Indian in traditional clothes would appear to a New Yorker visiting Arizona.

---

[2]Sidra Ezrahi, "Our Homeland, the Text . . . Our Text the Homeland: Exile and Homecoming in the Modern Jewish Imagination," *Michigan Quarterly Review*, Vol. 31, No. 4 (Fall 1992), p. 484. Much of the present discussion is informed by the recent work of Sidra DeKoven Ezrahi, in which she shows that the Holy Land as an imagined place has always eclipsed the Holy Land as a geographical space. See her *Exile and Return in Modern Jewish Literature* (Berkeley: University of California Press, 1997).

I came to appreciate the subtle cultural mechanisms that
mediate our notions of the picturesque years later when I visited the Museum of Natural History in New York City. Among
the various kinds of birds and deer I discovered figures of
native Indians in their traditional clothes. Indians in the Museum of Natural History! Some years later, in the short summer between finishing high school and being conscripted into
the Israeli army, my son Ariel and I went on a trip into a
shared dream, the American West, where we discovered yet
other ways of placing native Americans in authentic landscapes. After rafting on the Colorado River and admiring the
Petrified Forest, we drove through Arizona and many Indian
villages to Monument Valley in Utah in search of relics of ancient Indian culture. Upon arriving we met a very "native"-
looking man who offered us a drive through some local
landmarks. It looked very promising and we and a few other
tourists crowded into the rugged-looking van. The "native"
man drove us to a nearby hill, where we stepped out to observe
and photograph a spectacular giant piece of sheer rock. "You
see this?" asked our guide. "This is where the famous GM
television commercial was made, where a helicopter placed its
new GMC model on the top of this rock." Some members of
our group seemed deeply appreciative. But this was just the
first station. The next one in our three-hour tour was in front
of a striking narrow, tall stone pillar which was carved at the
edges. I thought it must be the totem pole used in ancient
Indian rituals. "This," said our guide, as my hand rushed to
the camera, "is where John Ford shot the movie *Fort Apache*
with John Wayne." "Yeah, yeah," cried the companion at my
side with obvious enthusiasm. At the end of this trip, I was not
sure what this Monument Valley was a monument to. Were we

looking for real places and finding just the places where our fantasies of the real were created? And is the futile pursuit of the match between the place and the fantasy what feeds the children of this native American? Is this what makes him collaborate in the effacement of his own culture by the marketplace?

How different is the Holy Land? Aren't the Christians, Jews, and Muslims who roam this country also looking in vain for the "real places" of their respective Scriptures? In this region, how far can archaeology function as science and how much as ideology? Hasn't this land seen how stories come and go, each people remaking the place in its own image and enlisting the survivors of the defeated story, those who were bumped from history back to "nature," to serve as a backdrop for the monuments of the victorious one?

As a child, I innocently integrated the abandoned houses of the Arabs at the entrance to Jerusalem with my imagination of authentic ancient Oriental landscapes; the Oriental buildings, together with the olive trees spread in the valley below Lifta, came to suggest "biblical nature." Any Israeli who passed through the West Bank in the years following the Six-Day War must have encountered Orthodox Jewish settlers fully armed and dressed in the religious uniforms of their redemptive drama, who would point out the "blessed divine beauty of that biblical landscape" as if beauty alone confers a divine right to be living there.

For many years, my favorite Israeli nature authority was Azaria Alon, whose historical-poetical accounts of various nature sites over the Israeli radio had become widely popular. One sad day I discovered that Alon is a leading ideologue of the Greater Eretz Israel movement, a right-wing association which holds it sinful to concede any territory, any part of "our" nature, to the Arab side. Since then, Alon's compelling and illuminating nature talks have been tainted in my eyes by their political subtext. This was an important moment in my loss of innocence about nature, a loss of the possibility of refuge in an ideologically or politically neutral landscape.

Israel's costly battles over so many of our most precious local treasures has interrupted the dream of nature as well. I am certainly not the only Israeli who cannot enjoy, as I once did, the snowcapped slopes of Mount Hermon in the Golan. Ever since the bloody battles that took place on this mountain during the Yom Kippur War in 1973, I have been unable to see the white without the red. Nature in Israel can hardly be privatized without monumental acts of denying the dead, effacing those we have transferred from history to nature, or ignoring the ancient texts, which are used as flags to stake claims of group ownership. Like fiction, nature can live here only in the suspension of history. No doubt some Israelis can escape to someplace else, but mostly through ignorance. And those Israelis for whom being at home ended "exile" as a place can escape to a place relatively new for Jews: "abroad." The merit of being abroad is in being neither in Zion nor in exile. Being abroad is different from being in exile because it is more self-consciously temporary and it gives the Israeli Jew the neutral status of the tourist. Tourists are allowed to be ignorant of or forget the battles, the claims, and the injustices that keep them from experiencing pure nature.

The awareness of the occupation eventually made it impossible for me to enjoy the engaging beauty of the landscapes on the West Bank. The settlement of our conflict with the Arabs will, no doubt, make it possible for us to visit these landscapes as tourists. The peace with Jordan transformed Petra, previously considered a dangerous place just beyond the border, into a magnificent tourist site. Agreed-upon and peaceful borders are also likely to restore to us ways of encountering nature at home. But during Israel's first half century, Israelis have been raised to recognize that on our "native grounds," this battered land where competing stories have deposited their relics side by side or one on top of the other, there is no such thing as pure nature.

As a nine-year-old boy, in 1949, I would wander with my friends into an abandoned *pardes*, a citrus orchard near our neighborhood on the northern outskirts of Tel Aviv. It served us as a hideout. As if in defiance of long years of neglect, wildly growing branches blocked the paths between the trees and sealed off the sky, forming a cool, shady retreat from the summer's heat. The orchard was both inviting and threatening. The barbed wire around it was a warning, but against what was never clear to us. Was it to protect us from mines somebody said the Arabs might have left behind or just to protect the fruit from invaders like us? In winter the trees were loaded with oranges, mostly rotten but with a few good ones which would not last long. I remember the moment when, amidst those half-cultivated, half-wild trees, my hand reached up to pick the forbidden fruit. I bit into it. The sweetness of the orange was mixed with anxiety as I recalled those Arabs who had worked there some years before. Such anxiety must have made us invent our favorite game. We would sneak into the orchard, moving swiftly among the trees, imagining ourselves as commando units trying to pick some good oranges, until suddenly one of us would shout, "The Arabs are coming! The Arabs are coming!" As soon as the scream was sounded, all of us would run out of the orchard in a frenzy, as if our lives depended on it, jumping over the barbed wire and then, upon reaching safe ground, bursting into laughter in relief.

The yellow sands of Tel Aviv's Mediterranean beach, a twenty-minute walk west of my house, were destined to be more neutral grounds. For years, my visits to that beach were dominated by the ominous presence of a huge, black, burnt piece of shipwreck sticking out of the water some thirty meters offshore. This was the remains of the *Altalena*, the ammunition ship brought to this shore in 1948 by the ultranationalist Irgun Zvai Leumi, an armed Jewish underground organization that advocated and practiced military activism against the Arabs and the British Mandatory authorities. The newly installed first Prime Minister of Israel, David Ben-Gurion, had ordered the army to fire on the ammunition ship, ostensibly to prevent a violation of the cease-fire agreement by the Israeli side and, even more important, in order to assert the supremacy of the newly established state over private military organizations from the pre-state period. This bloody incident, a reminder of how close we were to a civil war, left a deep scar on the Israeli psyche. But in time the burnt shipwreck disappeared below the soothing green waters of the sea as the straight line of the Mediterranean horizon took over the scene.

In later years I realized that the magic of this place, the power it exerted on me, did not come so much from the spectacular sunsets, the warm sand, or even the woman who once swam toward me in its waters. It came from the clean straight line of the horizon, beyond which there were worlds too far away to limit my imagination. Just a pure straight line and a clean canvas stretching above it, a seductive empty space with no Jews or Arabs, no churches, no synagogues, no ruins, no abandoned orchards; a perfect private airport for the wildest flights of fancy. The straight clean line of the Mediterranean horizon became my private hideout, an intimate ally, a secret exit that I have used a thousand times, a place from which I could first look beyond the edges of our story and then look back inside from without.

> > *4*

The Precariousness of
Autobiographical Time

Martyrs live and die in eternal time, heroes live and die in historical time, and regular people like us live and die in the extended present. The human passion for immortality, the secret desire to transcend the mundane, to touch eternity or become a part of history, has created a paradox. Since time began, ordinary people have traded their lives, a safe present, for a promised fragment of the immortal, dying by the millions in uplifting religious and historical wars.

In many respects it is only when autobiographical time begins—when the individual can resist the call of immortality to make his or her life shorter in return for making it loftier and more meaningful—that the democratic citizen is born. While citizenship defines the relations of the individual to the state, in the liberal-democratic state the citizen is largely a public extension of the private person, rather than the individual's reflection of the state or the group. Liberal-democratic politics rests on the individual's judgment of the state, rather than on the state's evaluation of the individual.

As a political fact in democratic societies, the value of each individual life as a singular unrepeatable human experience is largely the result of many struggles fought by the modern self. The self struggled first against the attempts of religions to subordinate the individual's personal calendar to a cosmic calendar stretching from creation to revelation and redemption. From the perspective of the cosmic calendar, autobiographical time is too transient and partial to be a worthy vessel of experience. In modern times, democratic individualism is the consequence of no less serious struggles against Marxist and nationalist ideologies and the political attempts to enlist the temporal duration of individual life in the larger projects of class and nation.

In modern Israel, the liberal individual has somewhat anachronistically struggled to protect the integrity of autobiographical time against the converging armies of martyrs and heroes, against the temporal claims of religion and ideology, which for many years collaborated in sanctifying the sacrifice of the individual for the land. Liberal-democratic individualism has been confronting the formidable forces of nationalism and religion in their attempt to turn the state from an instrument of self-government serving the necessities of individual and collective lives into a means of realizing a religiously—or ideologically—inspired historical vision of wholeness and greatness.

By welding into the annual ceremonial schedule of memorial days, holidays, and festivals events of a few thousand years ago (the destruction of the Temple, the Exodus from Egypt) and events of more recent epic Jewish history (the Holocaust, the creation of the State of Israel), the Israeli calendar fuses historical and religious time. The anthropologist Robert Paine has suggested that the concept of time invoked in Israel is in fact totemic rather than historical or religious. Don Handelman and Elihu Katz of the Hebrew University of Jerusalem indicate further how the decision to structure the Israeli calendar so that Holocaust Day precedes the memorial day for the fallen Israeli soldiers, and is succeeded by Independence Day, gave the calendar a narrative sequence: from mourning to rebirth, from fall to redemption. They discern in this sequence a rhythmic progression embedded in both religious and secular Jewish culture, a movement from fragmentation to integration, darkness to light, corruption to moral bliss, slavery to freedom. "The abstract formation of time in Jewish culture," they observe, "is, generally speaking, that of directional development and that of collective becoming."[1]

This radical appropriation of time for the narratives of collective history dwarfs and marginalizes autobiographical time, and renders what has been cast as public time resistant to its use as a resource of the Israeli self. Time in Israel has been too sacred to be responsive to the needs of the individual: too emotionally loaded by endless commemorations; too scarce, given the urgency and the size of the effort of nation building and the limited number of people who participate; too politicized by ideology.

Among members of the early generations of those born in Israel (and probably among those born later as well), an adult birthday—a celebration of the beginning of autobiographical time—has been a relatively insignificant event. A comparison with American attitudes can be instructive. While eating out with friends during my first visit to North America in 1963, I saw how an intimate birthday celebration at another table became a public event, as the people at the other tables joined

---

[1] Don Handelman, *Models and Mirrors: Towards an Anthropology of Public Events* (Cambridge, England: Cambridge University Press, 1990), p. 227.

in singing and applauding when the waitress brought a cake with lit candles. In time I came to realize that this ritual is common, a kind of social gesture acknowledging the significance of personal time, which even strangers can identify with and reinforce. Being married to an American has made the Israeli in me keenly aware of the culture of personal calendars—the reciprocal gestures among friends and intimates who acknowledge significant dates on the personal calendar.

It is hard to imagine such a culture flourishing in the absence of liberal-democratic individualism and an elaborate culture of the self. In modern Israel, adult birthdays have characteristically been downplayed as bringing too much attention to the individual, who is expected to be self-effacing and indifferent to private needs and delights. For decades birthdays were generally for children, and then celebrated in school with a party for several children at once, rather than as a separate one for each.[2] While this is no doubt more economical, the notion that a separate birthday party celebrates individuality and uniqueness has been too weak to induce a sense of deprivation among teachers and parents alike.

Historically, in the West, biographical and autobiographical time has been reinforced by Christian traditions of individual spiritual progress and confessional practice. The concern for the salvation of the individual soul integrated key elements of the personal calendar into the collective calendar of the com-

---

[2]Lea Shamgar-Handelman and Don Handelman, "Celebrations of Bureaucracy: Birthday Parties in Israeli Kindergartens," *Ethnology*, Vol. 30 (1991), pp. 293–312.

munity. However, the predisposition to view and frame the life of the individual within the temporal confines of the span between birth and death has grown as time has been secularized. In the early fourteenth century, churches in Western Europe displayed astronomical clocks to represent the links between the movement of celestial bodies and the orderliness of God's cosmos. The development of timepieces—from these early church clocks to the cheap personal wristwatch of our time—reflects the history of the desacralization and the democratization of time in the West. Moreover, each society has evolved its own particular culture of time. Most relevant to our purpose, perhaps, is American society, because of its advanced forms of democratic individualism.

Time in America seems particularly malleable and flexible, something plastic to be molded and shaped to meet diverse institutional and individual needs.[3] Especially interesting are the economic considerations guiding the buying and selling of "airtime" on American radio and television. Because airtime is such an expensive resource for advertising, cadres of talented Americans have devised very effective methods to use it economically and have trained American viewers to practice high-speed reading (of subtitles), high-speed viewing, and high-speed hearing.[4] The connection between speed and at-

---

[3] An instructive illustration is the readiness of Americans to make the birthdays of leaders such as Washington and Lincoln national holidays and then shift them from the original dates to allow for longer weekends, better to accommodate American vacationers.

[4] See Yaron Ezrahi, *The Descent of Icarus: Science and the Transformation of Contemporary Democracy* (Cambridge, Mass.: Harvard University Press, 1990), pp. 254–62.

tention may actually have revolutionalized political communications in the American democracy, privileging contents
which can be instantly communicated over those requiring
more time, more concentration, and longer sentences. In addition, the frequent distracting injection of commercials in TV
movies as well as news programs has probably affected American viewers' orientation toward narratives, facts, and public
discourse, and at a deeper level their very notions of time and
reality.

In Israel, where for decades the "news" has been treated as
an unfolding collective drama, until recently interrupting a
news broadcast with commercials would have appeared scandalous. With the introduction of commercial television in
1993, and against the background of the moves to defuse the
Arab–Israeli conflict, puncturing the epic narrative of the news
with commercials may actually have the salutary effect of re-
laxing the grip of public affairs on Israelis and shrinking the
use of public time for mobilizing the citizens.

The grip of public affairs on the average Israeli persists, of
course, through his or her army service. During Israel's first
half century, the regular army service (which until recently
lasted at least three years for males and two for females) and
the reserve military service (which adds up approximately to
another two to three years for Israeli males) have been a major
claim on personal time. Due to extended periods of army service many Israelis feel they never have enough time—that they
are always behind in their studies, work, business, or personal
affairs. An Israeli male.is asked to give time to public service
during the years when a young person needs time to be alone
so as to develop his sense of self. In requiring extended periods of army service of men, especially between the ages of

eighteen and thirty, the state, of course, is not deliberately or consciously aiming to diminish their time for personal affairs, for reflection, and for self-examination away from the demands of the group. But it has had these effects. An Israeli high school student normally has but two months between graduation and army service and as a result does not have the opportunity to make the personal choices which in other societies involve self-probing and individualization. On the contrary, because for half a century young Israelis have enlisted in an army which has sent them to fight dangerous wars, they have been preoccupied with the prospect of untimely death, not personal growth. While there are, of course, many diverse responses to the fear of death among the young, probably the most common is a sense of camaraderie and group attachments which characteristically defy individuation.

By the relatively late age of twenty-one, when newly demobilized soldiers are free to start making personal choices, time to explore and reflect is short because higher education and professional training are expensive and most students need to work to finance at least part of their studies. Under these pressures of "life," students often become "pragmatic," acquiring a skill or taking a job that will allow them to make money, rather than developing their talents and interests. The Israeli university system has from the very beginning structured the undergraduate curriculum in such a way that from the first or the second year of studies students are expected to commit themselves to their major rather than devote themselves first to a more general education, which could empower them as persons. In the absence, until very recently, of comprehensive liberal arts programs, undergraduate education in Israel has usually been more a form of professional training than higher

education, and therefore much less congenial to the intellectual, cultural, and psychological processes that foster the
growth of the individual self. As a result, the opportunities for
young Israelis to acquire and employ what Foucault aptly
called "technologies of the self" have been quite poor. Maturation has been seen as a coming to terms with the harshness
of army service, war, scarcity, and the generally adverse conditions of collective existence. Only rarely has it been associated with the development of the individual as a feeling,
thinking, or judging self or the mastery of the rich repertory
of the self's cultural techniques.

It is a symptom of the poverty of Israeli individualism—
whether conceived as ideology, a state of mind, or a cultural
form—that such massive strictures on private time have not
been resisted. There are always, of course, some people who
through a mixture of circumstances and willpower have escaped these constraints and developed genuine private lives.
Such exceptions do not form a culture, but they do form a
situation that is beginning to make inroads in the society at
large. Since the 1970s, more and more Israelis have begun to
use leisure time—especially holidays and the Sabbath—to pursue personal rather than communal activities.[5] Moreover, in
Israel as elsewhere, the marked increase in mass travel abroad
(even by less affluent Israelis) and the spread of television have
exposed more and more Israelis to present-oriented consum-
erist culture.

------

[5]See Elihu Katz and Hadassa Haas, eds., *The Culture of Leisure Time in Israel:
Changes in Patterns of Cultural Activity, 1970–1990* (Jerusalem: The Guttman
Institute of Applied Social Research, 1992) (in Hebrew).

Nevertheless, only with deeper cultural, social, and political changes will a culture of the self, with its autobiographical time, be able to resist the invasive calendar of totemic, mythical, religious, and epic-historical time in modern Israel. The Catholic theologian Jacques Maritain used the most common strategy of attacking autobiographical time in comparison with religious or social time when he insisted that individual present-orientedness is a form of egotism. "Immediate success," he wrote, "is success for a man . . . not for a state or a nation according to the duration proper to state vicissitudes." But the measure of time according to individual vicissitudes, rather than state or religious ones, is precisely the aim of liberal democracy. Mortality—the inescapable end of every individual life—defines the present (which encompasses the recent past and the near future) as the temporal domain of politics in the modern democratic state. Democratic publics characteristically demand that their leaders facilitate or provide a variety of instant (usually material) gratifications. Such pressures typically entrap democratic governments between the inherent limitations on their ability to deliver such gratifications and the criticism of their attempts as shortsighted political opportunism. Where possible, governors prefer the temporal scales of states and nations, of history and of eschatology. Israeli leaders are no exception. They prefer to be accountable to God, to the dead or the unborn, to destiny or history in order to escape the pressures of democratic accountability to the living. This is, at least in part, why nationalistic and ideological politicians are much more often at war with journalists than with historians, with the press and not with theology. Ironically, however, because we the living are often unable to face the harsh implications of our mortality, we are prone to collaborate with our governors in deferring their accountability to the future. We cooperate with their attempts to "theologize" or "historicize" political time in the name of idealism, to exchange the present for posterity.

The modern nation-state has often presented itself as an enterprise which depends on the contributions and sacrifices of individuals who in return achieve the sense (if not the reality) of life "more prolonged." Thus a life of sacrifice—and at the extreme, the sacrifice of one's life for the state—has been understood as a way of extending and deepening life rather than as a denial of life.

Jean-Pierre Vernant refers to early versions of this strategy of transcending the limits of one's lifetime in his comments on Homer's *Iliad*. He observes that "Achilles is the model of the heroic warrior; in choosing a short life and deathless glory, he embodies an ideal of honor so elevated that, in its name, he will reject both the gifts of the King and the honor of his own companions in arms." Greek culture created ingenious cultural devices to turn ordinary persons into heroes. For the Greeks, as Vernant shows, to die young in battle was to escape the more dreadful and humiliating decay or deterioration of the human body through the aging process. A "beautiful death" was preferable to ugly, emasculating degeneration; one lost one's "youth and beauty in a heroic death in order to acquire them definitively in the world beyond, to eternalize and extol youthful beauty in art and memory."[6]

Judaism, Christianity, and Islam have added to this reper-

---

[6]Jean-Pierre Vernant, *Mortals and Immortals* (collected essays), Froma I. Zeitlin, ed. (Princeton: Princeton University Press, 1991), pp. 50–74.

toire important ideas and forms of the spiritualized sacrifice of life, of glorified death that sanctifies the name of God.[7] In modern societies, secular ideologies like socialism, fascism, nationalism, and republicanism have provided powerful symbolic devices for coding and sanctioning the sacrifice of individual lives, for exchanging this passing life for the glory of fighting for noble ideas of justice and liberation. These ideologies were used by modern states to rationalize the creation of armies and the wars in which they fight. Like the great religions, these ideologies have downgraded the individual life left to itself, reducing it to a disconnected fragment, lost without purpose or direction. Dictatorial regimes cannot afford, of course, to dehistoricize politics completely because they justify the sacrifice of the liberties and resources of the living for the sake of some good or amelioration in the distant elusive future. Throughout the twentieth century Communist regimes in Eastern Europe often enlisted Marxist–Enlightenment theories of progress to back up the claim that a better future depends to a large extent on the willingness to make great sacrifices in the present.

St. Augustine gave powerful expression to this idea, comparing the individual life to a word in a sentence whose end is unknown. Only God can know the words that will complete the sentence; thus no single person can fully comprehend the meaning of his or her own life. Only a life of faith and worship can allow the individual to connect his or her life with the

---

[7]For the Jewish context, see discussion in *Zion: Quarterly for Research in Jewish History* (Jerusalem: The Historical Society of Israel), Vol. 59, Nos. 2–3 (1994).

cosmic narrative. Religion and ideology link the "words" of individual lives into historical "sentences," then into a meaningful narrative that extends in time from the past through the present to the future. It is probably one of the principal secrets of the recruiting powers of religions and ideologies that they draw on the aesthetic and cognitive attraction of a holistic conception of time and meaning, on the superior force of the whole relative to its parts. Except for the very few talented people for whom the promise of "eternal reputation" may be achieved through extraordinary intellectual or artistic achievements, for the masses the promise of immortality, of entering the pantheon of the great, is transmitted through army service and the possibility of heroism on the battlefield. It involves, therefore, a more direct invitation to exchange life in the present for the possibility of eternal memory. In all these exchanges, human time, energies, and other resources are invested in projects that transcend the life of the individual and therefore supposedly invest it with deeper meaning. As Ernst Jünger, the ideologue of German militarism remarked on the battle of Langemarck, which took the lives of 145,000 men in World War I: "Who would have thought that the sons of a materialist generation could have greeted death so ardently? . . . The result of this war cannot be anything but the recovery of a deeper Germany."

In the liberal-democratic tradition, the purpose of the attempts to separate religion from the state, and the state from hegemonic ideology, has been to emancipate the present, to resist the impulse to theologize or historicize political time, or at least to check the capacity of the government to replace accountability to the citizens with accountability to God, History, or an ideal of greatness. The basic liberal-democratic impulse (with a few important exceptions during major crises) has been to dehistoricize politics. The preoccupation of liberal-democratic governments with economic issues—unemployment, inflation, production, commerce, taxation, and public services—has drastically shortened the time frame for political action and accountability, tying political power and authority to here-and-now aspects of public affairs. As Thomas Jefferson observed to James Madison in a letter of September 6, 1789: "No society can make a perpetual constitution or even a perpetual law. The earth belongs always to the living generation."

Modern Israel has been beset by a bitter struggle between those who believe that the earth belongs to the living and those who believe that the living "belong to the earth"—that it is their duty to make sacrifices to ensure that the land under Israeli control will remain the land of the Jewish people. These opposing perspectives were most clearly articulated during the swearing-in of the Labor-led government on July 13, 1992. "We are determined to place the citizen at the top of our concerns," Yitzhak Rabin, then the new Prime Minister, told the Knesset; he went on to declare peace with the Arabs the best way to advance the security and welfare of the Israelis. It was in light of this commitment to place the individual citizen at the center that the Rabin government's emphasis on the peace process and readiness to make territorial concessions made sense. Rabin was committed to benefits that would be manifest in individual lives, not just in historic time. In his reply, Yitzhak Shamir, the outgoing Prime Minister, articulated the characteristic collectivist position, insisting that Israel is "an ideological country" guided by a vision. "We would not be able to survive for long like any other state just by concen-

trating on the welfare of the citizens," he said, and went on
to criticize the "tendency to sacrifice the future for short-term
and shortsighted achievements." Praising the political alliance
between the right wing and the religious parties during almost
fifteen years of right-wing-led coalition governments, Shamir
noted the affinities between the nationalist and the religious
worldviews, especially concerning the status of the land. The
Land of Israel, he said, "is a sacred thing," and Israelis must
guard and secure the land "entrusted to us in its entirety as
the eternal inheritance of the Jewish people." Attaching the
word "sacred" to the land, not to the life of the individual
citizen, and referring to the contested land as "*eternal* inheritance" (my emphasis), characteristically downgrades the
"present" as the context of government action. It elevates politics beyond the structures of democratic accountability to the
living. In Israel's highly ideological society, the politics of
"high missions," of "sacred principles," of "destiny," has often had greater appeal for the masses than the politics of pragmatism and present-day accountability, which for a long time
has been characteristic only of certain elites. There have always
been individuals and groups wary of idealism, mindful of the
limits of human enterprise, skeptical about promises for the
future, and therefore not disposed to seek immortality
through "noble deeds" or "noble sacrifices" on the battlefield. While, for centuries, such skepticism was confined to
limited circles in Western societies, during the later decades
of the twentieth century it has expanded to wider social circles
and penetrated more deeply into contemporary philosophy,
literature, art, and (mainly social) science. While such developments have provoked sharp political and religious reactions,
the dominant movement has been away from eschatological

politics and toward a politics attentive to the present. Although this movement has often been condemned as a symptom of selfish materialism and cultural decadence, it has in fact roots in long-standing intellectual and cultural traditions, including legal theories of natural rights and social contract, secular philosophical critiques of religion, anarchistic political ideas, ethical concepts of individual agency and autonomy, and artistic expressions of the inner, subjective self. Such cultural forms have provided spiritual rationales for this-worldly individualism, which, thus strengthened, has been less vulnerable to religious and ideological attacks.

These developments in Western culture and politics have, of course, penetrated modern Israeli society through its roots in European culture, and alliances with the United States and other Western nations. Their impact in Israel has nevertheless been severely restricted by the powerful collectivist counter-liberal orientations toward language, space, and, time. The burden of the past may be the most significant of these. While, as Alexis de Tocqueville anticipated, democratic sensibilities tend to dehistoricize politics, this process is unlikely in a Jewish polity, for throughout Jewish history in exile, the past has been the real "home" of the Jewish people, and it was this past that was used to justify the very creation of the State of Israel in the Holy Land. Thus, while an immigrant society like the United States of America has been characterized as a new beginning, a break with the European past, the "Jewish state," although founded as a break with the condition of nearly two thousand years of exile, has depended for its very legitimation upon claims of historical and cultural continuities leaping over these thousands of years back to biblical Israel.

Modern Israel, therefore, faces a dilemma: how can the present be empowered as the temporal home of democratic politics within a society that has turned collective history into civil-political theodicy and religion? In such a society the emancipation and protection of private time is almost an affront to social solidarity and an abdication of responsibility to serve the public.

While the process of dehistoricizing and de-ideologizing time has just begun, in the longer run it will deepen the foundations of freedom. An Israeli culture of the self, an Israeli individualism, and ultimately an Israeli democratic polity will depend on the extent to which forms of private time, private space, and private language become available so that the Israeli individual can develop distinctly from the group, as a voice and an agency. Ultimately a resilient Israeli democratic culture would have to be nourished by emancipated Israeli individuals capable of creating, or living in, personal narrative spaces resistant to the imperial power of the epic narratives of religion, ideology, and history.

> > > *II*

The Battle of the Stories

Self-narration as Self-defense

In *The Social Contract,* Rousseau wondered why human beings, who are naturally born free, are everywhere in chains. Part of the answer to this persistent question may be found in the great power of communal narratives. Perhaps nothing enslaves the individual more than the "high," elevating meanings a community attaches to a life of devotion to collective goals. There is no more daring and difficult act for an individual to undertake than to step outside the bounds of the prevailing universe of meaning, the institutionalized modes of ordering and interpreting experience, of reward and penalty, praise and blame. While authoritarian societies do not hesitate to use force to discipline "deviants," a subtler but no less effective way of keeping the individual in line is to downgrade the individual life which is not integrated into the communal narrative. Epic narratives do not generally encourage the expression of confusion, weakness, and fragmentation, which find their way into authentic autobiography.

Where the life of the individual is regarded as a vital resource for realizing the monumental projects of the community, where society makes the sacrifice of the individual life richly meaningful as a spiritual, ideological, or patriotic act, narratives about the private self—a perishable being, unique and precious, independent of his or her connections to the collective—can become a means of self-defense. While from the perspective of normative communal narratives the separate individual is characteristically cast as an aimlessly fallen fragment, from the perspective of democratic individualism it is the individual who is primary and the whole that is derivative. A story told in the first person singular "I" expresses the distinct reality of the individual; of the unique inward voice and language. It asserts the presence of a distinct, nonderivative perspective and, therefore, also of the claims of the individual apart from the group. In highly culturally and psychologically collectivized societies where communal narratives are often internalized through a voluntary self-effacement that facilitates the symbolic incorporation of the individual into the higher "reality" of the group, self-inscription is a subversive method of inhibiting the recruiting powers of the community. Where society forces or seduces the individual into surrendering self-authorship to the collective order, individualism may constitute what George Kateb has aptly called "defensive idealism."[1] As "defensive idealism," individualism moralizes and spiritualizes—even ontologizes—the self as a limit to what may be called the "offensive idealism" of the collective. In its deeper sense, then, self-narration expresses the claim of each of us to be the author of our own life. It implies the cultivation of the self, of the subjective person, as a protection against the moral and spiritual imperialism of society.

Although the cultivation of the self is a complex process, with-

---

[1]George Kateb, *The Inner Ocean: Individualism and Democratic Culture* (Princeton: Princeton University Press, 1993).

out it the liberal experience of freedom is inconceivable. Individuals are not born individuals. Like communities or nations, individuals too must be imagined and brought into being. As contemporary critics of individualism like to stress, each of us is born into a particular race, community, language, culture, and possibly a religion. We learn to speak a native language and think, imagine, feel, or remember within communally available forms. But the necessary role of the community in the genealogy of the individual does not foreclose the possibility of a "second birth" of the individual as a distinct voice, with its own sensibilities and moral agency. Selfhood often starts merely as an imagined possibility that gradually takes on a life of its own, like a sculpture that starts walking.

Such a "second birth," of course, is only part of the process of individuation. No less vital are the individual's acts of selection and organization of the polyphony of the voices he or she hears from within. A liberal-democratic polity depends on such acts. While even liberal societies require that the autonomy and freedom of individual citizens be balanced against minimal requirements of solidarity, the presence of a culture of individualism protects the private domain of the self from the powers of collectivism. In a society like Israel, where until recently a formal commitment to legal and political principles of individual freedom has coexisted with an impoverished culture of selfhood, the liberal-democratic façade often conceals quite an invasive collectivism.

In the context of a rich liberal-democratic culture, individualism need not be defensive. The individual can allow itself to have looser boundaries and greater internal fluidity. Not surprisingly, the more reflexive, underdetermined types of selfhood seem to flourish in free societies with long

traditions of individualism. Israel has not yet reached this
stage. It remains a society in which the multi-vocal self, or what
we have come to understand as the postmodern self, is characteristically resisted as subversive or decadent. In many respects, to be sure, the more rigidly coherent and bound the
modern self is, the more effective it is in countering invasive
collectivism. Strong individuals are better able to challenge or
check a strong group. In the long run, however, the unfixed,
reflexive, postmodern self is even more deeply resistant to un-
liberal ideological blueprints and political "engineering." As
the symbolic expression of individualism as a principle of liberal-democratic political order, the autobiographical perspective rests on the democratization of uniqueness, on the idea
that as an unrepeatable configuration of experience, emotions, sensations, thoughts, memories, biological traits, contingencies, aspirations, beliefs, and relations, each life is unique
and, therefore, invaluable; the passing of each individual is,
therefore, an irretrievable loss. The democratization of
uniqueness also means that autobiography or self-narration
presupposes the liberal aesthetic conception of each life as a
whole story unto itself, a complete self-sufficient story, not just
a fragment or a chapter in the wider, larger story of the group.
The idea of self-narration assumes that a whole universe of
meaning can reside in the identification of the narrating and
narrated "I" independent of the community of which that "I"
is also a part. When, by contrast, the individual is conceived
only as a building block of the larger collective whole, like the
soldier, the individual becomes inherently replaceable, an in-
terchangeable part and therefore ultimately dispensable. The
liberal-democratic commitment to the individual resists the
tendency to define the social whole as greater and more per-

fect than its parts. "In the sum of the parts," writes Wallace Stevens, "there are only the parts."

In the secular age, society attempts to inherit the privileged status of the divine and, as Durkheim indicated, claims to speak to the mortal individual in the voice of the immortal. From the perspective of society, therefore, the birth of the individual is not a beginning nor his death an end. Inasmuch as epic narratives are essentially social, they coax the individual into collaborating with the obliteration of his or her particularity, the silencing of his or her voice. Humility before God is replaced by humility before society or the state.

The most likely candidates for such collaboration are, of course, the tender, unformed and vulnerable young persons and the socially and educationally deprived. The former have not as yet developed a sufficient sense of self to resist the colonizing power of imperial collective narratives, while the latter have had no access to the cultural resources and technologies of individuation. Autobiographical consciousness is rarely an option of the young or the socially and culturally deprived. As a weapon of self-defense, self-narration is usually lacking where it is needed the most.

Although Israel is committed to basic liberal-democratic principles of order, such as the dignity and freedom of persons, the value of self-narration has been limited not only by the poverty of personal space, personal time, or personal language but also by the omnipresence of the collective social voice. The monumental epic of the restoration of a Jewish Kingdom in the Holy Land has generated at least three principal variants of the communal epic, each of which equates individualism with its own distinct notion of the breakdown of a lofty, idealistic enterprise. The first communal epic felt every-

where in Israel nowadays is that of Orthodox religious Zionism, which draws upon the long Judaic tradition of viewing the
individual as a member of a community of faith designated by
God to carry out a divine mission. In this narrative, the lives
of the multitude are cemented by a single superhuman author
who inscribes both nature and history; one God, one King,
one Kingdom. As a direct challenge to paganism, with its idea
of a multiplicity of gods, and kingdoms, Judaism has been a
paradigmatic expression of the attempt to privilege a single
all-encompassing master narrative, even as it attaches a unique
and universal mission to the Jews as a particular people.

Like religious Zionism, a second collective narrative—that
of national Zionism—focuses on the Jewish return to the ancient homeland. While clearly inspired by classical Jewish texts
and ideas, nationalist Zionism has drawn much of its inspira-
tion from secular European nationalism. In this narrative a Jew
is a member of a persecuted minority, and the fate of the
individual is determined by his or her membership in the
group rather than by personal resources, talents, or chance.
This Zionism cultivates the view—widely believed to have been
confirmed by the Holocaust—that individual Jews (even fully
assimilated ones) are not likely to escape persecution and even
annihilation except through a resolution of the "Jewish problem": that is, the emancipation of the Jewish people from dependence upon other, often hostile, peoples. National Zionism,
which replaces God with the nation as the principal actor, is no
more hospitable to the individual than religious Zionism. For
national Zionists, Israel is a collective enterprise of the Jewish
people, an answer to the "Jewish problem," a guard against persecution and genocide. Only secondarily is Israel a response to
or a condition for a personal quest. The liberal-democratic no-

tion of the state as the instrument of its individual citizens, a power which is constitutionally checked in order to protect rights, among other things, has certainly been present but not central in Israeli politics during its first five decades.

While the religious Zionist narrative invests the idea of return with religious significance, and the national Zionist narrative equates return with liberation as a necessary condition of Jewish survival, the third Zionist master narrative is that of socialist Zionism, which integrates the idea of Jewish return with the ideal of a socialist community. Drawing upon the traditions and texts of European socialism, socialist Zionism has brought to Israel a conception of history as a record of class wars. Partly socializing nationalist Zionism, partly nationalizing Jewish socialism, this Zionism has added another, socialist category of the collective to the religious and the secular nationalist ones.[2]

By elevating the spiritual and moral significance of the collective narrative, the religious, nationalist, and socialist Zionisms have converged in diminishing the individual. In all of these narratives, the individual in modern Israel is variously portrayed as misguided, culturally ignorant, assimilated, faithless, degenerate, materialistic, and egotistical. Against the lofty communal narratives of return, national liberation, or the building of a socialist utopia, middle-class Israeli culture has developed a bad conscience. In this view, the middle-class consists of persons who have succumbed to the lower culture of instant material gratification, corrupted by Western (particularly American) mass culture and consumerism. Inasmuch as

---

[2]On the affinities between Israeli socialism and nationalism, see Zeev Sternhell, *Nation Building or a New Society: Labor Zionism and the Origins of Israel* (Princeton University Press, forthcoming).

all three Zionist narratives have enlisted history on their side, the individual who rejects their ideals is condemned for choosing a life without purpose or vision, a life spent chained to the insignificant present.

The well-known record of Jewish liberalism in Western countries and the prominence of Jewish intellectuals among liberalism's most articulate spokespersons have encouraged the expectation that liberal-democratic individualism would flourish in a Jewish state as well. During Israel's first half century, these expectations have remained largely unfulfilled. Indeed, they may have been baseless. In many respects, Jewish liberals in the West have supported what may be called "external individualism": consisting of demands for legal rights and economic opportunities in civil society, not affirming the reality or significance of the self. These liberals characteristically drew many of their ideas from Enlightenment political and legal theories of natural rights, economic individualism, and free-market competition.

As such, in the Jewish context liberalism was more a phase in a collective national narrative about the emancipation of the Jews as a persecuted minority than a dimension of evolution within Jewish culture of the modern narrative of the self. European Jewish advocates of liberal individualism, like the prominent German Jewish philosopher Moses Mendelssohn, who fought for Jewish civil rights in the 1770s, Eduard Lasker, the German liberal leader of the end of the nineteenth century, and leading English liberals at the turn of the century like Sir Rufus Isaacs and Herbert Samuel, focused on the external legal and political emancipation of the Jew as a citizen, not on the cultivation of an internal culture of individualism among Jews. In concentrating on the legal and economic status of the individual as a bearer of rights, Jewish liberal-democratic spokespersons have often ignored the individual as a subjective self. Because of restrictions on public, social expressions of Jewish group consciousness, identity, or culture, the Jewish private home, which in normal circumstances would have been the sanctuary of the individual and the family, became the only safe space for the expression or socialization of the individual Jew as an actor in the collective narrative. This condition encouraged the nationalization of the private sphere in the Jewish context. The religious school in the Jewish Diaspora community was called *heder* (room), because it developed as an activity at the private home of the *melamed* (teacher). Hence, in a Jewish context liberalism characteristically lacked the deeper roots liberalism had in movements such as Protestantism and Romanticism, which stressed the internal, spiritual, moral, and cultural life of the self. As a matter of historical record, the identification of Jews with the legal-economic vocabularies of external individualism has made Jews a convenient target of anti-liberal critics, who have regarded liberalism as a soulless, divisive, alienating cultural or political form.

While the internal poverty of Jewish liberal individualism has persisted in its Israeli versions, the majority status of Jews has meant that the advocacy and defense of citizens' rights have been more characteristically associated with the rights of Arabs and other minorities against the Jewish majority. In Israel, then—unlike in the Diaspora—liberal positions have often been incompatible with and positively opposed to ethnocentric Jewish concerns. The Jewish commitment to the primacy of collective group narratives has also undermined liberal temporal orientations toward the present. If the life of an individual cannot be considered meaningful except in the context of collective history, one is deprived of the capacity or the right to define or represent the meaning of his or her own life. If collective memory upholds the memory of fathers and ancestors, democracy, observed Tocqueville, not only "makes every man forget his ancestors, but it hides his descendants and separates his contemporaries from him." Democratic individualism, by privileging the present, the temporal frame of the living, tends to dehistoricize the narratives of individuals and communities and their political orientations.

Together, religious, nationalist, and socialist Zionisms have combined the power of various modern Jewish epic narratives to depreciate the story of individual life and the claim that it is intrinsically valuable and complete. They have furnished a particularly rich array of orientations that obliterate the cultural resources of democratic individualism—personal languages, private calendars, private spaces, and the like. The most salient of these anti-liberal orientations include political messianism, historical determinism, utopian political engineering, and Darwinian nationalism.

Most recently, Israeli religious and political forms of messianism combined in the settlers' movement in the West Bank. Led by Gush Emunim (Bloc of the Faithful), the leaders of this movement have claimed to be the only authentic heirs of the original Zionist epic, demanding that their followers make great personal sacrifices and take great risks, including endangering the very safety of their own children, in order to settle amid a hostile Arab population in the contested territories that comprise the map of ancient ("Greater") Israel. Members of Gush Emunim have interpreted their lives and actions in terms of a redemptive communal narrative that unfolds in broad theological or eschatological time.

Not surprisingly, this disposition has involved a diminished accountability to current state law and to the government, and a profound disregard for the rules of liberal-democratic politics. Individual members of the movement often sound as if they were self-enlisted soldiers in an elite army fighting to realize a divine plan. This kind of religious-political messianism denies the very idea of the democratic state as a political organization in which the government is accountable first and foremost to its live citizens.

Historical determinism, elements of which were imported to Zionism through its socialist–Marxist wing, also undermines the integrity of the lived present by casting it as the inexorable expression of sociohistorical laws discernible in the past. The past is, in this view, pregnant with clues to the inevitable future in relation to which the present is just a bridge. Living individuals cannot usually change the course of history. The present is not a domain of creative actions that can lead to alternative possible futures. Individuals may accelerate or slow the process of change but they cannot radically alter it.

Hence also historical determinists tend to reject the voluntary theory of democratic action as an illusion. Since past events, like past class struggles in the Marxist perspective, are supposed to have foreshadowed future events, historical determinists are often engaged in reading the present or the recent past into the more distant past. Michael André Bernstein defines the intellectual operation of looking backward at the past as necessarily leading to what we know to have followed as ''backshadowing.'' ''Backshadowing is a kind of retroactive foreshadowing in which the shared knowledge of the outcome of a series of events by narrator and listener is used to judge the participants in those events as though they too should have known what was to come."[3] Based on the unwarrantable claim that the clues to what would turn out to be the future of earlier generations were already unmistakably discernable in their present, "backshadowing" serves to blame actors for actions which led to self-destruction or to credit them for actions whose effects proved salutary. As a variant of historical determinism, backshadowing, therefore, denies the conditions of voluntary and moral actions and the uncertainties and contingencies that humanize actors whose actions can both be rational and defy their intentions, actors as historically or socially situated individuals facing largely unpredictable futures. Maurice Merleau-Ponty notes that the issue of our responsibility or our irresponsibility for actions whose meaning changes over time because of new information or unanticipated contingencies is at the center of Greek Tragedy. "Oedipus did not want to marry his mother nor kill his father but he did it and what he did stands as a crime. The whole of Greek Tragedy assumes this idea of an essential contingency through which we are all guilty and all innocent because we do not know what we are doing"[4] Bernstein argues persuasively that the assumption that there are knowable deterministic causal connections between actions and events over time corrupts the value of historical accounts as descriptions of morally and psychologically credible human agencies, of actors who can act freely and responsibly, given the circumstances and levels of attainable knowledge, and still be undermined by the consequences. Ob-

---

[3]Michael André Bernstein, *Foregone Conclusions: Against the Apocalyptic History* (Berkeley: University of California Press, 1994).
[4]See citation and discussion in Timothy J. Reiss, *Tragedy and Truth* (New Haven: Yale University Press, 1980), pp. 286–90.

viously both messianism and historical determinism are profoundly antagonistic to modern democratic individualism and to the possibility and value of life as a voluntary self-narration.

Utopian political engineering, although it is basically collectivist in orientation, is less distant from democratic individualism insofar as it is open to the engagement of living individuals in actions directed to the sociopolitical order. It is, of course, incompatible with individualism to the degree that it imposes on the future a single, all-encompassing ideal. Its fixation on the future undermines the present as an open situation subject to human choices as well as to the contingencies of society, history, and nature. It denigrates life in the present as falling short of the ideal, which has not yet been realized. The rhetoric of utopianism draws much of its strength from its view of the present as a corrupt condition from which the perfect redeemed future is the only escape. While the sacrifices political utopianism demands are very real, the ideal state that it promises is remote, elusive, and mostly unrealizable.

The fourth orientation, Darwinian nationalism, obliterates the present by appropriating it as a resource for a collective war of survival. If utopian engineering has been a central element in socialist Zionist ideology, Darwinian nationalism has been a major element in right-wing Zionist movements. Because it tends to be constantly preoccupied with threats to the survival of the nation, it gives little attention to the individual as such. Its military orientation encourages constant alertness and mobilization. The life of a community organized along the lines of Darwinian nationalism resembles that of Sparta more than that of Athens. In such a society the requirements of security are always used to defer the present, to delay all the wonderful opportunities and possibilities which appear to compete for resources, which are, almost by definition, insufficient to cope with the problems of security. For the Darwinian nationalist the state is primarily a tool, a weapon of the group, not a continually created and re-created instrument of the self-government of free individuals.

The other side of the tendency of this orientation to treat the citizens as an army is to exclude members of groups whose loyalty is questionable. Darwinian nationalists are inclined to extend the war of survival from the battle against outside groups to a struggle against real or imagined internal enemies. In Israel, leaders of several right-wing parties have very frequently treated Arabs living in the state not as Israeli citizens, a minority group living among us, but as the internal arm of the external enemy. A Darwinian–nationalist conception of power and history does not cultivate much faith in the possibilities of stable compromises among nations. It tends therefore to consider peace agreements as modes of deception designed to improve one's position in the longer run. Darwinian nationalists examine history as a record of successful and unsuccessful strategies of survival. They often tend to blame those who did not survive for failing to pursue the "correct" course. Like historical determinists, Darwinian nationalists usually ignore the inherent uncertainties and contingencies which in retrospect could make actions that in fact led to failure seem rational under the circumstances. They also tend therefore to dehumanize individual human agency and question the very premises of autobiography except as a genre describing the history of the collective from the perspective of individual experience. Blanket allegations of the kind that Jews died in the Holocaust largely because they failed to read the available signs, that they were victims of their own innocence or ignorance, are, as Bernstein aptly points out, both intellectually unwarranted and morally reprehensible. They are flagrant cases of backshadowing, of retrospective determinism which in fact denies the humanity of past individual actors in relation to whom the future was, as it always is for human actors, inherently uncertain. Machiavelli, no naive observer of human affairs, had, in fact, a deeply humanistic conception of action as something always taken in the face of great uncertainties. He held, therefore, that in light of continually changing and largely unpredictable circumstances, the wisest actors could do no better than be flexible and adaptable. Anticipation is important, according to Machiavelli, but long-range planning without taking Fortuna into account is folly.

Nevertheless, the power of collective narratives to invest individual life with dense meaning that weaves it into larger forces over which the individual has little control often proves irresistible. Much of this power resides in the weaknesses and vulnerabilities of the individual, the fear of life without enduring purpose or direction, without connections to past or future generations, without criteria for positioning one's being in relation to other people, to society, or the world. Monotheistic religions and their derivative universalistic ideologies have had the compelling force of master stories that could connect the lives and times of individuals to the grander march of societies and world history.

Even where such communal narratives have recognized the tensions or conflicts between the individual and the group, they tend to treat them as failures of socialization, as problems for educators and leaders.

Against this background, the narrative structure of Greek tragedy appears again particularly intriguing. As Bernard Williams has suggested, there is an element of liberal sensibility in the refusal of the Greek tragedian to accept either a given or an achievable harmony between the individual and the world.[5] If one substitutes social reality for supernatural necessity as the inexorable constraint on the ability of the individual to control his own fate, the tragic hero represents the vulnerability of the individual to the overwhelming and often incomprehensible social forces which threaten to crush him from the outside, to the sense that there is no inherent purpose or good in terms of which the lives of all individuals can necessarily or voluntarily be harmonized, that society and politics may doom the individual to an unjust fate. Such a notion of primordial individual alienation was important for the eventual development of liberal democratic conceptions of the individual as a distinct entity. Against this alternative, the tensions between the narrative structure of monotheism and that of liberal democracy become particularly suggestive.

From the perspective of each individual, the temptation to anchor the meaning of one's life in a safe, fixed point in time—to draw a straight line from a point in the past or the future which connects that life with a larger continual narrative—is often compelling. Messianists, utopian engineers, historical determinists, and Darwinian nationalists differ only in where they place this fixed point in the flow of time and how they relate it to the present. It is as if each group started to write the book of existence in a different place. The messianists place the source of meaning in the final chapter (although

---

[5]Bernard Williams, *Shame and Necessity* (Berkeley: University of California Press, 1993), pp. 164–65.

there is some throwback to a primordial state of perfection); they start from the state of perfection at the end of time and work their way back to their lives in the present. The perfect messianic moment loads their lives with meaning, a sense of direction and hope, thus becoming the organizing principle of lived experience. The historical determinists fix the source of meaning in the past, in the first chapters of the book of existence. These early chapters determine and anticipate the logic of the present and all future historical narratives. The past reveals the laws of the unfolding narrative of life. While the messianists write their book from the end backward, the historical determinists write their book from the past into the future. The utopian engineers are, of course, closer to the messianists in measuring their lives in light of the progress toward an ideal state of affairs. The two groups tend to differ, however, with respect to the question of whether or not the ultimate state depends on the active efforts of the living. While some schools of messianism consider the devotion and conduct of the faithful causally related to the prospects of redemption, utopian engineers usually rely on a much more ideologically directed political activism. In this, Darwinian nationalists are closer to the historical determinists. They also believe in a law of history, but see it as an extension of the laws of nature. While the laws of survival are fixed, the consequences of their operation are nevertheless influenced by what human groups do or do not do. Darwinian nationalists thus have a deterministic view of the past and a more open view of the future.

By comparison with all these groups—with those who base the Book of Life on the last chapters and those who ground it in the early chapters—liberal democrats anchor the mean-

ing of the narrative in the middle chapters, in the present.
They continually rewrite the past and the future from the perspective of the present. They are the only group that has an
open conception of meaning directed simultaneously toward
the past and the future. This, of course, is the strategy that
subordinates the narrative of life to the autonomous present
and a maximalistic conception of human freedom. Such a concept of freedom sponsors a multitude of narratives of the past,
of the present, and of possible futures. The sheer plurality of
perspectives and stories undermines the mobilizing power and
authority of any single master narrative and upholds the status
of the individual as a free agency who will make choices from
among alternative forms of life.

The lack of anchorage and the absence of closure in the
liberal-democratic outlook often seem to be deeply at odds
with human needs. For most people, the tendency has been
to absorb the present within an all-encompassing view of time
as a movement extending from the past into the future—defining the present as merely the moving line separating the
two. At least until relatively recently, the notion of the present
as the temporal domain of individual lives—the notion of
"lived time"—has had very little support in the metaphysics
of dominant world cultures. And yet it is the normative superiority of the present, the care for the integrity and wholeness
of the life of the individual, that underlies liberal democracy
and its implicit conceptions of authority, accountability, and
action.

In modern Israel, the weakness and fragility of such liberal-
democratic sensibilities have left the individual particularly sus-
ceptible to the compelling force of collective religious,
nationalistic, and ideological narratives. Against such odds,

self-narration has for a long time appeared to be a losing option. It has been pointed out that, by comparison with other Western cultures, Hebrew culture from its classical period to the present, including the recent Israeli chapter, has a distinct poverty of autobiography as a viable literary genre. There are exceptions, of course: Leon Modena's *Life of Judah* (written in Venice in the seventeenth century and published only in the twentieth), the memoirs of Gluckel von Hameln, a Jewish woman living in Hamburg (written between 1691 and 1719), and Salomon Maimon's autobiography (written shortly after Rousseau's *Confessions* and under his influence). As Allen Mintz has pointed out, during the period of crisis and transition in modern Jewish culture and history—the late nineteenth and early twentieth centuries—Hebrew writers such as Feierberg, Berdichevsky, and Brenner also wrote autobiographies. Still, autobiography—as the voice of the first person singular, of the self-reflecting, self-narrating individual, not as a soldier or missionary of a particular collective—has not flourished in Jewish or Zionist culture. The most typical form of "autobiography" in modern Israel has been the political autobiography of a public figure, often composed with the help of a ghostwriter, in which the principal theme is some variant of "How I Helped Build the Country." The "autobiographies" of Moshe Dayan, Abba Eban, Shimon Peres, Golda Meir, and Yitzhak Shamir do not address the inner life of their author nor do they provide honest, reflective narrative of the writing, or speaking, self.

Alan Mintz attributes "the relative alienness of autobiography to Jewish culture" to "the secondary status of the individual in Judaism. Although the individual is responsible for his actions," he observes, "the meaning of his life is absorbed in collective structures and in collective myths. With the partial exceptions of mystical testimonies in the Kabbalistic tradition, Judaism, unlike Christianity, does not know the deeply personal experience of conversion, nor the nuanced inner drama of individual salvation."[6] As part of Western culture, many Jews were, of course, exposed to non-Jewish literary genres of self-narration. Some Jews or half-Jews, including Marcel Proust (1871–1922), have contributed to this Jewishly "external" body of Western literature. The point, however, is the poverty of this genre as an internally available form.

The Israeli "I" has generally connoted a collectivized self, a "we" of the peer group; this self's story characteristically refers to historic, not emotional, psychological, or spiritual, events. Yael Feldman, who examined the "autobiographical impulse" among modern Israeli women writers, suggests that in the 1970s and early 1980s women still preferred autobiographies disguised as fiction, and even in this tempered form "the 'self' currently constructed in Israeli fictional or disguised autobiographies is far from being 'alienated' . . . it is communal and collective rather than purely individual."[7]

In Christian societies, the idea of individual salvation—so closely associated with St. Augustine's *Confessions*, the paradigm of Christian spiritual-moral autobiography since the third century—and the preoccupation with individual acts of conversion have encouraged modes of introspection, reflection, self-examination, and moral and spiritual self-narration which

---

[6]Alan L. Mintz, *Banished from Their Father's Table: Loss of Faith and Hebrew Autobiography* (Bloomington: Indiana University Press, 1989), p. 206.

[7]"Gender Difference in Contemporary Hebrew Fictional Autobiographies," *Biography*, Vol. 2, No. 3 (Summer 1988).

enriched and consolidated the Western conception of the interior, inward self; liberal and democratic thinkers like Locke, Rousseau, and John Stuart Mill could elaborate on these "technologies of the self" as the basis of modern conceptions of individual freedoms, rights, and citizenship. Where such traditions of spiritual individualism are weak, invariably liberal-democratic individualism is depicted negatively as a form of degenerative, narcissistic, or materialistic egotism.

In modern Israel, expressions of individualism have been perceived as symptoms of the breakdown of high ideals and the disintegration of communal life, not as the inner spiritual dramas of the individual and the issues of his or her social authenticity. Studies of Israeli society and culture reinforce the observation that transparency and honesty have been connected more with an external, more social, idea of the individual than with a notion of the individual as having infinite subjective depth. Tamar Katriel, who studied Israeli "straight talk,"[8] notes that while "self-disclosure" in the course of agonizing soul talks was a known form of speech among the pioneering generation, most of whose members came to Israel from Europe and were steeped in European culture, the "straight talk," the "plain speaking," of the Israeli-born generations has been socially assertive and confrontational. *Dugri*—the Arab word adapted to signify straight talk among the Israeli-born—has by no means been a form of self-exposed soul-searching. Rather, Katriel suggests, it is characteristically simple, direct, undiplomatic, often action-oriented behavior

---

[8]Tamar Katriel, *Talking Straight: Dugri Speech in Israeli Sabra Culture* (Cambridge, England: Cambridge University Press, 1986).

innocent of probing reflection. Direct *dugri* speech has many forms. A typical illustration is: "I'll tell you *dugri* I did not like your lecture." Another example comes from an Israeli newspaper referring to the *sabra* quality of General Mordecai Gur, who was in the habit of "saying *dugri* whatever [he] thought and paid for it dearly more than once." Israeli "straight talk" seems to presuppose a trust like that of an extended family rather than inviting potentially shocking revelations among strangers-turned-intimates. It is a form of speech that is more social than personal, and its linguistic media are highly standardized.

Beyond the fact that the epic narrative of the return of the Jewish people to its ancient homeland has been thoroughly uncongenial for the evolution of an advanced culture of the self, a consciousness shaped by the tragedy of the mass destruction of European Jewry during World War II and the bloody wars of modern Israel has been particularly antagonistic to liberal-democratic conceptions of life and death. The burden of mass death seems to counter the impulse to individualize or particularize one's life and see its choices as made voluntarily. In such a climate, it is much easier to collectivize the meanings of life and death as the results of larger forces.[9]

Ruth Firer's examination of history textbooks used by Israeli grammar and high school students during the first decades of Israel's existence—roughly the years when I was a grammar

---

[9]Sidra Ezrahi has shown how the impulse to collectivize the meaning of the death of the Jews in the Holocaust underlies Israeli forms of memory and commemoration. See her "Revisioning the Past: The Changing Legacy of the Holocaust in Hebrew Literature," *Salmagundi*, special issue on "A Sense of the Past," Fall 1985–Winter 1986, pp. 245–70.

and high school student—indicates the overwhelming influence of collectivist, Zionist notions of Jewish history. Their principal theme is the hatred of Gentiles for the Jews as the primary force shaping Jewish history throughout the ages. Only following the Six-Day War does Firer discern a move toward a more pluralistic and interpretive approach to Jewish (as well as world) history, an approach that reflects a greater balance between ethnocentric and cosmopolitan views of the past.[10]

I remember my high school teacher discussing the lessons of the Dreyfus Affair, the public scandal in France between 1894 and 1906 based on the false accusation and trial of an assimilated Jewish officer who was charged with treason. It demonstrated, according to my teacher, that even Jews who want to leave their own traditions and become full members of their host society cannot escape their Jewish identity and the fate it brings them. This "lesson" was later reinforced a thousand times by other historical accounts, culminating in the Holocaust. Zionist ideology has enlisted Jewish history very selectively. The only way to escape Jewish fate was to create a Jewish state and a Jewish army, which would transform the Jews from helpless prey into citizen-soldiers capable of self-defense. In such a universe, life as self-narration, the very idea of self-authorship, could only suggest blindness or narcissism. Both death at the hands of the Nazis and liberation by means of a Jewish army were too monumental to be regarded as autobiographical events. They were not personal but collective ex-

---

[10]Ruth Firer, *The Agents of Zionist Education* (Tel Aviv: Hakibbutz Hameuchad Publishers, 1985) (in Hebrew).

periences. Perceived in such terms, Jewish history does not have much space for autobiography. The circumstances of birth, death, and survival were, of course, diverse. Often individual ingenuity and resiliency would be rewarded by survival in defiance of the general trend. But these cases were extraordinary. Like my friends, I was born into this story and took it for granted, like the sun above my head and the sea below. While it appeared to me as a rather dangerous story, a story in which a lot of innocent victims are buried, to imagine myself totally outside of that story filled me with the anxiety of the loss of home.

I was probably no older than twelve when one summer afternoon I was lying on my bed, with my eyes open but not fully awake. Suddenly I felt as if everything inside and around me had become chaotic. For a few chilling moments I must have lost my sense of time, place, and meaning. I did not recognize anything around me or remember who I was and why I was there. I'll never forget the terror as I felt I was moving in the void, without a tree, a rock, or anything to hold on to. Then, as if by a superhuman effort, I fixed my eyes first on a chair, then on a picture on the wall: a portrait of my mother as a student in Paris wearing a round hat. Bit by bit, the pieces of the puzzle began to come back together again: my father, my sister, my violin, the voices of my friends across the street, our house, Tel Aviv, the Jews, the Arabs, my anger at the Nazis, my new shoes. My anxiety gradually subsided. I knew I was saved. As an adult, I have recalled this incident again and again, but with reverse significance—as a liberating moment, a fleeting escape from my dense collectivized and historicized consciousness, a seductive invitation to a trip outside the Jewish–Zionist epic. I have remembered that moment together with the moment when I pondered the straight horizon of the sea as if they were, respectively, my flying machine and my imaginary airport, the means of temporarily becoming an outsider within my own community.

When one is ready to move away from the master narrative of one's culture, one must be prepared, in Petrarch's words, to "swim through a sea that has no floor or shore." While scary and painful, such a move is an important station on the way to the practice of life as a narrative of the self.

At first such a station appears as a lyrical niche in the epic consciousness of the age. But as the sensibilities and the appropriate linguistic means of self-expression emerge, the journey can take its fuller and longer course. One must leap through the dangerous no-man's-land of chaos and meaninglessness, to even become momentarily insane, to lose control, before one can become someone else beyond or even within one's own community. Dreading this moment and its potential implications is what keeps most human beings tightly bound to their respective communal stories.

Descartes compared the first phase of his solitary intellectual journey to the anxious experience of a lost swimmer desperately searching for a rock to stand on. The freedom and the strength to change course can sometimes be a gift provided by the contingencies of birth or social circumstances. (Some people are free because of wealth; others are marginalized because their selves are grounded in perceived anomalies such as homosexuality.) For others it may take an enormous drive, an almost masochistic effort to make themselves at least temporarily outsiders to their own communities.

The acute anxiety of the aimless fall into the void and the sense of warmth and exhilaration I felt when I recovered my anchoring narrative suggest to me the extent to which a young person is vulnerable to the seductive recruiting force of one's communal narrative, the story into which each of us is born. Like the landscapes of one's early childhood, such a narrative becomes the inner homeland. It is precisely because these stories organize our experience and become identified with our ideas of a floor or a shore that they become our means of combating chaos and emptiness. But at the same time they can easily deny us the moral and emotional powers of self-authorship. A highly developed individualism can, to be sure, contain affinities and bonds to one's own society. But without an inner space reserved for the reflexive self and the technologies of subjectification, the individual has no way to experience personal life as part of social life without denying the personal and the subjective.

In the Zionist context, the individual, the familial, and the national have all too often flowed into each other so freely as to erase the demarcation lines between "subjective" and "objective," "private" and "public."

I wonder whether my grandfather Mordechai, the Hebrew scholar-educator, was aware of the implications of his decision, soon after his arrival in Palestine from Russia at the end of the nineteenth century, to replace the Russian family name Krichevsky with the Hebrew name Ezrahi. He said to his family that whereas in Russia he was arrested and deprived of his elementary citizen's rights because of his political activities, now, in his real home, he hoped to become a full citizen (*ezraḥ*). My grandfather must have thought it important to weld his family name to the idea of citizenship. In choosing to connect the private and the public in such a way he probably could not have anticipated the ambivalence of at least one of his grandsons, who would share his enthusiasm for and commitment to the privileges of citizenship for Jews but would feel an equally insistent impulse to keep the family domain separate from the public space and public duties. Like most of his peers, my grandfather idealized the idea of the Jewish state, not exactly recognizing the value (indeed, the necessity) of the separation between family and state, individual and society, the subjective self and the citizen.

Despite a thick culture of collective consciousness, indoctrinating school textbooks, and a family name that means citizen, I had early moments of grace when I was able to transcend them. In later years, I collected these moments like pearls reserved for a precious necklace. One of them occurred around 1956, when the Israeli press (and the world press as well) was preoccupied with the Cold War and the danger of a nuclear apocalypse. One day my high school classmate Isaac (a Hungarian Jewish orphan who had miraculously survived World War II) approached me during recess and asked me in a teasing tone, "What is the difference between partial and total annihilation?" When he saw that I was hesitating to take up this riddle, he said triumphantly, "Partial annihilation is when everyone dies and I am the only survivor. Total extinction is when I die!" We both laughed. This was not a particularly grim or serious conversation. But these words stuck in my memory with a special force. They contained the inescapable thought that, from the perspective of the individual, one's own death can be imagined as the end of everything. In the Israel of those days, even to think of one's own death in apocalyptic terms could only be regarded as subversive, a bad joke.

And yet it is precisely where the individual is the ultimate source of value, where the self narrates its own life, that the death of an individual can be understood as the end of a whole story. Because death is the last chapter in one's own narrative, the chapter one can never write, there is perhaps no deeper expression of the death of the self-narrating voice than the absence of that last chapter, the absence of the last word and the silence that follows. Those who have perceived and understood the life of the individual as a kind of self-narration would be reluctant to rush in to fill this absence, to write the last chapter of the dead self on his or her behalf, or worse still, to present the form or meaning of someone's death as the key to the meaning of that person's life. Insofar as the act of dying is usually involuntary, viewing the form or circumstances of a death as a clue to the "real" meaning of a life is in fact to impose meaning on a life retrospectively, when the author is no longer alive to resist. It is the refusal to arrogate the authority to fix the meaning of someone's life and death which expresses the deepest sense of loss, the mourning of an irreplaceable singular voice. Imagine mourning Mozart by a performance of the *Requiem* which abruptly stops before the end with the last note Mozart actually composed before he was cut off by his own death. The pain of the incomplete composition, without the parts added by Franz Süssmayr, would have violated his peers' need for closure. It would have also been irreligious and aesthetically risky. But could any alternative be more human, more respectful of Mozart's unique voice, more expressive of our loss of Mozart?

It is probably a symptom of the poverty of Israeli individualism that society and its spokespersons are rarely reluctant to fix the meaning of the deaths of individual Israelis, turning the death of the individual into an event in the life of the community.[11]

The tendency to erase the self as an autonomous unit of meaning, to employ the individual in the service of the community in death just as it supposedly was in life, is, of course, more pronounced among fiercely nationalist (often also religiously committed) than among more individualistic liberal-democratic Israelis. The responses to the death of fourteen-year-old Tirza Porath, the daughter of a family of Jewish settlers in the West Bank, are revealing. In April 1988, early in the Palestinian uprising, Tirza joined a group of young Jewish settlers for a hiking trip in the surroundings. While such hikes were a natural part of the life of Israeli youth, they had taken on added significance in the West Bank as bold assertions of the settlers' claims to make their home on these lands taken by the Israeli army during the Six-Day War (1967). From the beginning of the Intifada, such trips became much more risky for the children but ideologically much more important in the eyes of the settlers. It was common, therefore, to make sure that the young hikers were accompanied by armed guards, and so they were in this case.

Within a few minutes of the hikers' approach to the Arab village of Beita, some Palestinian youths attacked them with a barrage of stones. The confrontation between the two groups

---

[11] By comparison with death in war the victims of car accidents usually provide the perfect example of meaningless death unmarked by monuments and commemorations. Recently, however, Israeli media started to recite the names of accident victims and print detailed stories of their life and death, enlisting their personal tragedy in socially meaningful campaigns for road safety.

quickly escalated into a shooting incident which left one Arab and one Jew dead. The Jew was Tirza Porath. Her death caused shock throughout the country. Leading spokesmen for the settlers and the right insisted that the incident demonstrated that the Intifada was not prolonged civil disorder but war. Thus it warranted the full application of the IDF's military force—a policy basically rejected by the Israeli army on the grounds that the rebellious Palestinians were civilians (children and women by and large), not soldiers in uniform.

Tirza Porath's funeral was held shortly afterward. It turned out to be a major media event. Thomas L. Friedman, the chief *New York Times* correspondent in Israel at the time, covered the funeral and phoned me shortly afterward to share his puzzlement. The key speaker at the funeral, the right-wing Knesset member Rabbi Haim Druckman, had delivered a fiery, ideological speech attacking the Arabs and declaring that "the village of Beita must be wiped off the face of the earth." When he finished, the mourners responded with a storm of applause. This response struck Friedman as extremely odd. "Applause at a Jewish funeral?" he asked. "What is going on here?" Friedman's report appeared in *The New York Times*. With reference to the applause, he wrote that "it is not that they did not genuinely mourn the girl" but they were celebrating "the birth of a symbol." Within a few hours of the incident, Tirza became a flag of the settlers' "army," a martyr in the settlers' war to appropriate the occupied territories as their home.

After the seven days of mourning for the dead girl, Tirza's father was interviewed on Israeli television. He looked grim, talking to the reporter while walking on the contested land of his settlement. In response to a question, he said that his daughter was born there fourteen years ago, to make the point that the settlers intended to stay there, and that she had died there for the same cause. I found myself wondering whether anyone had mourned for Tirza's private self. What had she been like as a person, aside from the ideological significance of her birth and death? What/whom had she loved? What had she liked to do? What sort of personality did she have? None of those aspects of her life was conveyed in the news report. The symbolism of her birth and death eclipsed everything else.

I have no doubt, of course, that Tirza's close relatives and friends mourned for the real person behind the symbol. The point is that the impulse to convert Tirza Porath into a martyr of the settlers' movement was overtly checked neither by an impulse to see and present the person behind the symbol nor by any attention to the details of Tirza's death. If the settlers and other nationalist spokesmen had been more restrained in their rush to convert the dead girl into a flag, they would not have been so humiliated when the army published its report on the incident. The report established that Tirza was not killed by a bullet shot by an Arab, but by "friendly fire" accidentally shot from the gun of a settler who served as the hikers' guard. Since the girl had been shot to death by a Jew, she could not continue as a symbol of the settlers' plight as victims of Palestinian aggression. The loss of Tirza Porath the symbol was so sudden and painful that a few ministers of the incumbent right-wing government, unwilling to accept the army report, decided to undertake an investigation of their own.

The sad story of this innocent girl illustrates the power of collective narratives—in this case, a narrative of the radical Israeli right—to impose themselves on reality. It indicates the speed with which those who promulgate these narratives cull the facts that do not fit so that the narratives have clarity and force as well as symbolic import. The contradictions between the story that mobilized the settlers and the irrefutable facts made public by the army a few days later did not give the settlers' story a chance. In time, of course, a series of brutal killings of Israeli settlers in the West Bank provided genuine alternatives to the story of Tirza's death. But the story of Tirza Porath illustrates the resiliency of the settlers' narrative as a source of meaning for individual lives and deaths.

The propensity to turn the dead into political symbols does not exist only within the Israeli right. On the left, the assassination of Yitzhak Rabin involved a two-stage process of symbolization—before his death and after it. Before the assassination, the extreme right had launched a comprehensive campaign of vilification against Rabin, welding the private person and the public personality into a composite symbol of betrayal. Then the slaying of this leader who had been made into a symbol of evil generated counter-acts of canonization. The reconversion of Rabin into a martyr in the battle for peace and an icon of democratic values was too widespread and spontaneous to be attributed strictly to his supporters on the left. The left played a leading role in this process; nevertheless, at least among Israelis committed to liberal-democratic ideas, such a tendency is restrained by aversion to the transfiguration of dead persons into symbols. The cult of martyrs in politics involves the kind of emotional appeal that subverts the liberal political temper and undermines liberal-democratic norms of discourse and solidarity. The canonization of Yitzhak Rabin, therefore, will meet with some resistance in liberal-democratic circles.

The assassination of a leader of the Peace Now movement during a demonstration in front of Prime Minister Menachem

Begin's office on February 10, 1983, furnished an earlier illustration of the point. (The reader should be aware of the
fact that I was personally involved in this case.) Following
the Sabra and Shatila massacre, in which Lebanese Christians
murdered Palestinian refugees in a region under the control
of the invading Israeli army, the Begin government was
compelled by domestic and international public opinion to
appoint a national commission of inquiry under the
chairmanship of Supreme Court Justice Yitzhak Kahan. The
report of the Kahan Commission a few months later asserted
that while Christian Lebanese Arabs had done the actual killing, the IDF Regional Command, which controlled the area,
bore some indirect responsibility. The commission also
strongly criticized Defense Minister Ariel Sharon for his conduct in the affair, thus increasing already mounting public demand for his removal from office. The Israeli cabinet was
scheduled to meet on February 10 amid rumors that the opposition to his removal within the cabinet might prevail. Leaders of the Peace Now movement decided to demonstrate in
front of the Prime Minister's office during the meeting in order to call for Sharon's resignation. I personally objected to
the timing of the demonstration, thinking it wiser to wait for
the cabinet decision and then respond to it if necessary, and
elected to stay home. Those who did march to the Prime Minister's office later reported that antagonistic crowds had attacked them all along the way. Shaken by outraged domestic
and world public opinion provoked by the Sabra and Shatila
massacre, leaders of the right who had initiated the Lebanese
invasion accused the Israeli peace movement of betrayal. The
deep rift and hostility between these opposing factions in the
Israeli public raised fears of imminent violence.

Still, the early reports on that evening's news bulletin were shocking. A hand grenade thrown into the Peace Now demonstration exploded, killing one demonstrator and wounding scores of others. I drove immediately to the nearby hospital which had admitted the casualties. Many of my friends were standing near the reception area, where we learned that the dead person was Emil Grunzweig, an active leader of the Peace Now movement and a graduate student of mine at the Hebrew University. At the site of the demonstration, hundreds of people stood silent, in shock, near the spot where Emil had been struck down. The stones were stained with his blood and that of his wounded friends. I stood there in disbelief. The pain of Emil's death (not yet officially confirmed) mingled with anger toward leaders of the right, who for months had incited public opinion against the peace movement. (Years later the murderer confirmed their influence on him.)

Looking at the pink Jerusalem stones which had turned red with blood, I recalled that just three days earlier Emil had come to my office at the Hebrew University of Jerusalem and submitted his master's thesis. The thought of reading it with the knowledge that he was dead made me sick. And yet I felt compelled to read it within the next few hours, as if there were still a chance to exchange a few last words with Emil before he left us altogether. The paper was a critique of positivist notions of discourse and objectivity and their relevance to resolving conflicts of opinion in the public sphere. Reading it in my office on Mount Scopus the next morning, I spotted, at the end of a brilliant discussion of the works of Jürgen Habermas and Karl Popper, a quote from Popper that Emil had highlighted: "The great tradition of Western rationalism is to fight our wars by means of words, not swords." Emil had glossed it as follows: "This sentence expresses the faith that without universal standards for rational choice among competing propositions, the speaker becomes the only source of authority for his own propositions, and a resolution of the conflict can be achieved only by annihilating or silencing adversary spokesmen."

I froze reading these lines. Emil had become an instant example of the substitution of swords for words, of the physical clash among people for the clash of ideas. It was almost impossible not to think of his assassination as a warning to an entire country facing a choice between persuasion and assassination.

In retrospect I realized that during the first few days following the killing I had unthinkingly collaborated with the demand to turn Emil into a martyr of the peace movement, a symbol of the excesses of the campaign of vilification waged by Israeli nationalists against Peace Now and its leaders. By commenting in interviews on the connection between Emil's essay and the form of his death, I was clearly building Emil as a hero of free speech and the peace movement. The impulse to infuse Emil's assassination with political significance was reinforced by continued attacks from the right. Even during the funeral procession from Jerusalem to Haifa, a few cars loaded with smiling, cheering youth passed by.

At the grave site, Emil's mother called on both the right and the left to respect the privacy of the family in mourning. It was as if the family felt it had to protect the space of personal bereavement against these overwhelming forces which were treating Emil as a political symbol—the forces that had prevailed in the case of Tirza Porath.

I realized the ill effects of making dead persons into symbols a few days after the killing. My daughter Talya, then twelve, came home from school with tears in her eyes. One of her classmates had told her that Emil was a traitor who deserved his lot. Another girl had told her she heard that "Emil was killed by a hand grenade he was hiding in his own pocket." Israeli newspapers reported similar voices in other places. Obviously the ideological imagination, the capacity to view Emil not as a member of "our family" but as an enemy, could stifle the flow of any feelings of sorrow over the dead person or of compassion for his relatives and friends. It was particularly shocking to see children dehumanizing the deaths of people by viewing them as symbols. The point is not only that we cannot feel anguish when the dead person is made a symbol of an enemy or adversary group. We efface their particular traits and ignore the circumstances of their lives that do not fit our image of them; by dressing them up in ideology against their will, we even find it easier to shoot them. It is as if our basic solidarity as mortal human beings is eclipsed by our narrow, contesting, factional claims as members of ideological or political groups. Talya, who had seen Emil at our home and who, like us, was shocked by the assassination, could not rest in the face of the discrepancy between her innermost feelings and the responses of her friends. I decided to call her teacher, who was aware of the conflicting reactions among the schoolchildren. She invited me to talk before Talya's class.

In the days before my appearance, I agonized over whether I could bridge the gap between the two Emils. It seemed a task beyond my powers. I decided to avoid the temptation to present Emil as a model citizen in order to counter the right-wing stereotypes of Emil as a typical left-wing traitor, a disloyal citizen who "loved Arabs more than his Jewish brothers." Granted, he had fought with a combat unit in Lebanon in a war to which he fiercely objected. He would insist in private conversations that our rights as citizens to protest and criticize government policies depend, among other things, upon our readiness to serve as regular and reserve soldiers and follow the orders of our democratically elected government even when we thoroughly disagree with them. But I wanted to take Emil out of this debate altogether. As arranged, I came to the school a couple of mornings later and was introduced to the schoolchildren as a friend and former teacher of Emil. I spoke for twenty minutes about the circumstances of Emil's birth in Romania just two years after the end of World War II, the wanderings of his family between several continents, his child-hood insistence that he come to Israel, a dream he had real-ized in 1963. I described Emil's work with underprivileged children, his relations with the four-year-old daughter he'd left behind, the objects and pictures I'd seen in his boyhood room (a room which his mother had left unaltered when he went into the army), his life in the kibbutz, his participation in my classes at the university, our short trips between classes to an Arab bread store near Nablus Gate. I recalled his anxieties, his hopes, his delicate handwriting; his piercing yet soft gaze—I described what it felt like to realize that all these had suddenly come to an end in that spot where Jerusalem stones were painted with his blood.

Then I stopped. All the students were silent. Some fixed their eyes on the wall. Others looked out the window or at the floor. Were there any questions or comments? the teacher asked. There were none. I quietly left the room. Later in the day Talya told me the two girls who had spoken scornfully of Emil earlier in the week came to her separately and apologized.

A year later, the Hebrew University of Jerusalem published a small book in Emil's memory, entitled *Truth, Free Speech, and Democracy*. It contained selections from Emil's articles, and essays by me and two other Hebrew University scholars. These were focused on the historical and philosophical issues raised by the assassination, not on Emil or the peace movement. Even so, during the time of the Likud governments, schoolteachers were advised not to use it in classes because of its "political connotations."

In subsequent years, memorials to Emil have been characterized by attempts to resist the conversion of this young man into a symbol. The peace movement spokespersons, for example, refrain from building up Emil's life story and fight the impulse to claim to speak on his behalf. His soul was too complex and restless, his mind a battlefield of competing ideas, his life a constant struggle between opposing voices, and Peace Now has been too individualistic to allow for the notion that Emil continues to live on in the spirit of the movement. It is as if his death has come to be perceived as silencing forever the only voice that could have spoken in his name.

Even those of us who have tried to rescue Emil the person from Emil the symbol are not just following personal feelings. We are also reacting against the symbolic appropriation of death as the most characteristic style of the nationalists. That is, we are acting on a shared ideological commitment of our own: a commitment to the idea that what is unique about a person, even the way a person dies, imposes limits on the authority of any person or group to interpret the meaning of that life. Like bereaved parents of fallen soldiers who protest state acts of appropriating their children's memory for "history" because they cannot bear to see them depersonalized, we have reacted against the pain of seeing Emil's memory turned into an abstraction. Ironically, then, in a sense we have made Emil into a symbol of our commitment to liberal-democratic values. On the one hand, deploying individual narratives enables us to resist the forces that would temper the harsh facts and pain of death by flooding it with moral, social, or ideological meaning. On the other hand, our attempts to preserve our personal recollections of the facts of Emil's life and death—unique, contingent, ambiguous, discrete, even trivial and accidental—have gained in significance for those of us who regard these features as fences against the invasion of communal narratives.

In the end the most intimate and painful moment of grief came to me not at Emil's funeral, nor when I spoke to Talya's classmates, nor when I stood where Emil was murdered and looked at the garden the city of Jerusalem had built in his memory, nor even when I read his brilliant paper a few hours following his death. It was a few months later, when one of Emil's closest friends opened my office door and handed me a book I had lent Emil three days before he was killed, following a discussion on his dissertation topic. The friend had found the book in Emil's Jerusalem apartment and inside it were several strips of paper on which Emil had jotted his reflections on the pages he had read. They were written in pencil in his delicate handwriting. These were the last traces of his thought. I closed the book with the notes inside and put it among my books on a shelf close to my desk. It has stood there for more than a decade now, unopened like a scar, my private commemoration of Emil's thoughts, of a conversation suddenly cut off.

> > *6*

Father's Milk: Father's Tales That Feed and Kill

"Mothers poison their infants with their milk," read a shocking newspaper headline some years ago. The newspaper reported the finding of dangerous levels of DDT and other pesticide-related poisonous chemicals in the milk of breast-feeding mothers in some regions of North America. Below the headline there was a drawing of a mother nursing her innocent-looking, totally trusting baby. In the delicate features of the mother gently pressing her baby's head against her nipple, her neck bent slightly in a graceful gesture of giving, her eyes half closed and her long hair casually falling on her exposed shoulders, there radiated love, youth, and serenity, which were violently shattered by an emblem of a skull and crossbones engraved on her breast. The notion that a mother's milk can be a deadly poison, the idea of "black milk," of nursing as killing, is jolting.[1] This was one of those moments when the Western public was moved to take environmental hazards seriously.

If the idea of poisonous mother's milk is so disturbing, why

---

[1] The oxymoron "black milk" is associated with Paul Celan's most-quoted poem, "Todesfuge."

do we accept as natural the poisonous "milk" on which fathers often nurse their sons: the tales they tell them about the great heroic wars they or their fathers fought, in which glorious warriors sacrificed their lives? Why has it been so easy to accept, even to celebrate, stories that bind the souls of tender, impressionable boys, stories in which these very boys, after just a few years, may die so meaningfully, so honorably, heroically? Haven't fathers always told their sons about storming horses in the night, about sailboats in the eye of the storm, about guns and honor, or, like Daedalus, about daring flights across the skies? Surely a father's tale, like a mother's milk, is the juice of life that nourishes a son's soul, that feeds a boy's dreams of glorious actions in great and trying times and places, that teaches the boy of love and hate, of friends and enemies, and shapes his emotions and notions about homeland and the past. Yet stories like these, the very stories that bind sons to their fathers, can also poison and kill.[2] Even fathers sometimes behave as if their children are meant to be merely the instruments or vessels of their stories. There is a Sanskrit saying, writes David Shulman, which goes: "A person

---

[2]In September 1995, when Tnuva, the largest Israeli dairy cooperative and symbol of the fathers' pioneering ethos, was charged with concealing the use of carcinogenic components, the metaphor of poisonous father's milk became almost literal. Decades of Tnuva commercials referred to the mythological, healthy-looking Israeli-born boy as a "product" of Tnuva's milk. In response to the scandalous exposure, Doron Rosenblum, a noted Israeli columnist, wrote: "We have nothing left of our dreams and desires, no socialism, no 'purity of arms,' no safe buses and no Tnuva. The children of Tnuva have forever lost their trust in the motherly company which nursed us as children." *Ha'aretz*, September 15, 1995, cited and discussed in Uri Ram, "Identity and Memory: The Sociology of the Debate among Israeli Historians," *Theory and Criticism* (Vol. 8, Summer 1996) (in Hebrew).

without a son has no path."[3] A man without a son to hear his story, writes Shakespeare, is but a "brief candle," like Macbeth, a man who can produce only "a tale told by an idiot, full of sound and fury, signifying nothing."

The other side of this broken bond is, of course, a son without a storytelling father. Hamlet is an orphan searching in vain for his father's story, for the clue to life, to action, to his own lost sense of direction. We learn from Odysseus' son, Telemachus, that sometimes a son has to find his father's story before he can find his father. When he does, the story is what binds them. "I count on you to bring no shame on your forefathers," says the returning father to his son at the end of the *Odyssey*. "If you are curious, Father," says the son, "watch and see." While mother and son bond physically and emotionally through the acts of birthing and nursing, fathers are more physically remote and uncertain. Whereas birth is often public, conception is characteristically hidden. When Telemachus is asked, "Are you Odysseus' son?" he answers, "My mother says I am but I do not know." This uncertainty that father and son share about their connection makes them anxious and leads them to search for evidence of that connection. The stories fathers tell and sons adopt are ways for them to constitute or confirm their bond. In the *Odyssey*, the son's search for evidence of filial links starts when friends or acquaintances make allusions to the physical resemblance of the son to the absent father. As Telemachus grows, claims of resemblance extend from physical traits to virtues, like the son's debating skill,

---

[3]David Shulman, *The Hungry God: Hindu Tales of Filicide and Devotion* (Chicago: University of Chicago Press, 1993), p. 53.

courage, and wisdom. Ultimately, Odysseus and Telemachus are bonded as the son joins the father's fight in the final episode of his story.

The tales fathers tell are the place where sons capture the wind that blows their sails; they are the way fathers seed their lives against death. When Medea wants revenge for Jason's infidelity, she puts an end to his story by killing his (their) children. She extinguishes his future both in his lifetime and beyond. Medea recognizes the relation between the stories of fathers and the deaths of sons. Fathers not only feed their sons on their tales;[4] they also feed their tales on their sons. A son who gives meaning and life to his father's story can be consumed in its enactment. Such stories are born out of loss.[5] Fathers' stories are born out of the sin of killing the sons.[6]

The trade-off between the enactment of powerful narratives and the risking of lives may reflect, in fact, a deep anxiety connected with the links between art and violence, the impulse to impose meaning on experience, to shape or transform reality, and the risks of the costs of using power to sculpt life. Children are the "coins" with which fathers buy the power to shape history and society. Isn't the binding of Isaac a tale of a father binding his son to his own story, a father ready to sacrifice his son to uphold the promise of a tale? Does this story

---

[4]See an excellent discussion on this theme in Bennett Simon, *Tragic Drama and the Family: Psychoanalytic Studies from Aeschylus to Beckett* (New Haven: Yale University Press, 1988). This book as well as many conversations with Bennett and his wife, Robbie, informed my reflections on the themes of this and other chapters.
[5]Shulman, *The Hungry God*, p. 116.
[6]With reference to Medea, it can be argued therefore that in enlisting the sacrifice of the children to her tale she is usurping a paternal prerogative.

suggest that life has a mission greater than life itself? At the least, it suggests that there are things more important to fathers than even the lives of their children.

Judaism invests the passing of "the story" from fathers to sons with a special urgency. The Passover Haggadah is an instructive illustration. It was composed, in fact, as a pedagogic device for telling "the story" of the Exodus to the very young. Words are joined to symbolically constructed food and ritual acts in order to ensure the passing on of the narrative. Cast as a tale fathers tell their sons, it directly addresses the questions sons may raise in order to instruct the fathers how to respond. The tale that binds fathers and sons is in turn nourished and upheld by the force of paternal authority. The centrality of the father in breeding both children and stories is embodied, of course, in the very language of the relations between "the Lord our Father and the children of Israel." The scene at the foot of Mount Sinai is about the binding of an entire people to a noble yet risky and burdensome story, a story they are compelled to accept by their fear of God, their father.

The convergence between a son's commitment to his father and to the stories his father tells weaves familial loyalties into tribal-religious ones. It is such convergence of the loyalty to our God, to "our father our King" (*Avinu malkenu*), to our ancestors, to our immediate fathers, and to our communal narrative (inscribed in the Bible) which has made the children of Abraham into the "people of the book." Modern Israel has tried to develop a secular version of this traditional Jewish model.

The fathers—whether Zionist pioneers, natives, or immigrants—came with an epic story which the children were expected to subscribe to and then enact as soldiers. Although Zionism was in the main a *secular* national liberation movement informed by a powerful Enlightenment criticism of religion and traditional Jewish society, the State of Israel has drawn much of its power and authority from the religious sources of Orthodox Judaism. Time and again political leaders have invoked religious texts, symbols, and approaches to substantiate the call for loyalty and sacrifice.

In the years prior to the establishment of the state, one could already discern the impulse to appropriate the Passover Haggadah for the secular Zionist ethos. In the 1930s, several kibbutzim rewrote the Haggadah as a spring nature festival. Immediately following the establishment of the state, the Israeli Ministry of Education suggested adapting the Passover Haggadah and the Passover dinner as a model for a festive family celebration of the theme of freedom on the eve of Independence Day. In 1952, the Israeli army asked the Israeli writer Aharon Megged to write a Haggadah for Independence Day for use in army ceremonies. He was expected to introduce new content into the traditional Haggadah form, rewriting the text as a secular modern epic of national liberation. In the long run, such deliberate attempts to develop secular Israeli cultural forms that are distinct from, or even alternative to, the traditional religious ones have not been successful. Independence Day did emerge as a civic holiday but one whose characteristics are closer to a street festival and a mass-media event than a home celebration. But Passover and the other traditional Jewish holidays maintained their supremacy. In retrospect, it appears that until very recently the attempts to use Judaism to legitimate and inspire the Jewish nation-state were more successful than the attempts to evolve a distinct culture that rests on secularized versions of collective identity.

The army Passover Haggadah is an illuminating example. As of this writing, the texts and rituals of Passover within the Israeli army reflect the convergence of the religious and the state narratives. While the text of the Haggadah distributed to Israeli soldiers reproduces the traditional text, it begins with an introduction in which the Chief Military Rabbi links the religious story with contemporary history. "This holiday of liberation has particular significance for you, Israeli soldiers," he writes, "since you are the vanguard carriers of the flag of the nation's freedom and the defenders of its values in this generation. This fact requires constant reflection on the part of the people, on how we can simultaneously realize our spiritual and national missions." This fusion of religion and recent political history within the Israeli army turns a classical religious text designed to impart Jewish fathers' notions of the holy history of the tribe to their children into a device for translating the fantasies of once powerless fathers into the actions of their armed sons. The sons are urged not just to know and "remember" but to act and so add another glorious chapter to the master narrative of the nation. The arming of the Jews suddenly literalizes a classical religious text and an ancient ritual, turning it into a call for action. For truly secular Israelis, this is scandalous, yet for the majority the convergence of the religious and national narratives has appeared natural. To most Israelis, to be Jewish means to be loyal to one's family, one's nation, and one's religion or culture. Thus the army rabbi who sits in his uniform at the head of the table during the Passover Seder on the military base is a composite persona constructed by Israeli culture that can speak to the soldiers in the combined voices of religion, the army, the state, and, most important, the father in whose chair he sits and whom he replaces at the head of the table for all those soldiers who do not celebrate the holiday at home.

When Israeli soldiers are sworn in at the end of basic training, they stand in rows holding a gun in one hand and "the Book" in the other. Like the Passover Haggadah, the Bible which the army distributes to Israeli soldiers contains an introduction by the Chief Military Rabbi. The title page is decorated with the insignia of the twelve army corps, alluding to the twelve tribes of Israel. The center of the page reads "To the Soldiers of the Israeli Defense Forces," and at the bottom the words "The Chief Military Rabbinate" appear around an illustration of the Tablets, the insignia of the military rabbinate. In the introduction, the Chief Military Rabbi asserts that "the Book of books, the treasure of the nation, and the source of its life is our ownership deed for this land, the property of our forefathers."

Even as the voices of God, state, and father have converged, modern Israel has also unleashed forces which work to keep them apart. The concepts of Israel as a Jewish state and as a democracy imply distinct relations of fathers, sons, and their stories. In a genuine democracy, all generations, indeed all individuals, are considered authors or co-authors of the stories of their lives. The state is charged with protecting the integrity of the public sphere as an arena for the free competition of alternative scenarios and narratives. In contrast to democracy, in what may be called an "ethnocracy," the rule of one people, sons are the servants, warriors charged with enacting the current chapter of a narrative authored by the fathers.

At the core of the Zionist movement as a revolution of sons against tradition and the authority of their fathers, there is profound anxiety. Can rebellious sons generate an authoritative alternative tradition? How can sons who abandoned their fathers have loyal sons? There is, of course, a striking analogy between the dilemma of the revolutionary as a father and the dilemma of Abraham, forefather of the Hebrews. Abraham is first Avram, the rebellious son who denounces the authority and the gods of his pagan father, Terah, and leaves to follow the voice of his own God to the Promised Land. Then Avram becomes *Avraham*, the sacrificing father. Does his binding of Isaac relate to his rebellion against his own father? A son who chose to abandon his father must be concerned with the possibility of facing the same break of intergenerational continuity and loss of progeny. Abraham's God addresses this issue in the principal theme of his blessing of the rebellious son: "I will make you into a great nation."

But Isaac is born to Abraham and Sarah only late in their lives, and the problem of faith in the creation of a new tradition remains. First Abraham fears having a story while lacking a son; then he is, perhaps, anxious about a son who, like himself, might not adopt his father's story. In the Akeda (the Binding of Isaac), Abraham symbolically binds his son to his story, at the very risk of the son's life. Henry Abramovitch aptly observes that Abraham has enacted "the symbolic death of Isaac as merely a biological son, but confirmed him in the role of a prophet successor chosen by God to carry out their covenant."[7] The Binding of Isaac is loaded with the tensions fathers have in keeping both their stories and

---

[7]Henry H. Abramovitch, *The First Father, Abraham: The Psychology and Culture of a Spiritual Revolutionary* (London: University Press of America, 1994).

their sons alive. The very stories that give life to the sons can also kill them.

Zionism has been a movement of rebellious sons who became sacrificing fathers, sons and daughters who broke away from their parents and became the pioneers and then the founding parents of the state, who created the army and sent their sons to fight on the battlefields of the Middle East. As the voices of the fathers and the state merged, to be a loyal son meant to be a loyal citizen, and family bonds became inseparable from the internalized national epic. During the early wars, as the children raised on the Zionist narrative began to die in the thousands, their own agony and ambivalence were largely repressed (although echoes are discernible in poems and stories written during the War of Independence of 1948 and shortly thereafter). As the fathers sought to glorify and aestheticize the sons' heroic sacrifices, among the surviving sons themselves there was a terrifying silence. Only a few resisted the celebratory praises of the proud parents; only a few acknowledged that the fathers' story of return, redemption, and liberation was also a story of conquest, displacement, oppression, and death.

Eventually—especially since the Yom Kippur War of 1973, and more dramatically since the invasion of Lebanon in 1982—the Israeli willingness to accept unqualified redemptive versions of Zionism has begun to erode. Younger generations of Israeli-born soldiers and citizens have begun to claim the right to co-author, even rewrite, the story rather than merely to enact it. But the convergence between the voices of the fathers and those of the state has imposed overwhelming difficulties on such claims. In the Israeli psyche, the weak boundaries between the family and the state have enabled the paternalist state to change places with the patriotic father and speak with his authority and presumed concern. This metaphoric shift has become quite literal at times. Joshua Durban and Phyllis Palgi describe an Israeli boy, Boaz, whose father was killed in the Lebanese war in 1982, when he was just three years old. The Ministry of Defense's department for the treatment of bereaved families characteristically showered much attention and support on the boy and his widowed mother, assigning a social worker to the boy, for example. Not surprisingly, Boaz developed a strong emotional attachment to the "Ministry." "His love and longing for his dead father," Durban and Palgi observed, "were projected on the Ministry of Defense personnel," who clearly had entered the space left empty by the death of his father. In later years, when the widow wanted to travel abroad with her son and a friend, Boaz was reluctant to leave behind "his Ministry of Defense."[8] When Golda Meir was Israel's Prime Minister, she referred to the soldiers whose lives she put at risk as "her children." She cultivated the image of the Prime Minister as a mother, seeing no tensions between the relations of mother and sons, and Prime Minister and soldiers. This harmony between the family and the state was first challenged when the negligence and tragic errors of Meir's government prior to the costly (and possibly preventable) Yom Kippur War were disclosed. The process only deepened during controversies under the successive Likud-led governments, which were responsible for both

---

[8]Joshua Durban and Phyllis Palgi, "The role and function of collective representations for the individual during the mourning process: a case of a war-orphaned young boy in Israel," an unpublished paper, Dept. of Behavioral Sciences, medical school, Tel Aviv University, 1990.

the tragic invasion of Lebanon and the deployment of massive military forces to back the controversial settlements in the West Bank. Labor, liberal, and democratic circles grew alienated from nationalist policies (especially in the West Bank), and this was later complemented by even deeper nationalist alienation from the policies of the peacemaking Labor government following the 1992 elections.

During the 1990s, then, convergence between the narratives of the state and the family have been questioned more and more. This process is probably one of the most significant developments in the culture and politics of modern Israel. It is instructive to see how such change has taken shape in the inner lives of individual Israelis. Individuals like Erez H.

One evening during the Six-Day War, Erez, nearly seven years old, was taken aside by his caretaker (*metapelet*) in the children's home in Kibbutz Ein Shemer and told, "Yesterday in the battle for Jerusalem your father, Amnon, was hit by a shell and killed!"[9] Erez went back to his room, slipped into his pajamas, and went to bed. He has no memory of anything in his life from that moment until several years later. Erez denied his father's death for many years. He refused to join the rest of the family and their friends in the annual visits to his father's grave at the military cemetery on Mount Herzl in Jerusalem. When Amnon was killed, Erez's mother, Edna, was twenty-seven years old and pregnant with Shlomit, the daughter Amnon would never see. Immediately and for a long time

---

[9]It was common at that time for children of the kibbutz to be raised as a group by the *metapelet* in the children's home, a practice that reflected the kibbutz movement's ideological commitment to weakening private family values and cultivating equality and communitarianism.

thereafter, the personnel of the Department of Rehabilitation and Immortalization (*mahleked shikum vehantzah*) of the Ministry of Defense and Amnon's comrades from the paratrooper unit showered their support on the family: moral support, financial support, medical help, and the advice of social workers and therapists. Because Amnon and Edna were kibbutz members, Amnon's death had not caused financial hardship. Still, the ministry's financial support was welcome. In addition, representatives of government and voluntary organizations began bringing Erez and his brother Tzuk and sister Shlomit presents and taking them to concerts and plays. The Ministry of Education sent books on Jewish heroism, and the army sent photo albums depicting monuments to fallen soldiers, important battles, and medals of honor. The paratrooper division organized trips, memorial meetings, and other gatherings for Amnon's and other bereaved families. Every year the Department of Rehabilitation and Immortalization sent the children birthday cards.

A birthday card the army sent to Erez on his thirteenth birthday—depicting the army as a mother or an older sister.

Ein Shemer erected a monument to Amnon and Hanan, another kibbutz member killed in the war. From that moment, all local commemoration ceremonies for Amnon were joined with those of Hanan. Erez notes in retrospect how his father's individuality was erased as the plural pronouns began to dominate the language of commemoration. "It was my father who died," says Erez, "but in the commemorations people did not say 'he died,' but 'they died, they sacrificed, they, they!' " On memorial days the two families became a sizable group of people who drove to Jerusalem in several cars as in a convoy.

Gradually Erez began reading about his father in memorial publications and in articles published in newspapers during memorial days. He actually began to look forward to radio and television programs which were likely to mention his father and the battle in which he died. Like Telemachus, he began to search for the details of the story of his absent father. He harbored a secret hope that warriors like his father could not really perish and would come back one happy day. His family and friends kept telling him how much he resembled his father. He wanted what everyone seemed to expect of him: to be like his father. As the oldest child, he gradually assumed some paternal responsibilities toward his younger brother and sister, and grew more and more protective of his mother and their home. He recalls writing a composition at school about the Six-Day War, referring to the combatants in the third person plural. He wrote about the hostility of the Arabs and the bravery of the Israelis, not mentioning his personal loss. "Very nice," wrote the teacher at the bottom of the page.

When he was eighteen, of course, Erez was conscripted to the Israeli Defense Forces. Although sons of fallen soldiers may choose to serve in noncombat units, Erez decided to become a paratrooper like his father. In such cases, the army requires the mother to give written permission for her son's decision. Nobody seemed able to oppose—no one wished to

oppose—Erez's almost deterministic journey in his dead father's footsteps. Edna signed the release. The convergence between Erez and Amnon seemed so complete that at times Erez
felt like a living statue of his father.

On the eve of his departure for basic training, Erez began
to sense a lingering fear that following in his father's footsteps
would inevitably lead him to his father's end—that a few stations ahead he too was fated to die. This thought did not stop
him, though, and he went on to excel in the army. He prepared to serve in a combat unit, although the times were relatively peaceful. But in June 1982, when the Israeli government, led by Prime Minister Begin and Defense Minister
Sharon, decided to invade Lebanon, Erez's elite paratrooper
unit was called from a training session in the south to join the
troops invading the northern border.

Erez and six comrades drove to the war zone in an army
vehicle. On their way they stopped, in the middle of the night,
at Erez's kibbutz. Edna got up to prepare a meal for them.
The invasion was ostensibly directed against PLO bases in
Southern Lebanon, but the prospect of an all-out clash with
the Syrian army deep in Lebanon was growing more likely
every hour. The young soldiers rose from the table and de-
parted in their vehicle, heading north to join the troops.

Everything seemed predestined: in early June, almost fifteen
years after the death of his father in the Six-Day War, Erez,
dressed in the same type of paratrooper uniform his father
had worn, marched onto the battlefield. Suddenly Erez
stopped. He stood frozen for a moment or two, then walked
with determination to his commander and told him, "I am
afraid. Perhaps I am a coward, but I do not want to die!" Erez's
stunned comrades urged him to "be a man" and continue.

But his decision was irrevocable. Within a short time he crossed the border back into Israel. Erez, who from the age of seven had lived so deeply and inescapably with the presence of death and the absence of his father, abruptly broke away from everything that bound him to his father's story. In refusing to deny his own fear, he had in an instant rejected the heroic military code, which had become a civic code, especially for kibbutz children. Erez committed a monumental act of defiance, discarding all of the emotional, psychological, and social forces that had enlisted him as a self-sacrificing soldier, as a son worthy of a heroic father. Can anyone imagine the *Odyssey* without the son ready to fight like his father? What if, following Odysseus's admonition, "I count on you to bring no shame on your forefathers," Telemachus had answered, "Sorry, Father, I am not going to fight, because I do not want to die"? By raising the subjective voice of his self, Erez broke with the epic narrative that had permeated his family and been sanctified by his father's ultimate sacrifice.

The differences between the Six-Day War and the invasion of Lebanon are not irrelevant, of course. The former war was almost universally justified within Israel as a war of self-defense; the latter, the most controversial and divisive war in Israel's history, came to be regarded as a tragedy that wasted many lives and undermined the leaders who had started it. But for Erez, the decision not to risk his life in the fighting—to extricate himself from his unit by taking advantage of his privilege as a war orphan—was connected in his mind with a deeper break from "the system." That system included even his family and friends, and certainly the kibbutz and the army—all those who had expected him to march in his father's footsteps. Fear of death became the wings on which Erez flew to his freedom.

To say, "I am afraid"—to confess what Israeli men have been trained to deny—is the most irrevocable act of leaping out and beyond the extended family of the paratroopers, the kibbutz members, and the bereaved survivors of the war dead.

When his sure march on the hero's path came suddenly to a halt, Erez started a painful struggle to restore his intimate bonds with his dead father. One of his first urges was to individualize his mourning for his father, to break away from the collective memorials with Hanan, Amnon's twin in death, and create a more personal ceremony. "This thing," he said, "happened to my father, to me, not to the kibbutz." Erez discovered, however, how difficult it was to excavate Amnon, the real father, the person he hardly knew, the hero who was embedded in state monuments and described in the epic language of state ceremonies. Erez desperately sought to reach beyond the abstract, stereotyped, idealized warrior and touch his "real father," imperfect but authentic, a man who could at times be a lousy father or lover, a disappointing friend.

Following this episode, as he planned his next move—to leave the kibbutz—Erez felt that behind Amnon the monument, who would remain in the kibbutz, there must be an Amnon he could take with him. He sought an alternative narrative to bind them, a story perhaps connected not with the way his father died but with the way he had lived. Amnon had been an amateur but very sensitive photographer; he left behind photographs of birds and flowers and, more important, his camera. At the point where Odysseus's son tried to take up his father's bow and arrow, Erez laid down his father's gun and picked up his camera. "Abba took pictures of pretty things," says Erez. "I took his camera and followed his style for a while. Then I felt as if I were photographing a closed world. But some of his photographs pointed to other possibilities. One was of a blooming cactus in a clay flowerpot broken at the rim. The juxtaposition of the beautiful plant and the broken flowerpot indicated that my father had appreciation for imperfection. He could have easily turned the flowerpot around so that the plant would hide the broken rim. But instead of the illusion of perfection, he

Amnon's photograph of the cactus in a clay flowerpot.

chose to leave the broken side exposed." It was this side, this photograph, to which Erez linked himself. Then for a "whole year I took only pictures of myself." The search for the repressed personal narrative of his father could not be separated from the quest for Erez's own selfhood and identity.

In anticipation of the fiftieth anniversary of his father's birth, Erez persuaded his mother to arrange a completely private family gathering, including Amnon's closest friends. Erez was eager to discover his real father, with the help of the people who knew Amnon best, to penetrate the official culture of bereaved families and get behind the idealizations and glorifications. He wanted to see the full cactus in the flowerpot with the broken rim. In the invitation, relatives and friends were instructed to prepare unabashedly honest stories they knew, "so that the children," said Edna, "could know their father."

Edna urged them not to hold back, to tell everything they knew. She endorsed Erez's new search to find the elements of another story, to "deconstruct" the dead soldier and recompose the private person, the father, who had lived Amnon's life.

Unfortunately, the effort to bring Amnon back by means of the party was a failure. The friends "could not remove the honey from their lips," Erez noted regretfully. There was still another chance, though. Edna had kept a box full of revealing intimate letters Amnon wrote to her, including his very last letters, written just prior to the battle for Jerusalem in which he was killed. Twenty years after his death, Edna offers the box to her son. In the letters Erez discovers what he was looking for, the fragments of the private person, the lover, the husband, the father Amnon was.

Erez's private journey takes a new turn when, in the third year of the Intifada, he joins several dozen other reservist soldiers in refusing to serve with his unit in the occupied territories. He is court-martialed and jailed in a military prison. Because he is a war orphan, his term is cut to two weeks. "Enough time to reflect," he says. From the son of the paratrooper killed during the Six-Day War to a young paratrooper merging his life with his father's and the state's narratives, Erez has become a citizen in opposition, challenging his army and his government by means of civil disobedience, refusing to collaborate with the occupation and the settlement policies of the government. When he gets out of jail, Erez—now the son of an amateur photographer—becomes an accomplished artist-photographer. Armed with a camera, he aims at the state, the army, the prison in which he was confined, even the kibbutz—"all in some sense parts of the same system." But, although he is outside the system now, he is no longer alone. "Abba and I are together now," says Erez, "both of us left the kibbutz, the army, both of us left Mother, he physically and I ideologically!" Erez's father, whom he almost literally saved from beneath tons of concrete, statues, and memorial war albums, could now join his son anywhere. In his solitary room in Tel Aviv, thirty-year-old Erez, who refused to visit his father's grave when he was eight years old, suddenly breaks down. For the first time he mourns alone the loss of his father, as the grief held inside for over twenty years breaks out. Now, not diverted by the well-meaning agencies of rehabilitation and immortalization which deny death, Erez, who knows the fear of death, has faced the irrevocable.

On January 1, 1990, an exhibition of photographs by Erez and his collaborator, Nir Nader, opened in the avant-garde Bograshov Gallery in Tel Aviv. The exhibition attracted wide attention and was reported and discussed extensively in the Israeli media. The gallery was set up as a series of interlocking installations, which cumulatively subjected the visitor to powerful, contradictory experiences. Upon entering the gallery, I immediately sensed the dignified, grave atmosphere of the familiar Israeli memorial for fallen soldiers. Ropes prevented the visitor from moving freely in all directions. One got the sensation of an authority directing one's steps and creating a distance between the visitor and the exhibits on display. Close to the entrance, the ropes separated the visitor from a row of chairs facing a bare wall. On the back of each chair was a plaque inscribed with the words "Reserved for the Heroes' Families." The floor was covered by a wall-to-wall carpet in the olive color of Israeli army uniforms. The highly polished wooden frames and pillars, the bright light bulbs, and a pile of mostly wooden boxes that seemed like coffins, all evoked the conditioned response of Israelis to sites of official rituals of commemoration. But upon recalling that it was not a commemorative but a gallery space, one could not escape the realization that one had been manipulated into acting as a participant in the theatrical reproduction of mourning. The sinking feeling of mourning, of loss, was suddenly replaced by a painful awareness of the means by which the experience of mourning and bereavement is induced. One had to face the teasing insight that grief and solemn sadness were produced in authentic commemorative settings by means similar to those used in the gallery; that mourning was, at least partly, a theatrically and aesthetically induced sensation. The boundaries between real mourning and its representations were blurred. The momentary transition from the sinking sensation of mourning to a critical reflection on the experience of bereavement as something artificially created by standard reproducible stimuli was profoundly disturbing. The artists had succeeded in establishing an eerie continuity between the dignity and sanctity of Israeli commemorative spaces and the space of the gallery. The movement between a sense of bereavement and a detached appreciation of its production by aesthetic means was, however, not linear. One was constantly fluctuating between grief and criticism, absorption and distance, authentic sadness and the sense of being an accomplice in its theatrical propagation; between solemnity and irony, grimness and black humor. One felt as if the safe vessels of mourning and commemorating could break down at any moment. Behind the rituals and the sites of commemoration the coordinating hand of the state, which, like the artist's hand, shaped the time and space of bereavement, had suddenly become transparent. The exhibition made you feel guarded against any attempt to attach excessive meaning to the death of these young Israelis, as if the meaning attached to their death was not passive but somehow an accomplice in their loss.

Erez and Nir's artistic strategy was to subvert the collective-official assignment of meaning as if in a gesture which enlisted the dead to resist it. In a glass case in one corner in the gallery they placed a book prepared for the exhibition. It contains a passport photograph of Erez's father, Amnon, as a young man, placed in the circular space of an absent medal of honor sent to the bereaved family by the Defense Ministry's Department of Rehabilitation and Immortalization. The pretty white ribbon that formerly held the medal now hangs over the head of the fallen soldier like a hangman's noose. A few pages later, another noose hangs ready for the neck, not of Amnon, but of his smiling fourteen-year-old son. "My father," says Erez in reference to the medal, "was always a winner, always first." The noose that holds the medal, that hung the father, like a narrative that can kill, now threatens to hang the son. The point is not that there is a conspiracy here. What is significant is rather the dualism, the close connection between winning and losing, meaning and death.

Erez had lost his father in the Six-Day War; his collaborator, Nir Nader, who had not suffered such a loss, responded similarly upon discovering the links between the official culture of bereavement and the role of the fathers as unconscious partners of the state in sending their sons to the battlefield. Nir included in their common book a photograph of himself at age six standing obediently in front of a towering monument to the fallen soldiers.

The wooden box became a central theme of the exhibition.

It seemed to stand for a variety of things: the body, the coffin, the darkroom, the camera, the studio. It also represented a private space insulated from the social gaze, a space in which the individual could freely confess and experiment, a sanctuary from the public spaces in which personal losses were made into elements in a national epic. The imagined, invisible, dark space within the wooden box could indicate the fear behind the socially celebrated heroic act, standing for the personal price, like the hidden, worn-out soles of the paratrooper's shoes, another object in the exhibition, whose tops were painted in gold, like a cult object, or like the teeth that bite the tongue behind pursed lips. The son who had run away from the gaze of the state and the fathers found his refuge in the studio, where he could look at himself through the eye of the camera, recompose, remake, and renarrate himself.

While the objects in the installations were often accompanied by fragments of texts, the symbolic stress on private space as a sanctuary of the self had the import of defying the invasiveness of state-controlled space, which as a vehicle of collective meaning is so inhospitable to personal reflections. The tensions and the symbolic dialogue between public and private spaces in Israel are aspects of an uphill struggle for a largely incipient Israeli culture of the self. For Jews, the lines in modern Israel between self and community or between individual and state do not divide between Jewish and non-Jewish spheres of life; in contrast with the conditions of the Jews in the Diaspora, the issue of private and public spaces appears in modern Israel as a domestic issue, a problem within a form of life directed and shaped by Jews, not a problem in the relations between Jews and non-Jews or between Jews who leave their community and Jews who stay behind. The responses to these tensions, then, may have formative effects on modern Jewish culture and politics.

Erez and Nir's works are, of course, only gestures (albeit important ones) in a much larger movement by means of which the sons of the founding fathers of Israel have been exploring the limits of the world they inherited. Such attempts indicate the potential of defying or reopening the official narratives, of opening paths to the future that are not automatically consistent with established scenarios.

The row of wooden boxes—open only on the side that faces the wall and therefore hidden from the visitor's eyes—suggests their defense of private spaces against the public gaze. The "vocabulary" of private spaces that has developed over hundreds of years in the West is of course accessible to Israeli artists. But in the context of a Jewish polity and a Jewish state it has novel, even revolutionary connotations. For Jews, Israel is the first modern state in which the lines separating private and public spaces do not correspond to the sociopolitical separation of Jews and non-Jews, and in which public space (like public power) is not basically off-limits to Jews. In a Jewish polity, where Jews are both the private citizens and the government, the assortment of individuals and the majority, the delineation of private space is sometimes a heroic gesture of self-limitation on the part of the collective, and sometimes an attempt to defend private values against the collective and the state. Private space also asserts the claims of self-narration against the collective epic of the nation. Such a move is particularly difficult in Israel, because of the powerful tendency to view the state and the Jewish society as two aspects of the same entity rather than as distinct and potentially antagonistic forms of association. Artists such as Erez and Nir represent a relatively novel Israeli awareness of the antagonism between state and citizens, an awareness that encourages ambivalence toward state power and seeks to draw clearer lines between the respective domains of voluntary and duty-bound conduct.

The impact and significance of Erez and Nir's exhibition did not escape Israeli art critics. One of them characterized the exhibition as a "protest against the nationalization of private bereavement in Israel." "The chairs reserved for the families of the heroes," wrote another, "generated shock." Erez and Nir were invited to face right-wing ideologues on the popular Israeli television show *Tonight*. When one of the ideologues denounced Erez as a "traitor," he responded by saying, "I am merely trying to make a contribution to Israeli culture." Erez and Nir's artistic questioning and protest directed at "sacred" military symbols was utterly unacceptable to Avigdor Kahalani, then a Labor Knesset member and a former war hero. "Why do you stay in this country?" he asked Erez. "Get up and leave!" "I will not leave," answered Erez, "just because there are people like you who think critics cannot be patriotic." The hostility to Erez, Nir, and their art has, among other things, led the Fund for the Bereaved Families of the Paratrooper Forces to withdraw an earlier offer to purchase wholesale quantities of the exhibition book to distribute to its members. Erez's art was not approved by the very organization that had bestowed so many good things on him and his family in the past.

Following several telephone threats from people supposedly defending the honor of the nation and the army, the gallery hired special guards. Edna, Erez's widowed mother, has basically remained a loyal kibbutz widow and her views have clearly and consistently differed from those of her son. Nevertheless, she has supported him all the way, saying she respects his independence and welcomes his attempts to mourn his father on his own terms. In the midst of a community that worships military heroes and soldiers' sacrifices, Erez's subversive acknowledgment of the fear of death does not remain a matter of personal exception. Through his art and the public response to it, Erez has helped consolidate alternative psychological and cultural facts, the kind of orientations that have come to be associated in late-twentieth-century Israel with the rise of individualism, the decline of military values, and the readiness to make hard concessions to the enemy in order to reach a settlement. In the final analysis, there was a striking connection between the demystification of death on the battlefield and the shifts in modern Israeli culture and politics during the early 1990s.

The Erez who stepped out of the official story and took his father with him is no longer the Erez who years ago could not enter the cemetery where his father was buried. On the eve of his own wedding, Erez visited his father's grave. His visit was not to a mute monument but to a father who, after years of silence, had started to talk. His younger brother-in-law, Gavri, captured Erez's spirit when he said to him, "Send my regards to your father!" When Erez returned, Gavri remembers Erez telling him, "Abba returns your greetings."

My Father, My Son

There is a moment in Book XXI of the *Odyssey* when Odysseus, the returning warrior, still in disguise in Ithaca, takes up again the bow he had left behind twenty years before. As he holds it—feeling the bow with assurance and familiarity, laying his fingers on the string—it is momentarily transformed into a harp, and Odysseus into a bard. "But the man skilled in all ways of contending, satisfied by the great bow's look and heft, like a musician, like a harper, when with quiet hand upon his instrument he draws between his thumb and forefinger a sweet new string upon a peg; so effortlessly Odysseus in one motion strung the bow. Then slid his right hand down the cord and plucked it so that the taut gut vibrating hummed and sang a swallow's note."[1]

The image of Odysseus holding his lyre between his thumb and forefinger always brings to my mind precious early memories of my father, a musician, standing over my bed, holding his violin, his eyes closed and his right hand effortlessly moving his bow over the strings. The link Homer makes between the warrior and the bard, the bow and the lyre, suggests, of course,

---

[1] Translated by Robert Fitzgerald (New York: Vintage Classics, 1990), p. 404.

the relation between power and narrative. Epic poems are written about what armed men do. But my father's bow, which connected us so deeply, could not shoot arrows. The bow and strings with which he spoke to me before I knew how to talk were purely a musical instrument.

While my father's bow was not good for shooting arrows, I would never underestimate the power of music. It must have been in 1946 when, as a six-year-old child, I was allowed to sit on a small bench in our living room in Tel Aviv while my father played chamber music with his friends and students. One morning they played a Haydn quartet and I was totally absorbed, first by the movements and expressions on the players' faces and then by the sounds themselves, which carried me great distances. On the top of a chest next to our piano there sat a blue glass bowl containing my three small goldfish, which reflected the sun's rays penetrating through the half-closed shutters. I was watching the beautiful fish, their rapid movements, wondering whether they were actually dancing to the sounds that filled the room, when suddenly I heard an explosion. The glass bowl cracked open and came apart as if by itself, and the water gushed to the floor with the fish. The four musicians leaped up, the chair near me fell backward, and the scores flew in the air. Amidst this chaos, the cellist and I rushed to save the fish on the floor. Only one survived.

Although Tel Aviv knew the sound of exploding bombs during those years, our little aquarium cracked open at the very moment in the quartet when, as Abba told me later, the four instruments sounded in unison and in fortissimo the same note in different registers. Since then the magic power of music has never died in my mind, nor have I ever forgotten those little dead goldfish on our floor at the eerie moment when the beauty, harmony, and gaiety of Haydn's music was punctured by a tragic note and the sight of death.

While Abba was already too old to become a soldier in the War of Independence in 1948, there was nevertheless an element of combat, of defiant affirmation of life, in his effort to continue to play, hold concerts, and teach music while a bloody war was raging around us. Abba's teaching violin in our shelter between air strikes, and the sound of Beethoven sonatas overcoming the distant screams of the sirens, seemed to me a part of the war effort; the boys and girls running with their violins in the empty streets of Tel Aviv were undoubtedly brave little soldiers. In fact, some of the older ones soon became real soldiers and appeared in uniform. We later learned that one of them, Daniel Benyamini, who served in the newly created IDF artillery battalion, had been wounded during the hostilities and was hospitalized. Once we were reassured that there was no danger to his life, we worried about his chances of playing again. This fear ended on the day Daniel appeared with his viola, still in uniform. He would go on to please thousands of admirers as one of the world's finest viola players. So there was, after all, some connection between playing and fighting, bows and arrows.

From my fifth year on, my father would take me to concerts of the Israel Philharmonic Orchestra, which always opened or closed with the playing of the national anthem, "Hatikva" ("Hope"). During Israel's wars, foreign artists such as Arthur Rubinstein or Leonard Bernstein would come to Israel in order to keep the concert series going, sometimes replacing less courageous artists who had canceled due to the emergency situation. When the audience applauded these guest artists at the end of a concert, it was often for much more than an inspiring performance. I remember a rendition of Beethoven's "Eroica" during which we held our breath, as if Israel's survival depended upon a flawless performance. The thunder of applause that shook the Ohel Shem Concert Hall in Tel Aviv at the end of these evenings celebrated, over and above the great music, the heroic acts of culture-making in defiance of fear and danger.

Even so, I had a powerful urge to see my father with bow *and* arrow, to see him as a soldier in uniform. I was, therefore, very proud when one day he was called to the military headquarters and inducted into the regional civil defense unit. Although his assignment was to help keep essential services going in our neighborhood in times of emergency, especially during air strikes, he returned home with an impressive green beret. Already I felt more protected, especially in facing some of the neighborhood kids, who would beat me up occasionally. One afternoon I came home bleeding from my ear and Abba rushed out to search for the little villains. I stood on the steps as he ran out and cried, "Abba, you forgot your hat!" The musician came back and reemerged in a few seconds as a warrior, completely transformed by his green beret. My adversaries ran away as if pursued by the devil himself.

The preoccupation with music and the revival of the Hebrew language in my home during my childhood must have tempered my exposure to the military aspects of the Zionist struggle during those years. Still, it is not difficult to see how a young boy in Tel Aviv could develop a romantic view of soldiers during the early struggle for independence. The enormous death toll of the war, the sense of danger, the constant dramatic radio announcements, speeches, and newscasts, the epic poems recited in public rituals, the military parades, the stories of heroic sacrifices—all these penetrated our lives and shaped our emotions. The unarticulated yet overwhelming knowledge of the destruction of European Jewry provided an eerie background for our sense that everything was at stake. As Ruth Firer points out in her study of Israeli textbooks published between 1948 and 1968,[2] *Kiddush Hashem*—the traditional Jewish idea of dying for the sanctification of the name of God—was translated in these books into a secular, nationalist ideal of self-sacrifice for the sake of the nation and the state. Shaul Tchernichovsky's poems were studied as celebrations of Jewish honor, strength, vitality, and heroism. Bialik's poem "The Dead of the Desert" ("Metei Midbar") was often read to welcome a new generation of powerful, self-confident Jews capable of taking their lives into their own hands. As is well documented, in the 1950s Jewish victims of the Holocaust were more often than not presented as the epitome of the Jew as helpless schlemiel, a counterexample to the new Israeli Jew. A few members of my own family seemed to fit this ideal of the new Jew. One was a pilot named Ezer, whom I first met in 1948 at a family gathering. He appeared in full military uniform and I must have been deeply impressed.

The home library had even a greater impact. The children's shelf included, among others, a book read by generations of young Israelis (as well as young people all over Europe), *The Heart* (*Il Cuoro*), written by the Italian author Edmondo De Amicis. De Amicis, who died in 1908, had been a soldier in the Italian army during the 1860s and fought the Austrian

---

[2]Ruth Firer, *The Agents of Zionist Education.*

army in the Custoza battle of 1866. His book, which appeared in English as *The Heart of a Boy*, was a worldwide success. It is a deeply moving story about love, devotion, and friendship in the life of Italian schoolchildren and their families. It celebrates nationalist military heroism and self-sacrifice for the nation as natural outgrowths of devotion to one's father, mother, and friends. Family loyalties naturally converge in *The Heart* with love and loyalty to one's country.

I realized only recently how deeply this book had affected me and my friends, when I came across an essay from 1932 by Abba Ahimeir, leader of the radical right-wing revisionist faction of the Zionist movement, and at the time a great admirer of Italian fascism. Ahimeir and his followers held that Jews must harden themselves in order to become effective soldiers, men who could survive by resorting to the power of the sword. In his essay, Ahimeir attacked the publishers of a children's paper, *Itonenu* (*Our Paper*), for exposing their young readers to articles, fiction, and illustrations that encouraged a too idealistic view of the world, innocent of the knowledge of evil, of violence, cruelty, and death, with which they would have to cope before long. He complained bitterly that while a writer like De Amicis told about Italian children who spied and died for their fatherland, for Israeli children the Israeli national poets wrote about rabbits. In his view, pictures of happy harvesters of grapes in the Valley of Jezreel were meant to conceal from Israeli youth the truth about the realities of their lives—the suffering, the danger, "the recent murder of a Jew in Bethlehem," and the attacks on the "Land of Israel." Such pastoral pictures clearly conveyed to him the wrong values and aesthetics. He urged teachers, rather, to inculcate in their students a sense of the heroic sacrifices of individuals like Joseph

Trumpeldor, the one-armed Jewish officer in the Russian army who came to Palestine and died while defending a distant Jewish settlement in the upper Galilee against Arab attackers. "The way to the Kingdom of Israel," Ahimeir wrote in a later essay, "would be paved by sacrifices that would kindle the enthusiasm of Israeli youth." We have to be a generation of "heroes, not saints," he wrote in 1936. While other people sacrificed thousands of their best children, he complained, our people failed to admire heroism. "The Arab," he wrote, has "proved he can despise death"; the Jew has not. During World War II, Ahimeir would even express his reservations about the march of the Jewish orphans (led by their teacher, Janusz Korczak) to their death in Treblinka.[3] He criticized the great educator for having taught his students to have faith in the fraternity of nations rather than recognizing that the world is ruled by the strong and that survival requires sacrifices. "Korczak," he wrote, "is not among the heroes I'll tell my son about."

Only now can I appreciate how much *The Heart* (which Ahimeir recommended to Israeli youth) was suffused with ardent nationalist values, romanticizing the heroic sacrifice and the death of young children for their nation. I have come to recognize the subliminal presence of De Amicis's stories in the deepest layers of my soul. Rereading these stories felt like discovering that the familiar soft drink I trustingly drank many

---

[3]When the Nazi deportation order was served in 1942, Korczak, suppressing the truth, told his children they were going on a picnic in the country. When he and some 200 orphans at last reached the cattle trucks waiting to carry them to Treblinka, he refused a last-minute offer of freedom and went with them to his death.

years ago was loaded with carcinogenic substances. My friends and I really loved and mourned for the twelve-year-old boy who, during the 1859 struggle for the liberation of Lombardy, volunteered to climb a tree and serve as a scout for an Italian battalion stranded on the battlefield. He spotted the enemy gunners and warned his compatriots just seconds before a hail of bullets killed him. De Amicis went on to describe the honors showered on the boy, the soldiers who saluted his corpse with their swords, the officer who tore off his medal of honor and threw it on the boy's coffin, and the soldier who bent to kiss the corpse's cold forehead. I remembered feeling envious of the dead boy's achievement. But now, several decades later, I pay attention to some other significant details.

De Amicis presents the boy as an orphan, thus removing the family as a potential obstacle to unqualified adoption by the state. In the absence of parents, it is easier for the "fatherland" or the "motherland" to take over.[4] Further aestheticizing the sacrifice, the author dwells on the flag that covers the boy's body and alludes to a faint smile on his face as if he were happy in his moment of glory, happy to have acted heroically and to return to the arms of the eternal motherland. De Amicis depicts the child's death as a comforting merger of the orphan with the nation. But even when—as in the case of the book's main hero, the schoolboy Enrico—a boy is blessed with

---

[4]Avner Ben-Amos has shown the centrality in French children's literature of the nationalist theme of the orphan child who discovers "motherland" as a surrogate mother (see, for instance, G. Bruno, *Le Tour de la France par Deux Enfants*, 1877). A. Ben-Amos, "A School for Democracy: The Rights of Man and Obligations to the Motherland," *Zmanim* (*Historical Quarterly*), Nos. 50–51 (Winter 1994), pp. 100–15 (in Hebrew).

a family, his father's voice is not significantly distinguishable from the voice of the nation. Both demand that the young boy sacrifice himself, and employ the power of love and respect between fathers and sons to encourage the son's love and devotion to his country.

"I love Italy because my mother is Italy," the father writes to his son. "My blood is Italian and its soil contains those whom my mother mourns and my father respects. When one day you see flags torn by bullets followed by soldiers who walk erect despite their wounds, their head bandages, or missing limbs, when you witness the cheering crowd showering these soldiers with flowers, you will suddenly recognize what the love of one's homeland is, you will understand how a homeland can be so lofty and sacred, and why if on some future day you return from the battlefield after you saved your life rather than courageously fight, I, your father, the one who cheers you every day upon your return from school, I would be crushed, I would never be able to love you anymore, and would die in shame."

In my own family, the resources of family love were not used to promote children's sacrifice for the nation. My father was distant from the Israeli military, totally devoted to music, and his own father's role in the Zionist revolution had been cultural and educational. The Zionist intelligentsia who followed Ahad-Haam had envisioned the Zionist enterprise primarily as a revolution of consciousness, and were ambivalent about the use of force and the cult of military prowess cultivated by other Zionist groups. Power, heroism, and sacrifice were largely foreign concepts to them. As for my late mother, Hannah (Diesenhaus) Ezrahi, she had come with her family as a teenager from Poland in 1923 as part of the "Fourth Aliyah"—the wave of European immigrants impelled largely by anti-Semitic persecution. They were the least ideological of the immigrants to Israel during that time—most of them middle-class, individualistic people who settled as small merchants and entrepreneurs in the big cities rather than in agricultural communities like the kibbutz. My mother was unsentimental and realistic, a survivalist who sought a safe haven for her family. Formed by the experience of anti-Semitism, and later by the news of the extermination of European Jews, she was skeptical of the romantic and cultural idealism of my father and his family, but she was too much concerned for her own family's security to expose us to the ethos of military heroism cultivated in other Zionist circles.

Despite these influences, my family, like almost all Jewish families in Palestine prior to 1948 (and certainly thereafter), was swayed by the spirit of citizens' mobilization and self-sacrifice in that time of great upheavals. The idea of self-sacrifice must have come to me from other sources: my friends, my teachers, the books I read, and the strong impressions left on me by soldiers dressed in uniform and the state military parades. My friends and I became very enthusiastic when we saw war veterans marching in the streets of Tel Aviv. Some of them were visibly wounded, while others appeared invincible. We admired them the way the youth admired the Italian infantry in De Amicis's novel. Still a boy, watching a military parade with my father one Independence Day, I asked myself whether my father would like me to be such a soldier. I felt, though, that he never could have written me a letter like the one written by the father in De Amicis's novel, tying his love for me to my exhibition of courage and self-sacrifice on the battlefield. Still, when I saw his admiration for the young soldiers marching in the streets of Tel Aviv, I wondered whether he did not, sometimes, think like the Italian father.

When I was conscripted into the Israeli army in August 1958, I felt both enthusiasm and anxiety, a sense of pride and power and fear of the dangers ahead. But my first discomfort, even anger, came only a few weeks later when, on the Eve of the High Holidays, the Chief Military Rabbi tried to convince us that our devotion and sacrifice were meant to serve not only the necessities of security but also the ideals of Judaism. I was not a sympathetic listener. I wondered whether such spiritualization of our mission, such glorification of our expected sacrifices, did not give license to a limitless use of power, a commitment to take risks unchecked by the specific demands of security. Still, I was uncritically responsive to secular-ideological versions of that call. We were boys who had just graduated from high school—children who believed even more than our parents in the official story imparted to us by our teachers. We knew that conflict with the Arabs was inevitable, we were taught that this was largely because the Arabs refused all compromise and wanted to "throw us into the sea," and we regarded our wars with them as necessary. In the dense collectivist culture in which we grew up, we had neither the resources nor the motivation to shake off the bonds of social and national solidarity. In those days, it was extraordinarily difficult and rare for a young Israeli to express ambivalence toward the demands for sacrifice in the struggle for security and independence which almost the entire society took for granted. It never occurred to us that our leaders could be unfair, mistaken, unjust, or reckless and they could lead us into wars and bloodshed by mistake. Only decades later were we able to recognize—with resentment—the extent to which our unguarded youthful credulity and innocence were taken advantage of.

For many of my generation, the rude awakening from youthful innocence came with the disclosure of the irresponsible conduct of Prime Minister Golda Meir, Israel's Prime Minister before and during the Yom Kippur War of 1973, and then the follies and misjudgments that led Prime Minister Menachem Begin to carry out the tragic invasion of Lebanon in 1982. Our reservations spread and deepened during the almost fifteen years of Likud governments between 1977 and 1992, in the course of which Israeli leaders officially backed Gush Emunim settlers in the occupied territories and sent Israeli soldiers to control crowds of rebellious Palestinian civilians.

In my case, reserve army service in a top military think tank had exposed me to decision-making processes I almost wished I had never observed. My disillusionment continued during the Gulf War, in the period between Saddam Hussein's invasion of Kuwait and the American-led intervention, and during the war itself, when I discovered the extent to which our leaders' thinking and policy about deterrence were muddy and confused. The top think tank dealing with this issue failed to organize systematic professional analysis of Israel's options and define clear criteria for choosing among alternative postures and responses.

In the meantime, my son Ariel had reached the age of army service, which he approached with innocent idealism. By 1991, there was already a huge gap between what Ariel and his peers took for granted and my own view: that the current policies of the Shamir government in the Arab-Israeli conflict were confrontational, profoundly unresponsive to the rapid changes in the international order, and most likely to lead to another unnecessary war, in which many idealistic, patriotic youths might die heroically but in vain.

Still, I recognized that the gap between Ariel's view (particularly his feelings of solidarity and unquestioning enthusiasm) and my informed skepticism and anxiety could not be easily narrowed. After all, my demystified view of the Israeli army and my disenchanted view of some Israeli leaders were inseparable from the richer and more complex sensibilities of adulthood, just as the emotional solidarity and idealism of Ariel were not easily separable from the optimism and vitality of youth. Even if I could, would it be wise to make my son skeptical and ambivalent? Might these traits—often the signs of reflexivity and complexity in adults—not prove confusing and even devastating to the young? Can an eighteen-year-old Israeli have the inner resources to stand, sometimes alone, against the enormous peer pressures of the group; can he or she resist the emotional solidarity and collective self-righteousness inculcated by parents, teachers, and peers? Given the poverty of the Israeli "culture of the self" and the persistent stress on the primacy of the group, how could I have expected in 1991 that a young high school graduate like Ariel would have sufficient sense of distance, even alienation, to reflect critically upon the premises of his obligation to take the ultimate risk in the name of the state? How much can such a young man allow himself to know about the ugly, unheroic realities of war, about gaps between the goals of leaders and the intentions of fighters, between actions and their consequences? And if genuine reservations lead a young person to question or even abandon the epic narrative of his nation, what life is likely to remain for him out there, where only the strong can walk alone?

As I was flooded by such thoughts in the months before Ariel's conscription into the army, I happened to assign an essay by the American philosopher Richard Rorty in one of my political theory classes. In the essay, entitled "Private Irony and Liberal Hope,"[5] Rorty recommends an ironic orientation toward public affairs as a way to combine distance and partic- ipation, to protect the freedom of the individual through de- tached engagement. In Rorty's view, ironic liberals are individuals whose commitment to critical thinking, pluralism, and diversity make them skeptical of the very attempt to regard any idea, narrative, or claim as unambiguously and decidedly superior to all others. For the ironist, "there is no such thing as a 'natural' order of justification for beliefs or desires." The "liberal ironist" is committed to opposing the use of force as well as to the coexistence of different, often competing, ideas and beliefs. I thought to myself how difficult it is for liberals who have an ironic perspective on the "missions" of the state to send their children (or defend their children's moral obli- gation) to risk their lives in a war cast in terms of a collective epic story and, at the same time, how difficult it is for us to encourage our children to shake off the bonds of the collective narrative which empowers them as young persons and soldiers.

This situation was not made any easier by a communiqué the Israeli army sent to Ariel, along with thousands of his peers, a few months before he turned seventeen. The letter notified him of his forthcoming induction into military service. Ariel read the letter very quickly and put it aside. I picked it

[5]Richard Rorty, *Contingency, Irony and Solidarity* (Cambridge, England: Cam- bridge University Press, 1989), pp. 73–95.

up and read it more closely, noticing things that must have escaped me years ago when I was Ariel's age. At the bottom of the page, a sentence in special print read as follows: "Draftees are called to the flag according to the law but come as volunteers." Ariel read the letter as another indication of his rite of passage into adulthood. This was the first time someone outside the family or the school had told him directly that he was expected to act responsibly and cooperatively. To me, suddenly the voice of the state had been injected into a world so far dominated by the voices of parents, teachers, and friends. I recognized the special power of the state to make a boy feel grown up, its ability to exploit the association the very young make between maturity, independence, and the sense of being counted on with uniforms and arms. The power of the state to make boys into soldiers gives it special advantages over parents. When parents exercise their power or authority with respect to adolescents, they may often only infantilize them, whereas the state makes them into citizens. The state can exploit the fact that, as Melville put it, "all wars are fought by boys."

Nothing in the official letter to Ariel suggested any awareness of the potential contradiction between the part which stated that "draftees are called according to the law" and the part which insisted that the draftees "join the army as volunteers." In fact, an accompanying booklet listed penalties that would be imposed on those who failed to "voluntarily" comply with the army directives. That the state had arrogated to itself the authority to define the act of enlisting as "voluntary" is, of course, an absurdity. No public authority can penetrate the sanctuary of the individual self and define his motives on his behalf. Still, this blurring of the distinction between a voluntary act and obedience to the law is very revealing. It betrays the difficulties the young state has faced in fully replacing the voluntarism that characterized military service (and, for that matter, all public service) in the Yishuv before the State of Israel was established. Even where military service is compulsory, voluntaristic behavior can, of course, persist—service in some high-risk units is a matter of choice, for example—and volunteering can become a powerful expression of one's identification with the army and its goals. By and large, however, the induction of citizens into the army simply signifies their compliance with the law, obedience to the state. The attempt to define conscription as both a duty regulated by the law and a voluntary act reflects the state's unwillingness to give up the symbolic significance of enlistment as the expression of solidarity and support for the army, the state, and their policies. In fact, by predefining the act of enlisting as "voluntary," the government actually deprives these young Israeli soldiers of their prerogative to distinguish between giving or withdrawing their voluntary support for the government and merely fulfilling their legal obligation.

Early in 1991, as Ariel's induction approached, I thought the Likud government was particularly vulnerable to the criticism implicit in the conduct of soldiers who served unenthusiastically, simply following their legal duty. Under the prime ministership of Yitzhak Shamir, Israel's diplomats did not receive a mandate to engage in serious negotiations with the Arabs, leaving the Israeli army almost the only available instrument to handle developments in the Arab-Israeli conflict. The government of a democratic society which does not zealously try to exhaust all the nonviolent, peaceful means at its disposal to settle violent conflict, which does not regard armed force only as a last resort, can lose the moral if not the legal authority to call the young to risk their lives in a war. It is in such situations that the voluntary expressions of ambivalence and criticism can carry special weight. In the course of bitter conflicts like the one between Israel and the Arabs, it takes great foresight and political courage on the part of leaders to choose a course that requires painful concessions to the other side and a radical change of attitudes toward the enemy. The use of armed force is often most costly to the citizens (some of whom must risk their lives), but cheap for the political leadership, which can more easily mobilize the passions of the people against a dangerous enemy. Diplomacy is often cheaper for the citizens (it spares their lives), but more costly to the leaders because it is associated with rarely popular compromises and concessions to the enemy. In 1990, I hoped that such an act of statesmanship could take place, but having observed this leadership for many years, I was skeptical.

For months, Ariel had expressed his reservations about his parents' opposition to the Shamir government's military policy. We had long been active members of the Israeli peace movement and relentless critics of governmental efforts to settle the occupied territories and foreclose future possibility of territorial compromise. Like other members of the peace movement, we regarded army service as a duty of all democratic citizens. But we also rejected government attempts to blur the distinction between policies guided by genuine security requirements and those guided by the logic of the occupation. When, for example, two generals in the Israeli army received decorations from West Bank Jewish settlers in a highly politicized ceremony a short time before the 1992 elections, I protested strongly on Israeli radio. The government and the settlers were clearly using the army in order to legitimate their controversial settlement policies. Lieutenant General Ehud Barak, Chief of Staff of the Israeli army, heard the interview and called to ask me to meet him. In our meeting, he explained that while the army needs to keep good working relations with the settlers, the generals who were decorated had been surprised when they were exploited to advance the political cause of the settlers. He promised that new instructions would prevent it from happening again. This incident suggests the atmosphere in which people like me were trying to draw a line between the legitimate and the illegitimate uses of our military power, a clear line where the government and the settlers preferred no lines at all.

While Ariel was generally sympathetic to our feelings and thinking on this matter, he was much less critical of the use of military force, and this led to considerable tensions between us. Anxieties about the prospect of another bloody war (a war in which we could lose him . . .) dominated our lives. In a way characteristic of Israeli families whose sons and daughters are about to serve in the army, we encouraged Ariel to take advantage of the short time between his graduation from high school and his induction to taste life and perhaps take a trip abroad. Sometimes jokingly and sometimes in earnest, Ariel spoke as if it might well be the last time he did this or that. Characteristically, his high school graduation party turned out to be a celebration of the end of his safe life as an Israeli.

It was in this atmosphere that Ariel and I planned a joint trip in order to spend time together. It was a trip to which I brought a specific agenda. We needed to talk about the gap between his perceptions of army service and mine. I also needed to clarify my own thoughts. I had no doubt that Ariel should serve his term in the regular army, as I had done a few decades earlier, but I wanted him to serve without my youthful enthusiasm, credulity, and innocence. Nevertheless, I needed to sort out and separate my fatherly anxiety about Ariel's safety from my conviction that the policies of the Shamir government were illegitimate, needlessly confrontational, and positively dangerous to the country. And he needed me to listen to him.

In early August, we flew together to Colorado, then rented a car to explore the Grand Canyon and the surrounding area. We drove along the canyon's rim, then parked the car and went walking until the late afternoon. We sat down to rest on a rock overlooking the enormous hole in the crust of our planet. The Grand Canyon was just about to collaborate with the setting sun in performing one of the most spectacular light-and-color shows on earth. Ariel was facing me. The abyss opening behind him created the optical illusion of a child about to fall. "I have been thinking about your army service," I started. "I am worried that the efforts of this government to annex the occupied territories by backing the spread of Jewish settlements will only increase the suffering and escalate the violence. When the Likud talks to religious Israelis, this policy is defended on religious and historical grounds. When they talk to secular Israelis they say the occupation serves our security needs." Ariel listened attentively but skeptically. "How could territories so close to Israeli population centers be useless from a military point of view?" he asked.

"Strictly militarily speaking, they are useless and even a liability," I said, "because of the hundreds of thousands of Palestinians who live there. Hasn't the Intifada shown that these are not docile Arab refugees but a nation? How long can we continue to consider the historic or even the military value this land has for us while ignoring the Palestinians who have made it their home? Wouldn't it be strategically wiser to assess the value of a piece of land for checking advancing enemy tank divisions against such gains as the effect of returning that piece of land on diminishing the aggressive intent of the enemy? Besides, in a war waged with ballistic missiles and with the introduction of sophisticated airborne early-warning systems, territory is devalued as a strategic asset."

Ariel was still not convinced. "You assume that we can return these territories to a reliable, stable adversary," he said. "But who is the other side? How can you trust them?"

"International agreements are not based on trust," answered the political scientist in me, "but on balances of powers and interests. When we negotiated our peace treaties with Egypt, much attention was paid by both sides to measures 'on the ground' which would increase the mutual costs of starting another war or violating the agreement." As I listened to myself speaking, I realized suddenly how slim my chances of convincing him were. The problem of this conversation had very little to do with the relative strength of the arguments exchanged. I was confronting Ariel with an impossible choice. Not yet eighteen years old, he lacked a sufficient basis for trusting his own judgment in such matters. His acceptance of what I said on my (parental) authority only—no matter how warranted—was bound to disempower him precisely when he was carving out his own personal space.

As I was looking into his blue eyes, the sun was moving behind him like a ball of fire, lighting the rocks and his face with an intense orange glow. I suddenly realized why I had gravitated to this place. There is a profound difference between sunsets in Jerusalem and those in the Grand Canyon. In Jerusalem the sun sets between towers, mosques, and ruins; the shifting sun's rays make the walls of the Old City dance. One feels humbled by the eerie presence of the past. In the Grand Canyon, one is dwarfed by the grandeur of nature, not history. I must have sought a retreat from Jewish history, a place where rocks and geological time humble us not as Jews but simply as human beings. Ariel and I went on to share the exhilaration of primordial landscapes on the Colorado River and the canyon. But this was just a brief interlude. In just a few days we would be back in the Jerusalem of towers, flags, and guns, and Ariel would put on his uniform and go to serve his country.

As I observed Ariel and his friends heading toward their army service before they had been able to distinguish themselves as individuals from the larger society or even from their own high school group, I realized that this "groupiness" has far-reaching consequences for the ways boys become and behave as soldiers.

Not only Israel but other modern states know well the advantages of enlisting the daring young before they mature. Social scientists have consistently found that group solidarity boosts fighting spirit. Strong and autonomous individuals can constrain the smooth working of a hierarchical military organization. In Israeli society, the history of Jewish persecution has reinforced the communitarian-collectivistic orientations already inherent in the religious, nationalist, and ideological sources of the polity, deepening already ingrained Jewish commitments to the primacy of the group. Since 1948, many Israelis have regarded the State of Israel primarily as a collective expression of the Jewish people, not as a creation based on a social contract among free, autonomous individuals. In this view, Israel was founded to secure the survival and self-fulfillment of the Jewish people, and only secondarily and within these premises can it address the issues of individual freedom and welfare. As Don Handelman has put it: "In general the 'Leom' (nation) as a category has been endowed with increasing authority to define a segment of the Israeli population in essentialist terms."[6] Thus, the army service as a civic duty tended to be submerged in ethnic solidarity and group loyalty.

The moral authority and the emotional power of the group vis-à-vis the individual have been manifest in many spheres of life in Israel. Students of the Israeli educational system have noted a tendency among Israeli teachers to ascribe great weight to the value of *gibbush*, of group cohesiveness in the school. Tamar Katriel, for one, discerns a policy of assigning the individual child in Israeli schools to a class which is preserved and cultivated as an internal group through the sixth grade. *Gibbush* continues as a policy in the higher grades as well, encouraging the submersion or repression of individual differences. She notes, for example, the expression of such valorization of the group in teachers' rhetoric and occasionally also in the employment of collective disciplinary measures that treat students as a group rather than as individual moral agents.[7]

The glorification of group solidarity persists after high

---

[6]Don Handelman, "Contradictions Between Citizenship and Nationality: Their Consequences for Ethnicity and Inequality in Israel," *International Journal of Politics, Culture and Society*, Vol. 7, No. 3 (1993), pp. 441–95.
[7]Tamar Katriel, *Communal Webs* (New York: State University of New York Press, 1991), pp. 11–34.

school in the army, where the core group becomes the "home" of the individual soldier. In close quarters, and often in danger, soldiers form unusually strong friendships. ("We few," says Shakespeare's King Henry V, "we happy few, we band of brothers; for he today that sheds his blood with me shall be my brother.") Writing about Israeli paratroopers, Gideon Aran records "the spirit of cooperation and intense awareness of belonging to one and the same whole. Each jumper must help the man in front of him and be helped by the one behind. Thus, a common pool of responsibility and trust is created, dramatizing critical interdependence and enhancing group solidarity."[8] In interviews with Israeli soldiers who fought in Lebanon, Amia Lieblich collected evidence of group bonding and an undifferentiated sense of self among them.[9] "All I thought of at that moment," one soldier recalled of his combat, "was that I wanted to join my buddies . . ." Another soldier said, "At first we just did what we were trained to do, not feeling much. But after the first man from my unit was injured, I felt that they had to pay the price. We all fought like animals afterwards." Buddies in a combat unit clearly fight more for one another than for the more abstract "country." Indeed, Israeli soldiers are known for their readiness to give their lives to save their wounded friends, or even just to retrieve their dead bodies under fire.

Like other modern states, Israel has capitalized on friendship and camaraderie as a precious military resource to en-

[8]Gideon Aran, "Parashooting," *The American Journal of Sociology*, Vol. 80, No. 1 (July 1974).
[9]Amia Lieblich, *Transition to Adulthood during Military Service: The Israeli Case* (New York: State University of New York Press, 1989).

hance the morale of the soldiers. Studies of the conduct of soldiers during World War II showed that soldiers could be both heroes on the battlefield and unaware of the causes or objectives of the war. Such soldiers presumably would have been scarce had army recruits been more fully formed as adult persons.

The readiness of young persons to make great sacrifices on the battlefield is connected with the natural propensity of young persons to take (sometimes extreme) risks in testing the limits of the body and psyche. Erik Erikson suggested in *Childhood and Society*[10] that the reckless behavior of youth reflects their tendency to experiment with various ways of life, identities, and opportunities, before committing themselves to a particular way of life and assuming family and professional responsibilities. By putting weapons in their hands and sending them to the battlefield, the modern state is harnessing this risk-prone behavior of the young to its military objectives. Army service, then, not only interrupts boyhood and the process of individuation; it also distorts youthful experimentalism into a military asset. The means of self-fashioning a unique person becomes ironically a vehicle of group solidarity. Thus the young Israeli high school graduate who is armed by the state undergoes the rite of passage from boyhood to adulthood through the collective experience of army service rather than through tests of individuation and independence. His firearms belong to the state and are entrusted to him by virtue of his membership in the national collective. Maturation is linked with integration rather than separation. It is not the individual

---

[10]Erik H. Erikson, *Childhood and Society* (New York: W. W. Norton, 1950).

as such who is empowered, but the individual as a soldier, as member of the nation, and as agent of the state.

Not surprisingly, in later years many Israeli men come to reflect on their army service with great anguish. "I was . . . a boy of a little over 20 . . . who did all kinds of things, all kinds of things that were fun . . . I was really daring . . . "one former soldier told Edna Lomsky-Feder in her series of illuminating interviews. "We would jump off, flip our motorcycles into the air and crash into a tree! I think I was just a boy. I didn't understand when I was in the war, I didn't feel anything, it didn't traumatize me." Another said, "All in all, when I did my regular army service I was not . . . at all aware of what was happening to us. We were fools . . . And when I started analyzing things after Lebanon with the help of a psychiatrist, I also, I really started to see . . . the true meaning of things."[11] I realized, however, that at this point I could not yet make Ariel see these things from such a perspective.

When Ariel came home from basic training with his M16 rifle, I suddenly saw my boy as a soldier. Something about his behavior suggested a hardening and discipline that I had not seen before. And although his gun belonged to the army and was to be used only in conflict with the enemy, the return of the son with arms has transformative effects. As a symbol of empowerment the gun cannot be neutral. I remember that when years ago I came home with a gun I expected my family to take me more seriously. Jokes about the possible risks of

---

[11]Edna Lomsky-Feder, *Patterns of Participation in War and the Construction of War in the Life Course: Life Stories of Israeli Veterans of the Yom Kippur War,* unpublished Ph.D. dissertation, Hebrew University of Jerusalem, 1994.

disagreeing with me which were made in good spirit reflected a kind of shift of consciousness. Now, several decades later, I could see it from the other side. The connection between suddenly being armed and being an adult manifests itself first and foremost in the family context.

Soon after that day, Ariel told me he'd had a dream in which he was guarding his mother and father by standing in front of our house in the middle of the night. The gun had turned him from a boy protected by his father and mother into our protector. A boy's adoption of this role, of course, reflects his growing physical strength and the narrowing gap between his strengths and his father's at that stage of life. Arming the young Israeli male, however, accelerates the process, and makes physical force more important relative to inner growth and maturing judgment.

The common sexual connotations of guns are, of course, not irrelevant. The Hebrew expression for arms (*klei zayin*) is also used as slang for the male organ, and this linguistic connection seems to reinforce the notion that by carrying a gun a boy becomes a potent male.

On the battlefield, soldiers who are afraid to fight are often reprimanded for behaving "like women"; linking shooting and potency fosters the fighting spirit. And during the Intifada, Palestinian youths often challenged the manhood of Israeli soldiers by shouting curses relating to their genitals and suggesting weak masculinity. Thus provoked, a few of the soldiers ordered not to shoot were unable to hold their fire. In trying to control such situations, the IDF command sometimes deliberately replaced units of young, recently recruited soldiers with reserve units made up of older, more mature soldiers. In this setting, the connection between masculinity and fighting (which on the battlefield contributed to the unit's fighting spirit) became a liability.

Less than a year into his army service, Ariel decided to carry a pistol rather than an M16 on his trips home, as it would be easier to carry and handle. Like other soldiers, he depended on hitchhiking to move between his base in the north and our home in Jerusalem. A number of soldiers had been kidnapped and even killed and he could easily fall prey to some of these sophisticated terrorists who would occasionally be dressed like bearded Orthodox Jews and use forged Israeli license plates on their cars. I supported his change of weapon, but it made me anxious. A pistol was clearly more flexible in a terrorist incident. Yet, for the same reason, a pistol could more easily trigger accidents. It could inculcate a false sense of safety which in fact would make him less cautious. A more profound argument against switching from the compulsory army rifle to the handy pistol was that a pistol is also easier to integrate and personalize. I was concerned that Ariel was making weapons a too significant component of his personal security. I thought the rifle would allow for a greater distance between his personality and his weapon, although both may inhibit the development of inner sources of security such as foresight and judgment. Moreover, the army did not usually encourage a switch to personal arms, and restricted it to officers or soldiers who lived in the occupied territories. According to army regulations, the M16 is owned by the state, while a pistol for the safety of the individual soldier outside of his military duty must be owned privately. As a weapon for self-defense it was thus designated also by the army as a more personal weapon.

Such doubts made me secretly hope that Ariel's request would not be approved by the army. In the end, his exceptional resourcefulness won out and he was able to carry his pistol everywhere. As he grew more mature and independent, he felt driven to personalize his weapon, to find a new balance between power and self.[12]

For most of Israel's history, Israeli soldiers have used their weapons more as members of a collective than as mobilized and disciplined individuals. During the critical period of maturation, the experience of Israeli male youth is marked by a special exposure to force and the responsibility for handling force. This exposure has fostered the development of a particular Israeli version of what I have called "external individualism," which lacks the internal dimension of "individuation."

For young men carrying arms without the internal constraints of a mature self—without the checks of self-knowledge and the ability to evaluate the complexities of the use of lethal force—shooting is a group act which is almost fully directed, perhaps even controlled, from the outside. Young soldiers carrying guns, therefore, have high stakes in the clarity of their missions and the unambiguous identity of their potential targets. The absence of the internal voice of the self is congenial for just such clarity. Armed youth are always prone to embrace the ideology and the emotional attitudes that render the use of their weapons clear and simple. At the other extreme, of course, reflective, mature individuals are likely to be trapped in Hamlet-like indecisiveness. Strong nationalist feelings and a propensity to take risks can allow young men to overcome such hesitations. But when a war's objectives are less than self-

---

[12]A few months following his release from the regular army, Ariel finally felt he was ready to rid himself of his pistol altogether.

evident or are even controversial, when soldiers are restrained by a more developed sense of individual selfhood and the enemy is not clearly defined and even a decisive military victory is not likely to be glorious, the use of force is transformed profoundly. Under such circumstances, bullets shot at the enemy may ricochet, so to speak, maybe even years later. They may inflict unanticipated wounds on the psyche of the man who fires them as he becomes more reflective and recognizes himself as an individual apart from the group of comrades or the nation. If only each soldier, I thought, reflecting on my own experience, would learn to play the violin before handling a gun; if only the boy had a chance to discover or make up his own tune, to recognize his own sound in the symphony of sounds around him, then he might handle his gun differently. In a truly liberal and democratic society, I thought, Odysseus's bow the musical instrument comes before his bow the instrument of war; the epic never eclipses the lyrical and the arrows are always invisibly attached to the strings of the lyre.

>   > >   *III*

Power and Conscience in Modern Israel

> > 8

Historicizing the Fantasy of Jewish Power

At the heart of the Zionist revolution that culminated in the creation of the State of Israel in 1948 was the transformation of the Jew from a member of a disempowered and vulnerable religious minority into an armed citizen-soldier of a sovereign state governed by a Jewish majority.

The use of military force by Jews; the need to cope with the inevitable, unanticipated effects and costs of state-sponsored violence; the need, before and after, to explain and defend its use to bereaved families, the larger society, and the tribunal of world public opinion—all these have influenced the fashioning of modern Israeli experience and distinguished it from the experience of Jewish communities in other times and places. Most important, it is this internal individual and communal dialogue with the power to kill that ultimately led Israel to renounce the idea of a military solution to its conflict with the Arabs, and persuaded most Israelis to pursue a peaceful settlement with their neighbors even at the cost of enormously painful compromises and domestic strife.

The antiheroic, militarily inexperienced Jews of the Diaspora characteristically have responded to the experience of power through irony and fantasy, two sometimes complementary ways of adapting to unchallengeable realities. In her illuminating literary study of the "schlemiel," the fool, as "modern Jewish hero," Ruth Wisse characterizes the ironic response of the powerless Jew to force directed at him by invoking a widely known Yiddish joke. Facing a Gentile policeman pointing his gun at him, the schlemiel cries, "What is the matter with you, are you crazy? Can't you see that this is a human being?" As a doomed victim the Jew can only hope for a momentary verbal triumph, an attitude which ironizes the truth of his imminent fall. Helpless to change his fate, the Jew can still sound the voice of humanity, still try to build a fragile verbal suspension bridge over the abyss between his absolute faith and his absolute vulnerability.[1]

Perhaps the most instructive expression of Jewish fantasy in the face of danger is the legend of the Golem. The Golem is an artificial man, created by magic, often for the purpose of defending the Jews. The roots of the Golem's legend are found in Talmudic tracts and later in medieval and Renaissance Jewish texts as well. The earlier, Talmudic versions of the Golem legend focus on the superior spiritual powers of the conjuring rabbi; the folk literature and art of later centuries shifts the focus to the supernatural physical force of the Golem as a giant capable of destroying the enemies of the Jews.[2]

The Golem is commonly depicted as a creature formed out of clay and animated by the magical manipulation of Hebrew

---

[1] Ruth Wisse, *The Schlemiel as Modern Hero* (Chicago: University of Chicago Press, 1971).
[2] Emily D. Bilski, *Golem! Danger, Deliverance and Art*, foreword by Isaac Bashevis Singer, with essays by Moshe Idel and Elfi Ledig (New York: The Jewish Museum, 1988) (in Hebrew).

letters and divine names. The most popular modern version of the legend is the one associated with Rabbi Yehuda Loew of Prague; toward the end of the sixteenth century, it is said, he used a secret recipe to create a Golem for the protection of the Jews of Prague. The Golem in this story is a blind artificial force directed from the outside by its master. In many versions of the legend, the Golem, created to serve its maker, grows beyond the maker's control and threatens to become destructive. As a Jewish Frankenstein, the Golem reflects a conception of force scarcely controllable by human agency. Isaac Bashevis Singer aptly observed that the Golem legend is a statement about the limitations of human agency and human control. "Our history," he writes, "is a preordained history of Golems. Freedom is and will remain an illusion."[3]

As a fantasy of power not subordinate to the free human will, the legend of the Golem reflects the Jewish condition and consciousness of powerlessness. It is pertinent, of course, that, as Jewish responses to power in the Diaspora, both irony and fantasy conceive force as something possessed and exercised by the "other." The ironic response to power is verbal, and the rabbi who knows the magic of power performs the miracle of the Golem by manipulating words. In this context irony and fantasy, as Jewish responses to powerlessness—the clever schlemiel and the Jewish master who creates an artificial giant—embody the deep Jewish faith in the word, in the superiority of language over physical force. Such a faith has been a key component of Diaspora Jewish culture. In the absence of sovereignty, military power, and territory, the word

---

[3]Ibid.

of God, the Holy Scriptures, and the words of the rabbis became the ultimate means of world-making, of acting and interpreting, of shaping and protecting life, of resurrecting the
ruined Temple, the conquered Holy Land, and the Lost Kingdom.

The Jewish religious imagination has produced an extraordinarily rich repertory of symbolic and ritualistic strategies, through which the Jews of exile, lacking access to the
instruments of military force, could nevertheless feel connected to the divine and cosmic power. The very organization of the life of the individual and the community
according to the injunctions of the religious law empowers
God as the supreme actor. Sometimes physical force was regarded as a manifestation of spiritual power to which
unique individuals (and, in some instances, the entire community) could have access. Jewish texts, prayers, and festivals often explicitly focused on the ways to influence the
conduct of divine powers. The ancient Jewish practice of regarding God as the ultimate King and warrior is, of course,
an integral part of this tradition.

Sometimes words and symbols were aimed directly at perceived sources of evil. Documentary evidence suggests that the
Jews of the fourth century in the Christianized Roman Empire
used to burn the effigy of Haman, the grand persecutor of the
Jews of Persia, and those of other enemies of the Jews as symbolic acts of revenge. The nineteenth-century Jewish historian
Heinrich Graetz saw a connection between the development
of such practices of symbolic aggression and Jewish powerlessness. Moshe Idel describes in detail Jewish Kabbalistic practices
during the early modern period, which rested on the belief
that the manipulation of divine names and secret word se-

quences could influence the course of divine, demonic, and cosmic forces.[4]

Zionism, the founding of paramilitary Jewish organizations before the establishment of the State of Israel, and the creation of the Israel Defense Forces embody a revolutionary change in the relations between words and works, language and power, in modern Jewish society. Military force has opened a new chapter in the history of the Jews and of Jewish culture; it has prompted Jews to redraw the established boundaries between force, language, action, and fantasy in Israel and in the Jewish Diaspora. In many respects the polarization between Israel and the Diaspora toward the end of the twentieth century reflects profoundly different interpretations of the meaning of force and its implications for Jews.

Since 1948, physical force has been entrusted to Jewish hands for the first time in the modern era, forcing the Israeli Jew to consider and experience power not as a passive spectator, a member of a tolerated minority or a defenseless victim, but as an actor in both the domestic and international arenas. From the moment an Israeli Jew held a loaded gun in his hands the relations between self and community, language and power, imagination and action were transformed. As responses to power, irony and fantasy in the universe of the weak and the helpless are profoundly different from irony and fantasy in the universe of armed citizens. The armed Israeli Jew who sees power from the sights of his rifle rather than facing the barrel of the gun is not likely to gravitate toward irony and

---

[4]Moshe Idel, *Studies in Ecstatic Kabbalah* (Jerusalem: Academon, The Hebrew University Students Printing and Publishing House, 1990) (in Hebrew).

fantasy as weapons of last resort. As Israel has gained and held force, the need to constantly guide and justify its uses and consequences has become a principal modern Jewish preoccupation.

While modern Israeli Jews have characteristically reacted to the schlemiel's ironic gesture in the face of overwhelming force with contempt, they have often been drawn to the fantasy of the Golem and the mystification of power. Since Zionist ideology has rested on a Jewish narrative of redemption, of return and liberation, it has encouraged fantasies of force as monumental as the dream itself. While Zionism as a secular ideology encouraged this-worldly and pragmatic rather than other-worldly messianic orientations toward power, the attempts to bring about liberation turned that fantasy into a potent evocative ideology. Jewish freedom fighters, soldiers, policemen, and spies were quickly mythologized as soldiers of the dream. Since the State of Israel was established, historical events have been enlisted to mystify Jewish power. The Mossad's kidnapping of the Nazi criminal Adolf Eichmann, the spectacular Six-Day War victory over Nasser's Egypt, the Entebbe rescue operation of Israeli passengers whose airplane was hijacked to Uganda, and the bombing of the nuclear reactor of Saddam Hussein's Iraq were such events. In these cases the uses of power seemed to uphold the fantasies of formerly powerless victims and feed the celebration of the new Jews as virtuosos in military strategy. The Zionist vision of Jewish progress—from persecution and annihilation to revolution, immigration, and liberation by means of the heroic exercise of force—presumed Israeli Jews' ability to acquire enough military might to enable them to shape their own destiny. It is certainly necessary to have power in order to enact an epic narrative of return and liberation. For Zionists, the possession of military force meant ultimately the opportunity to match "the real with the will," to regain the capacity to shape the collective history of the nation. In the Diaspora, Jews' allegiance to their traditions and practices in adverse circumstances depended largely upon their capacity to integrate failures and disasters into an edifying narrative of collective mission and ultimate messianic restoration. Zionism, in contrast, committed its followers to pragmatic tests of success, to the effective use of force—to the ability to win, at least part of the time. In the optimistic Zionist narrative, failed actions would devastate the morale of the whole society and affect the very future of the entire enterprise.

The commitment to building up and using force—to actually realizing the redemptive narrative of return—has compelled Zionists (and later Israelis) to reckon with a paradox. On the one hand, the creation of a "Jewish state" (with the risks to human lives it entailed) demanded a vision that could motivate people to make the ultimate sacrifice. Zionism required a redemptive narrative that could fuel a revolution. On the other hand, the use of physical force required a pragmatic, realistic approach that would check the self-destructive pursuit of unachievable, fantastic goals. No wonder the history of Israel has largely been a history of tensions and shifts between redemptive and pragmatic orientations toward power. Such tensions were discernible, of course, before the state was established, in the conflicts between the Irgun and the Haganah, the pre-state paramilitary Jewish organizations. As founder and first Prime Minister of the state, David Ben-Gurion had the exceptional ability both to engage the high rhetoric of Zionism and to use Israel's limited military power pragmatically.

With the founding of the Israel Defense Forces in 1948, these differences found their expressions in two alternative "philosophies" of power, sometimes allied with right-wing and left-wing Zionist parties and sometimes indifferent to party lines.

One of the most illuminating pre-state clashes between these two approaches occurred following what is known as the "*Patria* disaster" in November 1940. The *Patria* was a refugee boat carrying about 1,800 European Jews in flight from the Nazis; it anchored finally at the port of Haifa. The British authorities refused to let the "illegal" immigrants disembark and prepared to force the boat to leave the port and sail to the island of Mauritius. The frustrations of the Jewish refugees and of the Jewish leadership in Palestine were mounting when a bomb went off inside the boat, causing it to sink. About 250 refugees were drowned and scores of others were injured. The Jewish community in Palestine was shocked. At the time, only a few people knew that leaders of the Yishuv (the pre-state Jewish community in Palestine) and the Haganah had been involved in the decision to set off the bomb on the ship, and had supplied explosives to the refugees, who agreed to act on their behalf.

Apparently the Jewish leaders intended merely to disable the ship in order to gain more time to mobilize public opinion and pressure the British government to open the gates of Palestine to the Jewish refugees. The terrible unanticipated consequences of the operation stirred a painful debate within the leadership. In this case, the protagonists were members of the Labor camp (Mapai). One group, while regretting the terrible results of the bomb, justified the action as warranted by the objective of securing free Jewish immigration. Its members regarded the dead as martyrs who had sacrificed their lives for a noble cause. One of the involved commanders, referring to the action of detonating the bomb on the boat, later said that it was "our right and our determination to adhere to our purpose." On the other side, a group of critics focused mercilessly on the discrepancy between the goal and the consequences. One critic insisted that "if a few of us would have committed suicide at the door of the British High Commissioner to protest the torture of the refugees stranded on this and other boats one could at least commend the act as 'self sacrifice.' But an action that leads to the deaths of hundreds of other people is a hideous act."[5] The action's defenders characteristically insisted that the drowned refugees were victims of the British policy, while the critics focused on the tragic consequences of the Jewish decision to set off the bomb.

What makes the *Patria* affair so important in retrospect is not so much the polarization between the ideological and the pragmatic perspectives. It is that the *Patria* affair reveals the way actual experience of the use of physical force has affected the Israeli discourse on power and its uses. It gave Jews a very novel, if shocking, opportunity to experience the dark side of power from the perspective of those who apply it. Here, uncharacteristically, Jews were exposed to the tragic experience of power from the perspective of the armed persons who have to face the unintended consequences of their decisions to use force. While in the course of time an increasing number of Israelis witnessed the discontinuities between the intended and the unanticipated consequences of the application of

---

[5] Yigal Elam, *The Executors* (Jerusalem: Keter Publishing House, 1991), pp. 93–125 (in Hebrew).

force, the circumstances of the pre-state years encouraged the Jewish community of Palestine to resist doubts and criticism and to frame the *Patria* affair as another chapter in the heroic Jewish struggle for independence—a struggle Ben-Gurion summoned Israeli writers to extol. Leaders of a national liberation movement can hardly afford to dwell on the dark side of military power—on its great potential for self-destruction, its intrinsic ugliness, and its inherent uncertainties. In a recent study of Zionist conceptions of power in the pre-state period,[6] Anita Shapira points out that the dominant position in the pre-state Zionist discourse of power was consistent with the ethos of "self-defense," the attitude according to which military force was used merely in order to protect a threatened community fighting for its survival and liberation. While there were important differences between various Jewish organizations and political orientations, they shared the tendency to conceive and justify the uses of violence as means of coping with external threats to independence and security. The actual effects of force and its consequences for the victims were usually seen as necessary, inevitable results of pursuing these noble goals. The defensive ethos enabled Jewish leaders to attribute unanticipated consequences to external circumstances rather than taking responsibility for them.

Actions were judged by these leaders' intentions or ideological rationale rather than their effects. This was a tendency reinforced by a fundamental Zionist attitude toward Jewish power as a symbolic expression of the Jewish claim for free-

---

[6]Anita Shapira, *Land and Power* (Tel Aviv: Am Oved Publishers, 1992) (in Hebrew).

dom, independence, and justice. Particularly for nationalist Zionists, military power could express Jewish will, dignity, and pride. Sensitivity to its unanticipated consequences would encourage the kind of softness that could weaken the resolve of Jews to fight. They would characteristically invoke the history of the Jews as vulnerable victims while arguing that in order to enter history as fighters Jews must be hardened to the uses of force. In other words, among such groups an expressive symbolic conception of force seemed to restrain both pragmatic-instrumental and ethical considerations of its effects. It took a few decades of fighting before these considerations began to outweigh the symbolic-expressive rationale for the use of force among both Jews and Arabs—before the dualism of the necessary and the tragic aspects of force gave rise to truly sustained ambivalence toward idealizations of the use of military force in the Arab-Israeli conflict.

No matter how morally justified or retrospectively defensible the use of force may be, it was perhaps unrealistic to expect that during those early years of upheaval the soldiers of the Jewish liberation movement would become possessed or paralyzed by the subversive latent narratives of this conflict—narratives that depict what Zionism defined as liberation to be rather forms of colonization, displacement, and victimization of the local native population. Especially during a nation's formative phases, its redemptive narrative of liberation is usually powerful and intense enough to repress competing narratives and dim or erase the memory of accidental or "unnecessary" shootings or killings, of fatal failure of judgment or misguided action.

Occasionally, the experiences of those at whom Jewish force was directed—their suffering, displacement, humiliation, and death—did penetrate the consciousness and the discourse of the pre-state Jewish community. In the literature of the War of Independence, the stories of S. Yizhar, "Hirbet Hiza'h" and "The Prisoner," stand out as expressions of anguish and guilt in the face of the suffering of the local Arab population, the sight of burning houses in abandoned Arab villages, and the deaths of their inhabitants. Yizhar writes about the "screaming silence" which descends on the battered land after the battle, of the contrast between the vital presence of the Israeli fighters and the absence of the defeated Arabs. Most Israeli prose and poetry of the period, however, avoids the dualism between the internal narrative of liberation and the external narratives of defeat and between the high language of a struggle for independence and the realities of carnage. The redemptive Zionist epic (which saw the use of force by Jews as "defensive") was too strong to be permeable to the despair, disorientation, and sense of guilt or futility often experienced by the Jewish fighters. Israelis were also too preoccupied with the Holocaust, the internal dialogue of the Jewish people with its fate and destiny, and internal Zionist controversies to incorporate the distinct perspectives and voices of their victims.

Despite some important exceptions (whose significance increased over time), the sensibility reflected in the literary and journalistic writings during and after the War of Independence continued to ignore or repress the tragic experience of the fighters and the weight of the staggering number of casualties (6,000 dead Jewish Israelis out of a population of nearly 600,000). In retrospect it appears that the need to keep up the morale of the soldiers and the population prevailed. Dan Miron points out that wartime prose and poetry, by minimizing, denying, or aestheticizing death, resisted the shattering effects of combat on the surviving soldiers, the lingering potential of the sight of dismembered young bodies to induce nihilism, despair, and paralysis.[7] Authors, poets, journalists, and ideologues glorified the sacrifices of the young.

The influential poet Haim Guri, for example, composed poems that idealized Israeli youth as the children of their European pioneering parents' dreams, while denying the bleakness and finality of their deaths in the battles; in "Flowers of Fire," dead youths promise "to return as red flowers." Government agencies organized public ceremonies and produced albums "immortalizing" the dead as heroes who gave us "the state on a silver platter" in the words of the popular poet, Nathan Alterman. As Dan Horowitz recalled several decades later, combat itself was inglorious, depressing, and painful, but in retrospect heroic conceptions of war actually helped Israeli youth to cope with the death of friends and relatives.[8] Setbacks on the battlefield, such as the failure to gain control over the Jewish sector of the old city of Jerusalem, including the Western Wall, reinforced the heroic perception of the war as a war of survival, in which, despite many failures, the weaker Jewish side won due to the indomitable fighting spirit of the youngsters, many of them lacking adequate equipment or training.

The expanding shadow of the Holocaust, of course, reinforced this perception of the War of Independence as a de-

---

[7] Dan Miron, *Facing the Silent Brother: Essays on the Poetry of the War of Independence* (Jerusalem: Keter Publishing House, 1992) (in Hebrew).
[8] Dan Horowitz, *The Heavens and the Earth: A Self-Portrait of the 1948 Generation* (Jerusalem: Keter Publishing House, 1993) (in Hebrew).

fensive action waged by a persecuted minority resisting the threat of annihilation. The war thus portrayed the first massive modern Jewish exercise of power as an effort in which weakness and inexperience were compensated for by great courage, self-determination, solidarity, and intelligence. Ironically but understandably, in their first general war, Israeli Jews still seemed to perceive force from the point of view of victims rather than of fighters equal or even superior to their adversaries. The defensive orientation discouraged appreciation for the tragic character of the use of violence in the army.

All that began to change in the aftermath of the war of 1967. While during the period immediately preceding that war the Israeli public and its leaders were visibly gloomy and anxious because the impending battles appeared hard to win and were sure to be costly, the war ended after only six days with a spectacular Israeli victory. The almost total destruction of the Egyptian army and the liberation of East Jerusalem following a fierce battle against the Jordanian army was an unprecedented event in modern Jewish history. A people whose historical narrative is one of defenselessness had waged war with the skill expected of people with long military traditions. Israelis, and Diaspora Jews as well, had a rare taste of sufficient, even surplus, force. Suddenly the narrative of victimhood and the defensive conception of the use of force ceased to make sense. It was at this moment, I would like to suggest, that the Jewish-Israeli experience of the tragic aspect of applying lethal military force to one's adversaries—the kind of trauma that can be experienced by those who shoot rather than those who are shot at—began to penetrate the Israeli mind. Suddenly it dawned on these Jews that they might have used excessive force; that perhaps the miserable-looking Egyptian farmer-soldiers who ran for their lives, leaving their shoes behind, were not such an ominous threat; that although killing was perhaps necessary, it was not so glorious. To be sure, if the Israelis had lost the war, or incurred even a fraction of the anticipated casualties, such thoughts would have been unlikely. But this is precisely the point. Victory enabled Israeli Jews to revise their perceptions of war and power, to shift their focus from fear of a great hostile force to the tragedy of war as such. There was a rare moment of elemental human anguish across the dividing lines of the battlefield.

This condition facilitated the beginning of a long, gradual consolidation of more ambivalent orientations toward the use of force among soldiers, and through them among wider sectors of the Israeli society. Thus began a process of change that eventually broke the grip of the self-referential notions of force in modern Israel and replaced it with a more dualistic view. Israeli Jews continued to regard the use of military force as necessary. What changed was the notion that the use of force symbolized cherished elements of the Israeli's identity as a new Jew. The knowledge, ambiguities, and doubts that came with the actual experience of fighting (and, in the 1967 war, decisively winning) began to erode a view of force that until then had seemed self-evident and compelling.

Discussing their war experiences only a few months after the war, soldiers spoke of the tensions they had felt between the high, symbolic-expressive meanings attached to their conquests, the elevation of their deeds by a lofty, inspiring historical narrative, and the depressing, sometimes nauseating, shattering subjective experiences most of them had while fighting. Since this war ended in victory it was more difficult to ascribe losing one's friends or killing the enemy to a tragic necessity. The unprecedented triumph, the experience of surplus force, shattered the notion that insufficient military power endows the Israelis with special moral force and compels them to compensate with ferocity.

Ironically, the radical change the war brought in the perception of Israeli power had unsettling effects on the Israeli ethos of fighting. In a conversation among soldiers held at Kibbutz Ein Shemer in 1968, several spokesmen noted with anguish that while the deaths of their friends and enemies were final and irreversible, the arguments justifying these deaths would shift over time. In Ein Shemer and other socialist kibbutzim, this was dramatized at the time by (a rather belated) disenchantment with the Soviet Union and a rude awakening from the persistent dream in which Moscow had been the capital of the socialist utopia. Suddenly the idealism that had given meaning to the enormous sacrifices that paved the way to Communist regimes appeared as a cover for cruel and cynical power games. The irreversibility of death, and the apparent temporal fluidity of its meanings, cast doubts on the very ideas and beliefs that had motivated those who had been so willing to risk their lives.

The record of a series of probing conversations among soldiers who fought in the Six-Day War was published just four months after the war under the title *Siah Lohamim (A Conversation Among Comrades-in-Arms)*.[9] The conversations and the

---

[9]*Siah Lohamim*, published by a group of young members of the kibbutz movement (Tel Aviv: Ahdut Printing Cooperative, October 1967) (in Hebrew). The citations below are taken from conversations recorded both in *Siah Lohamim* and in *A Year after the War*, which was published by Kibbutz Ein Shemer in June 1968.

publication based on them (which were initiated by intellectuals from the kibbutz movement) were acclaimed at first as indicating the moral sensibilities of Israeli soldiers as reluctant fighters, youths who grieve over the necessity of using their arms against the enemy. The tendency of right-wing observers to see such ambivalence toward the use of military force as a sign of weakness, as the kind of sensitivity that could make Jews too soft to function as competent soldiers, could not be upheld in this case in light of the army's "historic" victory. In later years, a more powerful criticism of what this volume came to represent was heard from the radical left, which regarded the moral doubts of the fighters of the Six-Day War as a kind of dishonest attempt to remain clean and beautiful, as untainted as they were before killing thousands of enemy soldiers. Thus, in both these circles, *Siah Lohamim* became a common reference for critics who lashed out at the attempt to reconcile war and compassion, "shooting and crying," killing and regretting. In retrospect, however, I find this volume a remarkable record of the first bold expression of dualistic Israeli orientations toward the exercise of military force, a record of the emergence, at the very moment of modern Israel's most celebrated military victory, of ambivalent feelings toward the exercise of force by the fighters themselves. While this ambivalence was articulated immediately after the war within the elite group of soldiers coming from the kibbutz movement, it eventually expanded to other segments of the labor movement and Israeli society at large, a process later reinforced by further developments in the Arab-Israeli conflict. "I want to know," said Eli in a meeting held later at Kibbutz Ein Shemer, "why I fight? . . . History often discards the sacred thoughts which rationalized wars . . . but one cannot return the lives of the young fighters who died." Referring to enemy losses, Eli wondered aloud if "we can found our existence and continue to strive for a just life while inflicting such evil on another people." For another fighter, Haggai, the ambiguity of the arguments for waging such a war was accentuated by the monumental dimensions of the victory. It appears that he and his friends had great difficulties in marshaling justifications for such a stunning show of military force, justifications that would be as decisive as the victory itself.

Aharon remembered the moment when his unit entered the Old City of Jerusalem, near the Lions' Gate. We "did not have a sense of a historic moment," he said, acknowledging his and his friends' indifference when "the Chief IDF Rabbi, Rabbi Goren, suddenly appeared running around blowing the shofar." Aharon recalled being transfixed rather by a small funeral procession that took place nearby. "Four adult Arab males and one woman walked out of the Old City through the Lions' Gate carrying the body of a little girl in a blanket. They walked quietly to a site nearby outside the wall, where they dug a hole, lowered the girl's body, and covered it."

Shmuel belonged to a unit that had fought in Sinai. He recalled a moment when he thought it would be useful to take the ID card from the corpse of an Egyptian officer whom he had killed in the exchange with his unit. When he opened the wallet the first thing he saw was a photograph of two little smiling kids on a beach, and a letter written in a delicate handwriting, probably from the dead soldier's wife. "I suddenly thought of the pain felt by friends in my kibbutz who had lost their son, and here I killed a father of two children." A paratrooper who refused to give his name in the conversation recalled shooting an Arab to death at point-blank range in the Old City. "For a second we looked at each other. I knew I personally had to kill him, there was no one else there. I shot him with my automatic Uzi machine gun, which I pressed against my waist; my eyes followed the bullets, which hit first the wall on his right, and then slowly, as I moved my gun, his stomach. He fell on his knees and raised his head and I saw the pain and hatred on his face. I shot him in the head. There was so much blood . . . I threw up . . . until my friends came and gave me water."

Such shock, grief, and revulsion have, of course, been felt by soldiers everywhere. What was unique in the case of the Six-Day War was that an unprecedented sense of military prowess finally mitigated the sense of victimhood and vulnerability in which Jewish orientations to the uses of physical force had been encoded in the past. Now there was no fear or sense of vulnerability to filter the nauseating, brutal experience of destroying human lives. The ugliness of killing could penetrate directly into the Israeli mind, releasing there its long-term malignant effects on the romantic visions of Jewish military might, on the fantasies of triumphant victory fed by generations of feelings of powerlessness. The force which until then had been regarded mostly through the eyes of David was transformed when seen through those of Goliath. "Following the war," said Uri, "we became the strong ones as opposed to the 'ideal' of the weak, yet just party . . . Suddenly you see a parallel between yourself and other conquerors who came here. It creates the discomfort of guilt." "I returned without any sense of happiness," said another soldier. "I marched through the Mandelbaum Gate joyless, with no sense of the meaning ascribed to that victory. We could not even smile as the crowd cheered us from the sidewalks."

It would probably be wrong to describe such attitudes

among soldiers as representative of the entire fighting force. During and after the war relief and elation predominated. Yishai, who was stationed in a distant post in the south, far away from Jerusalem, remembered the tears pouring from his eyes as his transistor radio conveyed the sounds of the troops conquering East Jerusalem. Yet this elation was tempered by anguish. His unit had to face Arab villagers who would rather die than be evacuated from their homes when Israeli troops surrounded them. "I agreed that it was necessary to evacuate them," he recalled, "but I couldn't bring myself to be there."

As with religion, war depends on faith and on the faithful's willingness to accept the validity of a language that gives meaning to experience. The language of war divides the enemy and us, their soldiers and ours, their cause and ours; it must give us good arguments for why we fight, why we risk our lives. When the faith that upholds the language of war is weakened, when the experience of the war does not fit that language, when the boundaries between soldiers and civilians, fighting and murdering, become ambiguous, a people loses a clear sense of its motives and may lose its ability to act.

Because of the massive application of military force, the Israeli soldiers who fought in the Six-Day War had high stakes in the clarity with which the thousands of people shot at could be regarded as "the enemy." But soldiers talking about their experiences after the war repeatedly focused on moments when the perception of the other as "enemy" was ambiguous, when their confidence and certainty about the meaning of their actions were shaken. Such was the experience of the Israeli soldier who was jolted by a photograph of children in the pocket of the dead Egyptian officer. Clearly it was difficult for him at that moment to think only in terms of the public narrative of the war, to avoid seeing the human tragedy behind the official story, the killing behind the military victory. Even more shocking was the occasional discovery that the people shot at were not armed enemy soldiers but innocent civilians. This was Haggai's experience. "I gave an order and we killed a man. When I discovered it was just a local Arab peasant it was horrible. The fact that the act was committed according to the instructions we had been given did not solve the problem." It is a kind of inexorable re-enactment of Yizhar's story "The Prisoner." A soldier who fought in the armored division said his war experience was considerably easier than that of his friends in the artillery unit "because we do not see what happens inside the tanks we hit." "It is only when you get out of the tank," said Gad, "that you start having problems." "A forty-year-old man who could be my father's age approached me begging for his life, holding photographs of his wife and children." "Boys like us," he continued, "decide whether such people live or die. . . . I knew I had the right to conquer, but to kill?"

Hillel acknowledged that seeing hundreds of corpses of dead soldiers hardened him to the sight of death. But then, when one of his comrades frivolously shot a dog, killing it before his eyes, he was shocked. This killing, because it could not be part of the war narrative, must have confronted him with the horror of death unchecked by the rationale of the war. Underlying his reaction was an unspoken analogy between the mindless force that killed the dog and the force that kills the enemy. Since the dog was not an enemy or a threat, its death suddenly illuminated the ambiguities between combat and murder. Where a dog can die like that a soldier can die like a dog! Such experience of purposeless killing destroys the war—any war—narrative. Almost twenty years later, during the Intifada, when Israeli soldiers were forced to confront hundreds of thousands of rebellious civilians, the ambiguities between shooting at soldiers and firing on civilians defied all the rules and definitions of military encounters, thus triggering a profound change in the perceptions and in the course of the Arab-Israeli conflict.

The unprecedented sense of military prowess Israelis felt during and after the Six-Day War, lasting up to the Yom Kippur War of October 1973, provoked two opposing responses, two conflicting orientations, two distinct approaches to force, which have competed for hegemony ever since. One approach was influenced largely by the fighters' experience of the war as chaotic and disorienting and their traumatic discovery of the instability of official accounts of the causes and objectives of the war. This approach was ambivalent about the meaning of Israeli military force, and was made more so by the Yom Kippur and Lebanon wars and by the occupation. The other approach evolved among both Israelis and Diaspora Jews for whom the spectacular victory only boosted the mystification of Jewish force.

For the former, the eventual failure of the great military victory to deliver a political victory as well—as seen in the prolonged refusal of the Arab states to come to the negotiating table—demonstrated the limits of military force. For the latter, that military victory was read as a turning point, a license for Jews to historicize the fantasy of a resurrected Jewish kingdom, validation of the "Holy History" of the Jewish people. The idea that the schlemiel, the helpless Jew, the victim of the Nazi genocide, had become an invincible warrior fired the imagination of Jews and non-Jews around the world. Just as some Israeli soldiers began to speak openly of their demystified view of combat, they were glorified as the undefeatable soldiers of the rising Jewish state. Precisely when a group of reserve soldiers (many of whom came from the officer corps of the Israeli army) led by the aging founder of the state, David Ben-Gurion, insisted on the necessity of returning the occupied lands in exchange for peace, on dampening public expectations, and on lowering the lofty narrative of Israel's destiny in order to fit it to the limits of military force, they were opposed by a group of leading Israeli intellectuals and ideologues who sought to elevate the national narrative to new heights, to aggrandize and mystify Jewish military force in order to match it to reborn imperial aspirations. On September 22, 1967, a mere three months after the war, this group signed a declaration entitled "For Greater Eretz Israel," in which they asserted that the "victory" opened "a new and fateful era." Now that "the whole land of Israel is in the hands of the Jewish people," they declared, our history and destiny "command us to keep the entire land." "No Israeli government has a right to divide this whole," they proclaimed, placing the idea of a unified and "whole" Jewish state above both history and politics. In their view, not even a democratically elected Israeli government could legitimately make territorial concessions in the pursuit of peace for its citizens.

While the declaration, which became the charter of the Greater Eretz Israel movement, had been organized by activists from the labor movement, its leadership passed quickly to right-wing and national-religious ideologues and politicians. As Dan Miron indicated in an instructive discussion of this document twenty years later, it was significant that writers and poets were disproportionately represented among the signatories of the declaration, including such leading literati as Nathan Alterman, U. Z. Greenberg, Moshe Shamir, Haim Guri, and S. Y. Agnon. The declaration was upheld in fact by a coalition of intellectuals who welcomed the show of Jewish military prowess as an invitation to recast the mission of the state in terms of the Jewish visionary epic, to elevate politics from earth to heaven, to subordinate history to religious or secularized metaphysics, to poeticize politics and carve territories according to the aesthetics of the whole. While these poets and writers did not address the issue of force directly, their vision of the spiritual mission of the state was suffused with romantic conceptions of force.

So while for some soldiers the sense of surplus force called into question the applicability of the defensive conception of Israel's military operations, for these poets and ideologues no Jewish military force could possibly be excessive. By elevating the national narrative to epic new heights, they created a strategy that later supported settlers in the occupied territories who insisted that the Israel Defense Forces were not assertive enough in protecting them, that living in dangerous areas among a dense Arab population required greater force than the Israeli army or the Israeli government was willing to use. So while for many Israelis the experience of surplus force together with the swift gaining of control over vast lands complicated the boundaries between the Zionist narrative of liberation and the counternarrative of conquest, colonialization, and domination, for many other Israelis it was a call to go on to the higher narrative of redemption. The poets and ideologues of the Greater Eretz Yisrael movement and later the West Bank settlers thus found a way to be conquerors without losing the sense of unfinished liberation and victimhood that would justify the use of any and all available power.

Eventually, following the 1978 peace agreement with Egypt, these two conflicting orientations toward military power came to correspond with the rival views of the meaning of the Green Line, the pre-1967 war border between Israel and its eastern Arab neighbors, Jordanian and Palestinian. For the moderates or minimalists, the Green Line divides territories in relation to which the Israeli military is a defensive force, a guardian of independence and security, from territories in relation to which the Israeli military can be only a conquering force, an instrument of domination. For the maximalists (most, but not all, right-wing and Orthodox Jewish nationalists), the narrative of redemption renders the Green Line meaningless. For them, Tel Aviv and Hebron are equally valid spots on the map of the resurrected kingdom, and one cannot insist that Hebron is "occupied" without implying that Tel Aviv is as well.

In the conversations among soldiers (mainly those from the kibbutz movement) shortly after the Six-Day War, one can already see these two orientations taking hold. Some kibbutz members, overwhelmed by the emotional public responses to the conquest of the Old City of Jerusalem (and particularly the Western Wall), noted with pain, even anger, that the liberation of these stones was not worth the lives of their friends who were killed. Other fighters were driven to seek deeper knowledge of and connection to Jewish tradition, as if to claim for themselves the meanings that the Old City and the "Kotel" evoked among religious Jews. A soldier noted bitterly that none of the many victory albums published after the war appeared relevant to his feelings. "If I were religious," said another soldier, "all this would have been considerably easier." Another fighter reported on a conversation he had had with students in a Jerusalem yeshiva. "I found out that for them the issue of the war was much simpler. Judaism, at least as it is currently being interpreted, is apparently much less pacifistic than it appeared to us. There must be something in the formation of a religious person that facilitates identification with the national mission, a supreme imperative which subordinates the value of the individual . . . which binds him to the collective and renders his mission very clear and uncompromising.''

Reading these testimonies at the time, I wondered: Does religion blind us Jews to the tragic aspect of force when we are not its victims but its agents? Has a vital stage been passed over in this shift from our former fantasies of power—dreams we had in our darkest moments of suffering and vulnerability—to the sudden mastery of force? If our powerlessness allowed us to fly unrestrained on the wings of our imagination, what will check our fantasies now?

The answer that has evolved since the 1967 war is that we have gradually found our fantasies checked by the painful knowledge and responsibility born of the possession of power. We have discovered that bullets can ricochet; that violence is a double-edged sword that wounds the hand that holds it; that religion, nationalism, and epic poetry are not strong enough to overwhelm the counternarrative that speaks honestly of conquest, domination, and the tragic destruction of lives; and that even weak liberal, democratic, or humanistic sensibilities may be sufficient to expose the borders of the envisioned Jewish kingdom as emotionally, morally, and ideologically indefensible. At the end of the day, the bodies paving the way to the Western Wall alter the meaning of the mission; ultimately "the earth belongs to the living" and life, as the ultimate value, commits democracy to substitute the politics of compromise for the politics of utopian engineering. Moreover, in our short history we have learned the hard way that the exercise of military force depends on inherently fragile, uncertain, often erroneous human judgments, that the epic pattern of the Six-Day War was an exception that does not repeat itself, and that even that grand victory turned out to be inconclusive in retrospect. Thus the Yom Kippur War of 1973, which started with a devastating surprise attack on our troops, ended with an enormously costly military recovery and a political defeat followed by years of national depression and economic stress. The National Commission of Inquiry (the Agranat Commission) forced upon the Golda Meir government by an outraged public exposed the staggering incompetence of the army leadership and further evidence disclosed the misjudgments of Prime Minister Meir and Defense Minister Dayan, who were forced to resign. In 1982, Prime Minister Begin unsuccessfully tried to convince the Israeli public that although the military invasion of Lebanon could not be regarded as "a war of necessity" ("*Milhemet ein brera*"), it was a "just war." This war provoked unprecedented protests, particularly after another National Commission of Inquiry found some army officers and Minister of Defense Ariel Sharon indirectly responsible for not preventing the massacre committed by Lebanese Christians in the Sabra and Shatila refugee camps. The antiwar protests and demonstrations, reinforced by the spread of distrust and the decline in fighting spirit among select combative units of the IDF, gradually destroyed the leadership of Begin and Sharon. The public criticism of them served notice to all future Israeli governments that the rationales for going to war must be compelling and strictly guided by real, demonstrable security needs.

But perhaps no war taught Israelis the limits of power and the questionable association between security and the control of vast territories as did the Gulf War of 1991. When Iraq's Scud missiles landed in Tel Aviv, destroying hundreds of houses (though with surprisingly few casualties), Israelis sitting anxiously in sealed rooms wearing gas masks realized the gap between the heroic rhetoric of the Likud-led government and the government's humiliating inability to protect the civilian population. How innocent and credulous we were! When we realized that sealing our rooms with Scotch tape and donning malfunctioning gas masks and plastic bags as a de-

The Gulf War, in which the Israel Defense Forces were not engaged—despite massive Scud attacks on Israeli cities—left Israelis feeling helpless in the face of danger. It was a poignant reminder of what had been perceived as pre-Zionist Jewish vulnerability, and it provoked uncharacteristic black humor among Israelis. In the photograph, my younger daughter, Tehila, is wearing a T-shirt popular at the time, an ironic "souvenir" of the gas-mask experience.

fense against chemical warheads was ridiculous, when we learned how vast Saddam Hussein's arsenal of chemical and biological weapons was, how close Iraq was to realizing its atomic project, how inadequate our intelligence agencies' assessments had been, and how critical was the role of the United States and moderate Arab regimes in checking that danger, we learned yet another lesson about the empty rhetoric of the spokespersons of imperial Israel, and the risks of replacing rather than backing diplomacy by force.

During the Gulf War, the Israeli public knew that unless Saddam's missiles were equipped with atomic warheads, an Israeli nuclear response would simply be too extreme and destructive to be acceptable. Yet Israel and its allies had no adequate conventional military answer even to conventional Scud missiles. The U.S. Patriot missiles introduced with such fanfare were much more effective—and, from the testimony of former Chief of Staff of the Israel Defense Forces Dan Shomron, we now know were also more deliberately intended—for boosting public morale rather than for hunting Scud missiles. A retrospective analysis of their performance confirms expert assessments that they were not adequate for intercepting Scuds, which they almost consistently missed by several hundred meters.[10] In one of the rare cases where contact was made, the result was destructive. The intercepted Scud landed in a densely populated area in Ramat Gan, causing great damage.

Caught between the technical inadequacies of conventional responses to Saddam's missiles and the compelling political, moral, and psychological constraints on being the first to use nuclear weapons since Hiroshima, Israel learned another hard

---

[10]R. Pedatzur, *Ha'aretz*, October 24, 1991, and *Ha'aretz*, December 26, 1991. See also, by the same author, "Evolving Ballistic Missile Capabilities and Theater Missile Defence: The Israeli Predicament," *Security Studies*, Vol. 3, No. 3 (Spring 1994), pp. 521–70.

lesson about the weakness of excessive force. The Gulf War, and the scores of Lebanese civilians killed by Israeli artillery a few years later when the Israeli army was hunting for Hezbollah Katyusha rocket launchers installed near a United Nations safe area in Kana where these civilians had sought refuge, taught Israel what the Vietnam War had taught the United States: that an adversary can gain a great advantage when it chooses a level of violence that can be handled effectively only by a much larger force which cannot discriminate between military and civilian targets, and therefore is illegitimate in the post-Auschwitz and post-Hiroshima world.

Much more consequential and important for the Israeli-Palestinian conflict was, of course, the other, more prolonged experience with the limits of surplus force: the Palestinian revolt or Intifada. The spontaneous popular Palestinian uprising took the Israelis (as well as the Palestine Liberation Organization based in Tunis) completely by surprise. Perhaps the most significant fact about the revolt was the Palestinian discovery that stones can be much more eloquent than bullets. When tens of thousands of unarmed Palestinians (including many women and children) confronted armed Israeli soldiers, they trapped the Israeli army between the use of firearms against civilian demonstrators (which was not acceptable) and the use of other, more limited, measures to control the rebellious population (which were ineffective).

By eschewing firearms in favor of stones and broken bottles, the demonstrating Palestinians defined the use of firearms by Israeli soldiers as illegitimate surplus force. The demonstrations proved too large to be controlled by the Israeli police force and not violent enough to be handled by the Israeli army. The Intifada dramatized the ambiguities between the roles of Israeli military force as an instrument of defense and as a means of domination.

As such, the Intifada was a powerful attack on the Israeli defense ethos, which is the rationale for the very definition of Israel's military forces as "defense forces" (IDF). The Intifada also forced Israel to decide what distinguishes war from civil disorder and where and when the application of force serves to protect Israel's independence and security and where and when it is meant to serve, beyond such limited goals, the nationalistic objectives of "Greater Israel."

The Intifada provoked in Israel an unprecedented moral, legal, political, and ideological debate about the very purposes of Israeli military force and the limits of its legitimate use.

> > *9*

Rubber Bullets

The Palestinian revolt broke out in Gaza on December 8, 1987, and quickly spread to the West Bank. Unable to find effective and legitimate ways to handle the violent mass demonstrations, the Israeli military government in the occupied territories lost its control over the Palestinian population within just a few weeks. The frantic, confused Israeli military responses to the Palestinian revolt during the first few months of the Intifada reveal the extent to which this civilian uprising challenged established Israeli orientations toward the conflict. The extraordinary force with which the Palestinian uprising undermined entrenched military, political, and psychological Israeli responses to the conflict showed us our inability to classify the Intifada in familiar terms with the Palestinians as the enemy and military force as the appropriate response.

At the cabinet level and in the wider political arena, the Intifada provoked a debate about whether this outbreak of violence was a war or just an extreme form of civil disorder. A decision to classify the Intifada as a war would have licensed the use of military force against the demonstrators. Any reluctance to make such a decision would imply that

the laws of war did not apply in this case, and that the conflict was to be classified as a civil disturbance to be addressed by the Israeli police. The choice between the army
and the police implied not only alternative definitions of
the conflict and the appropriate Israeli responses but also
alternative notions of the Green Line separating the territories of Israel prior to the Six-Day War from the territories
occupied in June 1967. The ministers in Yitzhak Shamir's
Likud cabinet (retired General Ariel Sharon, in particular)
pressed for classifying the Intifada as a war, but the army
leadership objected, preferring to classify it as an extreme
form of civil violence. The army spokesmen recognized that
shooting civilian demonstrators could demoralize the Israeli
army. They knew better than many of the political leaders
that a policy of shooting civilians, including women and
children, would be not only illegal but morally unthinkable
for many soldiers (although by no means all), and that
such an action would redefine the Israeli army and its objectives in terms utterly unacceptable within the boundaries
of the national consensus.

In their book *Intifada*, Zeev Schiff and Ehud Ya'ari report
that at the end of December 1987, just a few weeks into
the Palestinian revolt, General Yitzhak Mordechai, who
served as chief of the Southern Command, gave a speech
asserting that the military response of Israeli soldiers was
constrained by the values inculcated in the Israeli army over
many years, which could not be changed radically during a
conflict. When one of Shamir's ministers challenged him,
General Mordechai warned that if the IDF gave orders to
fire indiscriminately on mass demonstrators, the Israeli

army—and Israeli society as a whole—would not be able to tolerate the consequences.[1]

This problem of definition was compounded by the inability of either the Israeli police or the army to keep the demonstrations under control. The police would have had to overwhelm the masses of demonstrators through sheer numbers, which turned out to be impossible because the Israeli police force was too small at the time and the demonstrators changed locations suddenly and unpredictably. The police force's inadequate response, in fact, weakened the case for defining the Intifada as civil disorder. But the inability to define it unambiguously as a war imposed serious constraints on what the Israel Defense Forces were permitted to do.

The "compromise" that emerged from this disarray was to send the army troops to act against the demonstrators, but limit their arms and instruct them to act like a police force. It was at this point that the Minister of Defense, Yitzhak Rabin, instructed the army to equip its soldiers with police clubs and urged the soldiers to "break the bones" of the rioters. The Israeli army and police had killed 26 demonstrators and wounded 320 Palestinians during the first month of the Intifada, and Rabin's declared intention was to decrease the level of violence on the Israeli side, in order to achieve some moral parity with the Palestinians, who were using mainly stones. But in the hands of the young recruits of the Israeli army, the clubs turned out to be brutal, at times lethal, weapons. As the young

---

[1] Zeev Schiff and Ehud Ya'ari, *Intifada* (Tel Aviv: Schocken Publishing House, 1990), p. 131.

rioters and the young soldiers provoked one another in face-to-face clashes, the license to beat up rioters with clubs resulted in violence far beyond anybody's expectations. The close physical contact between the demonstrators and the soldiers made control even more difficult. Israeli soldiers in the streets of West Bank cities complained that their instructions were both ambiguous and often inapplicable. The situations they confronted appeared too varied and unpredictable to allow for considered or anticipated responses.

Instead of using the clubs strictly as a measure to check the violence of the other side, some Israeli soldiers quickly began using their clubs to "punish" the Palestinian rioters who had thrown stones and shouted curses. In some cases, they beat and even killed Palestinians merely for not carrying the required papers. The face-to-face clashes immediately divided the army units into soldiers who were ready—even eager—to beat up the Palestinians and those who were tentative or revulsed by the very idea.

This first attempt to develop a response that combined police and military measures failed. Distraught soldiers returning from reserve duty were quick to transmit to the press accurate descriptions of beatings. CBS cameras captured one such incident and broadcast it to all the world, including Israel. These images quickly changed the public perception of beating from "something less than shooting" to "brutal violence." International and domestic criticism forced the army to reconsider the whole issue of using force against the demonstrators. This was just the beginning of a series of ad hoc adjustments and policy shifts which, in fact, never solved the problem, but just showed how hard it is to find an appropriate way to engage the army in coping with mass civil violence.

On February 23, 1988, the Chief of Staff of the Israel Defense Forces, Major General Dan Shomron, issued a communiqué to the High Command in an attempt to fix a set of clear directives that would balance legal restraint with an effective use of force. The Chief of Staff opened by stating the problem: the need to impose law and order in the face of spreading mass demonstrations and to ensure that the use of force by demonstrators "does not pay off." After defining this mission as unprecedented in complexity and sensitivity, he gave specific directives, stressing the need to act "assertively and decisively, but with restraint, self-control, and sensitivity." The use of force was restricted to the specific legally defined objectives of the army and under "no circumstances would force be allowed to be used as punishment." Force could be used only during violent demonstrations, in disorders, or in overcoming resistance to legal arrests. But the use of force in such cases should not exceed "the level necessary to accomplish the specifically designated objectives and only within the limits of the time and the place of the violent event." "No force will be used after the objectives of the intervention are achieved . . . and in each case the force used should be reasonable." Soldiers, the Chief of Staff warned, should "refrain as much as possible from beating people on the head or other sensitive parts." They should refrain from "abusing and humiliating the local population and avoid deliberately damaging property." Major General Shomron then concludes with the following words: "We shall continue to fulfill our tasks and overcome the violence directed at us while adhering, despite the difficulties, to the legal and moral norms as well as to the standards of disciplined conduct which were imparted to us."[2]

Many officers and soldiers responded to the communiqué with ambivalence and anger. They insisted that the instructions were applicable on paper but seldom in the field. They complained that a soldier operating in the middle of violent mass demonstrations cannot carefully balance an effective and restrained use of force or gauge the limits of "reasonable force." They found it unrealistic to expect eighteen-year-old soldiers to exercise self-restraint and judge the minimal force needed, which would be difficult even for mature policemen with long experience in crowd control.

A growing sense of incongruity between the principles enunciated by the army leadership and the actual mission of the soldiers in the occupied territories confronted the military and political leadership with a dilemma: Should they lower legal and moral standards to allow the soldiers to use force more effectively, or should they limit the use of force? Should they risk undermining the Israeli army's status as a defensive force, pursuing the just causes of independence and security within the Green Line, or should they risk defeat against the rebellious Palestinians? Because the leadership could neither abandon widely held restrictions on the use of force against civilians nor tolerate an ineffective use of force against the demonstrators, this gap could never be closed.

Facing this dilemma, the army leadership started to search for a technical solution: a perfect bullet that would stop the

---

[2]See source and discussion in Amnon Straschnov, *Justice Under Fire* (Tel Aviv: Yedioth Ahronoth Books, 1994) (in Hebrew).

demonstrators without killing or seriously wounding them. Enter the rubber bullet. Rubber and plastic bullets were designed, according to official spokesmen, to reduce fatalities and injuries. The "ideal" bullet would allow the army to achieve the desired balance between (in technical police parlance) "stopping effectiveness" and minimal injury to civilians. In order for rubber and plastic bullets to serve their purpose, however, they couldn't be fired from close range, where they could be injurious and lethal. But again, it was unrealistic to expect that soldiers who had failed to gauge the limits of "reasonable force" when holding clubs in their hands just a few weeks before would suddenly be able to do so when armed with rubber bullets. Like the Chief of Staff's communiqué and other directives issued in the course of the Intifada (such as those ordering soldiers to fire only at the legs of the rioters), this directive was rarely applicable in actual encounters with rebellious Palestinians.

At first, rubber bullets were released randomly from canisters shot from guns; the direct connection between the act of shooting and its consequence was broken. Since the canisters contained ten to fifteen rubber bullets and were directed at "crowds" rather than individuals, they depersonalized the use of force. But used this way, the rubber bullets proved to have little "stopping effectiveness." Israeli soldiers could not target the leaders of the demonstrations. Many demonstrators discovered that putting cardboard shields under their clothes significantly diminished the bullet's impact. At the same time, rubber bullets shot from close range caused serious injuries and even death. Army developers experimented with thicker and thinner rubber coating on the bullets' steel, but were unable to come up with a satisfactory formula. They then turned to plastic bullets, which were said to enable soldiers to aim more selectively at the riots' leaders but were not fatal when shot from a range greater than seventy meters. Well and good: but again, Israeli soldiers could not keep from firing at close range, especially because they believed plastic bullets were not as lethal as conventional ones. Even as the soldiers saw their behavior as more defensible, casualties remained relatively high, suggesting that the gap between a legitimate and an effective use of force was closed more at the level of rhetoric and appearances than in fact.[3]

The gap between army regulations and the behavior of soldiers on the ground is, of course, open to different interpretations. Avigdor Feldman, a leading Israeli lawyer who has represented many Palestinians in Israeli courts, noted that rubber bullets were a means to rubber-stamp the use of military force against Palestinians. Others likened the bullet's rubber coating to an ineffective prophylactic, or a mask meant to make brutal force appear gentle.

It is both plausible and easy to be skeptical of any attempt to "moderate" the force applied by soldiers to civilians. It would nevertheless be a huge mistake, in my opinion, to underestimate the symbolic significance of this effort to develop a weapon that allows the army to contain mass demonstrations while also limiting the scope and degree of

---

[3] Jay J. Schnitzer, M.D., and Dean Fitzgerald, M.D., who studied gunshot injuries with plastic bullets during the Intifada, reported that wounds caused by plastic bullets could be quite serious, although they were more comparable to the limited injuries produced by low-velocity bullets in civilian use than to injuries caused by high-velocity bullets normally used by armies.

injuries.[4] The impulse to restrain the use of lethal force against Palestinian civilians was no doubt motivated in part by Israel's desire to improve its image internationally. But it was also a response to growing domestic anxiety about the effects of the Intifada on the mores of the Israeli army and Israeli society at large. I would like to suggest that despite fatalities involving the use of rubber bullets, the choice of rubber and plastic bullets over ordinary ones represents a historic turning point in the Israeli–Palestinian conflict and a radical change in the Israeli understanding of the role of military force.

As I see it, the rubber bullet represents not only Israel's desire to reduce violence in the conflict but more significant, its readiness to actually reframe the conflict, to see it not as a war of survival but as a struggle between a civilian population and an occupying force. Even though, between September 1, 1988, and April 30, 1989, 1,955 Palestinians were seriously injured in the Gaza Strip alone by plastic bullets, and 497 by rubber bullets,[5] the very attempt to blunt the sword of the Israeli army reflects Israeli ambivalence toward the use of lethal force as a means to "solve" our problems with our neighbors. By recasting the conflict in terms of a clash between civilians and soldiers—a clash in which relative Palestinian

---

[4]A sample of 617 patients treated for wounds caused by plastic bullets showed that about 60 percent were leg, 2.2 percent head, and 7.2 percent chest injuries. There was apparently a very low percentage of fatalities. Jay J. Schnitzer, "Gunshot Injuries from Plastic Bullets Treated in a Small Community Hospital in the Gaza Strip," *Physicians for Social Responsibility Quarterly*, Vol. 2, No. 1 (March 1992), p. 29.

[5]Based on documents of the United Nations Relief and Works Agency in the Gaza Strip.

weakness turned out to be a most potent weapon—the Intifada forced Israelis to reassess the very meaning of military prowess in this conflict. Inasmuch as the army (unlike the police) usually represents the use of force vis-à-vis external enemies, the use of the army against the Intifada suggested that Israel was unwilling to treat it as a mere civil disorder in its own territories. Rather, the Palestinians—and the occupied territories—were still treated as *external*, thus reinforcing a perceptual distinction between most of the West Bank and internal Israeli space. But inasmuch as the soldiers were restricted in using their regular military arms, Palestinian demonstrators were treated as less than the enemy and more like members of a nation struggling for its independence. These balances between externalizing the problem and redefining the enemy in civilian terms as a nation constituted a major development. The rubber bullet was a metaphor of the compromise between military and police conceptions of force.

At the same time, there began the attempt to reinstate the Green Line (with a few adjustments, mostly in the Jerusalem area) as a marker separating the territories in relation to which the use of force can be conceived defensively from those in which force must be conceived offensively, as an act of occupation or conquest. In practice, this distinction means that we have come to regard the deployment of the Israeli army in most of the West Bank and the Gaza Strip as temporary. Religious Zionist settlers on the West Bank have argued that Israel must either regard both the West Bank and the land along the Mediterranean coast as redeemed "Eretz Israel" or else see all alike as occupied territory, thus condemning the entire Zionist project as colonial conquest. For most Israelis, however, the answer appeared to lie in drawing lines between territories necessary for survival, which came under Israeli control mostly in 1948, and other kinds of territories; between defensive and offensive uses of force; between our dreams of recovering the "lost whole" and the limits of our military power; between our religious and poetic visions of perfect return and our appreciation for the claims and rights of other peoples and the limits of politics as the imperfect "art of the possible." While the decision to divide the land did not make religious, historical, even moral sense to many Israelis, while the line dividing the land appeared arbitrary, the very decision to divide and to compromise—to live in and with only a part of the imagined whole—has had great moral consequences. It has inscribed into our history a democratic aversion to politics guided by the aesthetics of perfection and has created a border which would serve to limit our use of force. As a geographical line, such a border has not yet been fully determined as of this writing, but it corresponds roughly to the Green Line.

Again, the Six-Day War can be seen as a turning point. Until then, the conquered territories were treated as territories gained in the course of a war of survival. Although immediately before the '67 war broke out it was expected to be a war of survival, following the quick and decisive military victory and the conquest of extensive territories in just a few days, the Six-Day War was reclassified merely as a defensive war. Even though Israel's initial willingness to exchange the newly conquered territories for peace lost domestic support in the face of Arab refusal to negotiate and the growing influence of Israeli secular and religious nationalism, the difficulties of regarding these territories as parts of Israel persisted.

One of the most powerful cultural expressions of ambivalence toward the maximalists who talked about a "Greater Is-

rael" was the Hebrew play *The Queen of the Bathtub*, by Hanoch
Levin, written some three years after the Six-Day War. In the
play, whose performance stirred virulent protests from bereaved families and political leaders like Prime Minister Golda
Meir, a dead child speaks from his grave to his father, sarcas-
tically thanking him for sending him to sacrifice his life for
restoring the undivided Jewish kingdom. In retrospect, it appears more clearly that such skeptical voices rose to counter
the attempts to elevate the narrative of the war almost as soon
as the war was over. In wide circles the acceptance of the use
of military force beyond the minimal requirements of security,
the attempts in the aftermath of the Six-Day War to redefine
what was initially regarded as a war of survival as a redemptive
war restoring the imperial Jewish kingdom, the tendency to
elevate the narrative of war and idealize or spiritualize Israeli
military force, were almost immediately countered by voices
like Levin's, which spoke about the horror of sacrificing the
lives of children, of the reality of the people killed, and of the
false appeal of the grandiose, abstract visions invoked to legitimate such losses.

As it followed a surprise attack on Israel by its Arab neighbors, the 1973 Yom Kippur War was rightly seen from the very
beginning as a war of survival, and it restored to many Israelis
the sense of vulnerability they had had before the Six-Day War.
For a few years thereafter, the idea that the territories occupied during the Six-Day War were vital for Israeli security
gained credence. But when eventually the Palestinians living
in the occupied territories became assertive and violent, the
perception of those territories as a liability gained force as well.
The 1978 Camp David Agreement with Egypt, with its return
of the Sinai Peninsula, occupied in 1967, accentuated the

sense that there is somewhere a line between the territory of Israel and occupied lands that sooner or later would be exchanged for peace. There was no single moment when such a line was drawn. The debate between those who insisted on the need for such a line and those who denied it has persisted well into the 1990s. But attempts to limit the use of force against the Palestinians during the Intifada were crucial. The distinction between defensive and offensive uses of force began more clearly to correspond to the distinction between ensuring the security of Israelis within the Green Line and advancing the interests or security of Israelis beyond it.

Prompted by the Intifada and manifested in the shift to peace negotiations that followed it, then, in just a few years Israeli society gradually carved out its own identity by defining both the limits of its territorial integrity and the limits of its military force.

This process of setting limits on both territory and force—a process symbolized by the transformation of Rabin the warrior into Rabin the statesman of peace—was probably the most profound development in Israel since the establishment of the state in 1948. It was motivated by several distinct causes. Most significant was Israeli soldiers' firsthand experiences of the ugly, shocking, tragic consequences of using force even against dangerous enemies. Because the IDF has always been a citizens' army drawn heavily from reserve units, these experiences were shared by hundreds of thousands of Israelis, who were not insulated from Israeli society at large. When reserve Israeli soldiers return home after duty, they take off their uniforms and become civilians, free to talk about their experiences and even to demonstrate against government policies—including the decision to wage a war in which they have just fought. The

Israeli experience demonstrates that a citizens' army can be an effective constraint on the development of romantic conceptions of military force. Reserve soldiers and officers as well as retired top commanders have played central roles in the peace movement. While some military men have always identified with the cause of Israel's right-wing parties, the overwhelming majority of the top current and past military leaders advocate more moderate, minimalistic conceptions of the use of force in the conflict.

The campaign to distinguish between "homeland" and "occupied territory," between defensive and offensive military force, gained its focus in 1977 with Peace Now, a group initiated by a few reserve officers who were concerned that Begin's government would miss the opportunity to negotiate peace with Egypt. Peace Now quickly became the engine of the growing Israeli peace movement. In 1982 it led mass demonstrations against the Israeli invasion of Lebanon, and throughout the 1980s and the 1990s it headed the opposition to the Gush Emunim settlers' movement. With Rabin's victory in the 1992 elections, Peace Now's long-standing desire to curb the use of military force against the Palestinians and exchange land for peace became official Israeli policy.

Another significant factor in the great turn toward peace negotiations with the Palestinians has been Israel's persistent inability to find a weapon or a strategy that can quell the Palestinian revolt while meeting the criteria of the legitimate use of force. The stone-throwing Palestinian youths who confronted armed Israeli soldiers dramatized Israel's dilemma in this respect, and in response, widening segments of the Israeli public began to see the situation from the perspective of the Palestinian narrative of liberation, not just in terms of the Zi-

onist drama of return. The Palestinian counternarrative, even
before it was fully articulated or framed, was available, of
course, all along to any Israeli who wanted to consider it. But
only since the late 1980s has it persistently surfaced in the
literary, historical, and political discourses of Israeli society.
Israeli nationalists had tried to depict all the Palestinian pro-
testers as terrorists, but with the Intifada they failed. In a clash
of moral claims, not of physical powers, Palestinian stones
proved infinitely more painful and devastating than Palestinian bullets. In retrospect it is easy to see how the settlers
(comprising extreme right-wing nationalists and religious fanatics) lost ground as they were trying to thin down, indeed
to eliminate altogether, the rubber coating of our steel bullets.

Today, the refusal to acknowledge the claims of the other
side, the massive demonization of the Palestinians (and of Arabs generally), remain acceptable mostly among the devotees
of territorial maximalism. These are discernible, for example,
in the rhetoric of what could euphemistically be called "enlightened humanistic colonialism": in the speeches of the
rabbi from Efrat, who takes pride in Efrat's medical services
to individual Arab neighbors while denying their rights as a
group or a nation.

Over time, growing numbers of Israelis have discarded and
fiercely resisted long-term control of the Palestinians or actions against them. From the end of 1987, domestic moral,
legal, and political criticism of the operations of the Israeli
army in the occupied territories increased. The deployment of
regular army units for purposes of crowd control appeared to
weaken the morale of the soldiers and to undermine the ethos
of the Israeli army. Such organizations as B'Tselem—the Israeli Center for Human Rights in the Occupied Territories,

which collected and distributed information on the uses of force by Israeli authorities in the occupied territories—challenged official Israeli spokesmen by presenting alternative, and much grimmer, pictures of the situation in the West Bank and the Gaza Strip. A series of highly publicized military trials of soldiers charged with illegal use of their arms, as well as publicized incidents of soldiers refusing to serve in the occupied territories, increased the public awareness of the contradictory demands imposed on the individual Israeli soldier and the unfair responsibilities the "system" often places on him. Symbolically, the joining of steel bullets and rubber coating was paralleled in the attempts to weld military and legal considerations in the territories. In another bit of symbolism, army lawyers were instructed to wear the black lawyer's gown over their military uniforms when in civil courts; the two uniforms expressed Israel's dual commitment to the effective and the legal use of military force. The fact that the chief legal officer of the Israeli army is accountable to both the Chief of Staff and the legal profession as a whole indicates the potentially contradictory terms of reference deliberately established for the Israeli use of military force.

As Max Weber indicated, there is no standard, no authoritative criterion, that can guide us when the actions that correspond to our most cherished principles are likely to have terrible consequences, or the actions most likely to bring about desirable results appear inconsistent with our most cherished principles. In such cases, Weber observed, the individual must take responsibility for choosing between conflicting standards and causes of action. It is, of course, unfair and unrealistic to expect soldiers on the battlefield to do so during the few seconds when they must decide whether or not to shoot.

Still, it is in this very context that the poverty of Israeli individualism has its most disturbing consequences for the handling of military force. The emphasis on group cohesiveness in Israeli schools, the fact that young Israelis are not trained to make judgments and take individual responsibility for their actions in combat, and the value of collective solidarity in the society at large—all these have made it unreasonable to shift to the individual soldier the responsibility for coping with the inevitable gaps between ethical and legal norms, the flesh and blood specifics of real situations.

Despite the gaps between norms and practices, the use of military force is framed in Israel within a value system that refers to both principles and effects, and this suggests that military rhetoric at least recognizes the need for soldiers to cope with authoritative yet often contradictory commitments. In confronting dilemmas of power and conscience, Israelis cannot afford to mystify "Jewish power" or to spiritualize military force as a means of enacting redemptive Jewish fantasies.

The decision to draw a line between the defensive and offensive use of force and to translate that line into a border between the State of Israel and the "occupied territories" is a commitment to disentangle power and fantasy, politics and dreams. This decision reflects the sober realization that while "Homeland" (the territory of our dreams) cannot be divided, politics, pragmatism, and peace require that the land between the Jordan River and the Mediterranean Sea must be shared by two living nations.

Inasmuch as the affirmation of the condition of being armed and the ability to use force have been the basis of Israeli self-definition, reckoning with the responsibilities of power in limiting Jewish fantasies of empire and redemption is crucial for the development of modern Israeli-Jewish identity. Almost fifty years into independence, conquering the impulse to shoot, restraining the trigger finger, controlling one's panic in response to danger while learning to admit one's fear, seeing the tragic dimension of power not only with the eyes of the Jewish victim but with those of the armed person looking through the rifle sights—all these have challenged modern Israel's sense of itself. Gradually, they are shaping the psychology of the modern democratic citizenry and its conception of force.

This process has made it possible for Israelis to recognize that there is no military solution to the Palestinian-Israeli conflict, and that diplomacy may very well be a more potent *and* legitimate means to realize our objectives. As the assassination of Prime Minister Rabin indicates, the move to subordinate power to diplomacy—to use force as a means to empower diplomacy rather than diplomacy to back up force—has not been smooth. It has provoked a fierce, at times even violent opposition from the radical-secular nationalists, from right-wing religious Zionists, from non-Zionist *haredi* ultra-Orthodox Jews, and from a sizable group of Diaspora Zionists. All these factions share three characteristics.

First, they justify the use of force by reference to national and religious injunctions, rights, or motives, rather than with an eye to its costs or consequences. To all these groups the use of force has had a symbolic significance that extends beyond the instrumental considerations of security needs. Those who find rich symbolic-expressive meaning in violence characteristically pay very little attention to the need to justify the use of force with reference to its consequences. While these groups have often also advanced considerations of security and survival, such considerations are secondary and subordinate to arguments of religious mission, national obligation, or historic right.

Second, all these groups consider the decision to favor diplomatic rather than military measures and to vigorously pursue peace to be a sign of weakness, a failure of nerve, a degeneration in national solidarity; or they see it as a decline of Jewish religious or cultural values in the face of the corrupting influence of hedonistic individualism from America; the imperialism of consumer mass culture; the deluded notions of softheaded moralists from the left and the Israeli intelligentsia; or the influence of naive liberal universalists whose optimism is not informed by the Holocaust experience. Because of such weaknesses, these groups insist, those who are ready to exchange land for peace and prefer diplomacy to force only invite another catastrophe.

Third, these groups all demonize the Arabs and define the enemy abstractly as evil. Consciously or not, the demonization of the enemy is, of course, a way to give legitimacy to a maximalistic use of force. Because moral and religious absolutists have a concept of absolute evil as the eternal enemy of absolute good, evil is never a specific target and the war against evil can never reach a limit. Such an orientation licenses unlimited hatred and unlimited violence.

Because on both the Israeli and Arab sides moral and religious absolutists are inclined to combine demonization of the adversary and justification of extreme forms of violence, they tend to be mutually reinforcing. In early 1996, a series of suicide bombers who blew themselves up in loaded buses and shopping centers in Jerusalem and Tel Aviv temporarily inhibited the slow yet steady shift in Israeli conceptions of the Arabs from enemies who must be eradicated to negotiating partners and future neighbors. There is a symbolic connection between the act of a suicide bomber who turns his own body into a live bomb and the random death he inflicts on civilians. Although the terror is often carried out by a single person and its victims are individuals, it defines violence as something one group is doing to another. While on the battlefield armies usually clash as defined groups sent by their respective states or nations, the random death of civilians spreads a sense of danger, vulnerability, and solidarity to all members of the collective.[6] While the killing of civilians reinforces those trends that would demonize the enemy, as long as general war between Israel and the Arabs continues to be a remote prospect a process of change in Israelis' orientations toward the Palestinians and other neighboring Arabs, as well as in the Israeli conceptions of the meaning of force, is likely to persist.

Israel's gradual shift from faith in the military to faith in a diplomatic solution to the conflict—the shift that led Israel to opt for the peace process—is reinforced by the influence of a narrow, instrumental (relative to the rich, symbolic) conception of the role and meaning of Jewish military force. Not surprisingly, those opposed to a compromised settlement with the Arabs tend to view Jewish force beyond its role in ensuring security and stability also as an aspect of a new Jewish identity or as a sign of recovered masculinity, a repudiation of anti-Semitic stereotypes of the Jew as weak and impotent, a means

---

[6]As the Israeli army has learned, this also occurs when regular armies accidentally or deliberately kill civilians.

of restoring Jewish pride, a symbolic revenge for past crimes against the Jews or as the instrument of a redemptive messianic Jewish mission. Such tensions between an unsentimental-pragmatic, and a romantic-spiritual conception of Jewish force have nourished many debates in Israel and abroad. In an Israeli newspaper interview, Moshe Halbertal of the Hebrew University pointed out that the Scroll of Esther, which ends with a fantasy of the Jews taking revenge against all their enemies, was characteristic of the Diaspora condition of the Jews as a defenseless and dependent minority. Jewish fantasies of divine retribution were developed in this context as a means of coping with fear and humiliation. In Halbertal's view, for Israelis to give such acts literal meaning now that we have considerable military force can lead to actions like the one taken by Baruch Goldstein, who committed the Hebron massacre on the very holiday when the Scroll of Esther is read.[7]

Powerful as such fantasies are, their literalization has been checked by pragmatism inspired by a deepening sense of the enormous costs of the exercise of force which has developed as Israelis have gained experience in combat. In moments of great danger symbolic views of the use of force have had deep resonance within Israel, reinforcing a sense of domestic and worldwide Jewish solidarity, but when zealous leaders draw on such views to mandate Israeli military actions beyond the strict limits of necessary security needs, they alienate the Israeli public. Moreover, as Israeli governments have sent scores of generals and high officers in uniform to the American and other Jewish Diasporas, encouraging a world Jewish cult of the Israeli

---

[7] *Ha'aretz*, April 4, 1995, p. B4.

army as the embodiment of "Jewish power" in order to gain support, the gaps between Israeli and Diaspora conceptions of the role of power in modern Israel have grown. What was useful for firing the imagination of Diaspora Jews humiliated by a long history of anti-Semitism, what was congenial for boosting their pride and enlisting their support in the short run, has often contributed to a systematic misunderstanding between many Israeli and Diaspora Jews. In the long run, however, the mystique of Jewish power as an instrument of divine or historic justice or a source of identification cannot be reconciled with the restrictive logic of military power serving the interests of a modern democratic nation-state.

It was, therefore, no coincidence that while European-born Israeli leaders like Golda Meir, Menachem Begin, and Yitzhak Shamir drew pessimistic lessons from the Holocaust—that Jews can survive in such a world only by relying on their guns; that Jews can no longer afford to trust anyone no matter how strong Israel is—Rabin, the first native-born Prime Minister and a representative of the first generation of Israeli-born soldiers, came to embody a profoundly different attitude toward force. For Prime Ministers Meir and Shamir, armed Israeli soldiers were Jewish victims who merely react to imminent dangers, who wage the wars their unarmed grandfathers could not wage when they and their families were killed in Europe. For Rabin, Peres, and an increasing number of Israeli leaders and citizen-soldiers, power was or is no fantasy, nor is its exercise guided by a sense of victimhood. Rabin and his generation drew a completely different lesson from the Holocaust: that power gives one enough strength to compromise, to achieve goals without fighting; that power means, in fact, the ability *not* to use force on the battlefield; that the most effective and

least costly use of force is to deter the enemy or get him to the negotiating table, where you need strength to back up your diplomats.[8]

Contrary to the ideas of Jewish critics of Israel within and without, after the Intifada the armed Israeli soldier did not relapse into a vulnerable victim and lose the ability and will to fight. Rather, the Israeli soldier has become a more deliberative, less impulsive armed man. The ability to shift from guns to pens, or swords to words, from the battlefield to the negotiating table, has depended on a deeper and more tested knowledge of force, the inherent uncertainties and unpredictable costs of its use, its inevitable tragic effects for both sides, the false clarity of nationalist conceptions of the use of the military, and the dangers of decisive military victories against one's neighbors.

Ruth Wisse, one of the most articulate spokespersons of the Jewish Diaspora opposition to the peace process, has been unable to see the gap between the conception of force forged in Israel's wars and the conception of force shaped by the vulnerabilities, hopes, and fantasies of unarmed and powerless Jewish Diaspora minorities. In her account, Israeli ambivalence toward the use of force echoes naive, liberal, moralistic optimism, which she regards as the Jews' dangerous, self-deluding attempt to deflect the forces of hatred against them.[9] But there is, of course, a world of difference between the liberalism of

---

[8]Parts of this discussion are based on an interview with Thomas L. Friedman, cited in his article "The Brave New Middle East," *The New York Times*, September 10, 1993, pp. A1, A10.

[9]Ruth R. Wisse, *If I Am Not for Myself . . . The Liberal Betrayal of the Jews* (New York: The Free Press, 1992).

armed and unarmed persons, between the liberal optimism of members of an unarmed minority group and that of citizen-soldiers whose majority controls a sovereign state with a great army. The Israeli soldier who Ruth Wisse fears may be disappearing is not the soldier who fought in the Yom Kippur War or faced Palestinian demonstrators in the Intifada. It is the Israeli macho, the Swarthy Jew, who replaced the impotent schlemiel as distant hero in American Jewish fiction; it is the mystique of the soldier in the eyes of Jews who are filled with pride at the sight of an Israeli pilot or an agent of the Mossad.

But the real Israeli fighter may in fact be contemptuous of the kind of ethnic Jewish militarism that Wisse and others espouse. Colonel Yuval Neria would fully embody even the most militant idea of how a post-Holocaust Jew should behave on the battlefield. Yuval received Israel's highest decoration for heroism in the Yom Kippur War. The only survivor of his tank unit, he single-handedly waged his own personal war against Egyptian troops for twelve consecutive days in the 1973 war. But Yuval emerged from one of Israel's most costly wars angry and distrustful of the political and military leaders whose conception of Israel's security had collapsed only a few hours into the Egyptian surprise attack, when most of his friends were killed. This experience led him and other officers to found the Peace Now movement in 1977, pressing Prime Minister Begin to accept Sadat's peace initiative. The pain and bereavement caused by the Yom Kippur War, however, did not inhibit the inflated rhetoric of government officials. Asked by an interviewer to describe his feelings on the occasion of his decoration in the presence of the heads of the State of Israel and the army, Yuval confessed: "A sure way to drive a person mad is to make him go through such a war and then decorate him for heroism. . . . We stood there in the President's house . . . but I felt that the ceremony had nothing to do with the war. It belonged in the President's house." In his address, the President spoke abstractly about the noble moral and spiritual Jewish sources of the power of the brave fighters. But Yuval could only think of his own and his friends' tragedy. "I am sure the head of the army's Education Department knew exactly what we were supposed to represent in that ceremony. I certainly did not know. A decoration is for a success but we [the survivors of this war] represented a catastrophe."[10]

The armed, patriotic Israeli fighter who is, even so, deeply ambivalent about the use of force is alive and well—not only in the Israeli army but on the pages of modern Hebrew fiction. Wisse misconstrues the ambivalence toward the use of force found in such fiction as a dangerous sign of self-destructive weakness induced by credulous liberal moralism. Israeli novelists from S. Yizhar to David Grossman have been key participants in the Israeli struggle to discipline the use of force and to dissociate it from the symbolic or expressive values attached to it among some Jews in Israel and the Diaspora, or even to enlist the characteristic Diasporic critique of the culture of empowerment. But for Wisse such writers appear as solipsistic liberals who project a negative image of the Jew as a soldier, who weaken the Israeli resolve by naive moralism, and who "ascribe a guilt to the sins of Jewish soldiering and Jewish conquest" in the face of cruel and ruthless enemies.

Perhaps the most significant element in the Jewish opposi-

---

[10]"Shiv'a Yamim," *Yediot Ahronoth*, weekly cover story and interview with Yaron London, September 22, 1989, pp. 11–13.

tion's criticism of Israeli–Palestinian peace is the demonization of the enemy. And on this, too, Wisse is clearly a spokesperson of the Jewish right. She writes about evil as if it were an independent agency. "Evil," she observes, "selected the Jews as its target." But liberalism, she says, denies both death and evil. Liberal optimism after Auschwitz, according to this line of thought, is corrupt and self-destructive for Jews. Israelis should fight the Arabs as if they were Nazis. A deeply pessimistic and typological view of the world, a position which Jewish history privileges, does not permit the Jews to be too restrained or prudent. It wants Israeli soldiers to fight with the fervor and determination of Jews whose forebears were the victims of thousands of years of anti-Semitism, persecution, and genocide.

It is, of course, impossible for a post-Holocaust Jew not to have a concept of evil or not to feel hatred toward the Nazis. "When I was a boy," writes Leon Wieseltier in his reflections on the Holocaust Memorial Museum, "I was told of a Nazi satrap in Galicia, in Poland, in the early 1940s, who picked up a Jewish baby by his legs and tore it apart. My sense of the world has not yet recovered from that anecdote; I remember vividly my response. It was hatred. . . . I was, as I say, a boy; but when I reflect now upon that man, and that deed, and those circumstances, I do not conclude that my hatred was something that I must overcome, for the purpose of a more accurate or a more human analysis. Quite the contrary. Were I not to hate that man, and that deed . . . there would be a reason to wonder whether I had understood what I had been told."[11] As I read these lines sympathetically, it occurred to me

---

[11] *The New Republic,* May 3, 1993, p. 24.

that such memories, such thoughts, such intense feelings, which are quite natural for Jews in the Holocaust Memorial Museum in Washington, D.C., are very dangerous for the armed Jews of Israel. When, as an Israeli soldier facing Arabs on the battlefield or in the West Bank, I am holding in my hand a loaded Uzi machine gun with a finger on the trigger, such memories, such stories, such hatred can drive me into a rage of violence, in which I unload hundreds of bullets on the enemy, shooting at Arabs but thinking of that Nazi who tore a Jewish baby apart. Reflecting upon this possibility, I feel a powerful impulse, a counter-instinct to put my gun on the table. I realize that for the armed Israeli Jews understanding can emerge only from the struggle to keep hatred and action apart. Armed Jews cannot afford to be swept by such passions and the fantasies of revenge they incite. As armed Jews, we have tried to understand ourselves as fighting our Arab adversaries, not evil as such. We shoot our enemies, to be sure, but they are also our once and future neighbors. As Israelis, perhaps, we can afford a deeper understanding of the Nazis than can our Jewish counterparts in Europe and America, when we examine within ourselves the possible relations between hating and shooting, between the desire to avenge and the hand that holds the gun. Wisse's kind of ideological Zionism counsels that we should imagine ourselves as fighting evil, not only Arabs—that we should feel free to hate, that we should accept the pessimistic view of world history as an ongoing war of good and evil. This counsel, however, ignores the evolution of the internal dialogue with force in contemporary Israel.

This is why the rubber bullet is such an important token of modern Israeli civilization. Granted, Israeli soldiers wounded and killed Palestinians by shooting rubber bullets at them from close range; granted, the rubber bullet has often been a reflection of the Israeli liberal-humanistic self-image more than of Israeli practice; even so, the rubber bullet symbolizes a recognition of the tensions between the logic of force in the service of national interest and the repulsive destructive effects of its use, the hidden narrative of murder beneath the higher narrative of liberation. In retrospect we can recognize that the Israeli vision of the military as a defensive force blinded many Israelis to the counternarratives of colonization and subordination. The liberal-humanistic-universalistic self-image we Israelis have held for so many years was hardly consistent with our practice. But over time unrepresentative self-images can become causes. Perhaps at first the rubber bullet represented a desire to back up our self-image and appear on the world scene as the liberal, enlightened people we thought we were. But then, willy-nilly, the rubber bullet and what followed redefined in our eyes the conflict with the Arabs, until there emerged a commitment to victory without killing, to peace and security at last. As the conflicting reactions to the Rabin–Peres peace policy suggest, the characteristic Israeli dualism between pessimism and hope, distrust and trust, tribalism and cosmopolitanism, ensures that the movement toward peace will proceed along a zigzag path. Nevertheless, with this process we may have begun to literalize the fiction of our liberalism and to evolve a new equation, a new paradigm of power and conscience for modern Jews.

> > 10
Women as Agents of the Anti-epic

"Can a person who hasn't even been in battle say anything meaningful about war? Can a woman?" So wrote my friend Debbie Weissman in her "Woman's Diary of the Yom Kippur War 1973." If a woman cannot say anything meaningful about war, can a woman say anything meaningful at all in Israel, a country whose short history can be seen as one prolonged war with only a few interruptions? The voice of history as the narrative of battles, as epic, is, of course, not a female voice. "There is no reason to think," wrote Virginia Woolf in *A Room of One's Own* (1929), "that the form of epic . . . suits a woman."

Even where women are supposed to say nothing (meaningful) about war, history as epic designates crucial roles for them to play. Women are the mothers of all those boys who fight the wars or the wives or lovers of those men who march onto the battlefield. Women are the putative reasons we call our army our "defense forces." The soldier on the way to the war zone presumably thinks of a mother, a wife, a lover, or a daughter left behind, all those who need "protection." Conventionally, the woman is the very symbol of the home over which the battle is waged. She is meant to represent vulnerable, precious inner spaces of life and family, of intimacy and love—the very things that soldiers fight to defend and hope to return to. It is the photographs of women and children found on the bodies of dead soldiers that humanize the enemy in the eyes of the victors and make those among them not yet hardened by the war feel like murderers.

If women are meant to feel they cannot say anything meaningful about war in the public square, at home it is they who make war possible. It is the woman who washes and irons the uniforms, who makes love and who vows to be courageous, to take care of the children and not to worry. For days and nights she watches the battle from afar. One dead man can produce four primary female mourners: a mother, a wife or lover, a sister, and a daughter. Even in mourning a dead soldier, however, a woman may not be free to express the pain of war. She may be constrained and interrupted by another agency claiming to have lost that man: the state. In June 1993, Judge Maltz of the Israeli Supreme Court wrote the majority opinion that rejected a bereaved mother's request to inscribe a personal line on her son's tombstone, insisting that dead soldiers are dear not only to their family and friends; "they are dear to the entire nation and to the state." "Military cemeteries," he asserted, "are not private sites of bereavement. They are also historical sites." Epic death requires epic mourning. It cannot permit too much individuation. The woman can, of course, enter the military cemetery and mourn the private person she lost. But on the outside the headstones are standing in uniform straight rows as if in a military parade. This is unmistakably the sanctuary of epic events, not of individual persons.

Still, the state needs the woman to fashion a name for the soldier. The Israeli army created a special set of privileges for "solitary soldiers" (*hayalim bodedim*), those who have no home to go back to after duty, no woman who keeps the fires. This is the exception that illuminates the rule. It reveals how powerful is the need for soldiers to have a home to return to, a private place outside the battle zone. To serve in the army, especially in wartime, is to discover the almost mythical power of "home," of the little things everyone takes for granted in ordinary times. Ultimately the state too needs the home because it cannot stand on itself. There is no battlefield without home, no front without the rear, no dead heroes without mourning women. The centrality of the woman in the psychology of the warrior, her being as vital to the war effort, is symbolized in the earliest war epics by the loyalty of the woman who keeps the hero's home to the end. The value of Odysseus' many battles and adventures depends to a large extent on Penelope's perseverance and courage in preserving their home for twenty years, in making possible that climactic return when they reunite in the wooden bed Odysseus made for their love before his journey. When a woman, like Helen of Troy, does not keep the faith, her husband becomes a loser. Euripides's Medea is a particularly illuminating example of the powerful dependence of the warrior on his home. It is because an epic hero needs his sons for the battle to continue into the future that his woman has the power to dispossess him of that support. Medea dramatizes the tensions between war and the home, which the war itself puts at risk.

The military hero who returns to an empty home is either a tragic figure or a fool, but certainly not a celebrated warrior. What keeps the linear sense of purpose in the chaos of wars and adventures is the reliability of Ithaca, home, wife, and children as the anchor of the man who fights. The state and the army need the cooperation of wives, lovers, and mothers in order to maintain faith in the necessity for and the justification of the war. Soldiers who died in corrupt or frivolous wars cannot be idolized, only pitied. But those who sacrificed their lives while defending their homes are celebrated. Bereaved women can turn instantly from brave mothers and wives who mourn the dead men into the most subversive critics of the war. They can usurp from the state the emotional power of noble death and turn it into a lethal political weapon against the state. Bereaved women can act as victims of a government who sacrificed their men in an unnecessary or corrupt war. In their power to enhance or deflate the tensions between the private and the public spheres, women can be the ultimate ground of either the epic or the subversive, anti-epic voice. In the final analysis, in modern as in ancient societies, women can say a great deal, can speak meaningfully, even explosively, about war.

Even an epic needs limits, needs an anti-epic to delineate a real or an ideal end. As spokespersons of the anti-epic, of private lives within the epic framework, women can enlist the rhetoric of home and family to justify that war effort as necessary for the defense and welfare of society. When they follow this course they collaborate with the epic scenario of turning fallen soldiers into heroes of the nation. But they can also follow the "subversive" course of casting the state and the army as potential enemies of home and family, protesting the war as futile or frivolous, as the unnecessary sacrifice of private lives by an irresponsible government. In doing so, they can turn their black mourner's gowns into garments of protest defining the fallen—on both sides—as victims. Here women sub-

vert the epic by privileging the values of family and home—
not in order to rationalize wars and sacrifices but as a total
alternative to war as a way of life. In Aristophanes' *Lysistrata*
the wives of both winners and losers join in withholding their
sexual favors in order to force their men to disengage eros
and war and reengage eros and home. Aristophanes fully ex-
ploits the power of women to turn home into a potent weapon
against war.

Israeli women who were not aware of their power immediately following the Yom Kippur War learned it quickly
thereafter. Raya Harnik, who lost her son Guni on the first day
of the Israeli invasion of Lebanon (June 6, 1982), was one of
the early bold examples of a bereaved mother who channeled
her grief and moral voice into a biting criticism of the leaders
who sent "the boys" to the battlefield. Refusing to play her
designated role in the state-directed rituals of mourning for
and glorification of dead soldiers, she called the war in which
her son had died just a few days earlier a war brought about
by "cynical political calculation." In an interview for a wom-
en's weekly magazine, she insisted: "My son was murdered because of an unnecessary war."[1] Quickly becoming an
influential and outspoken critic of Prime Minister Menachem
Begin and his Defense Minister, Ariel Sharon, whom she held
personally responsible for a frivolous and costly war, Raya Harnik tried to expand the opposition to the Israeli invasion.
About three months after the beginning of the war, she called
upon the Hashomer Hatzair socialist kibbutz movement
(which had lost three other young men in the battle in which

---

[1] *La'Isha*, No. 1835 (June 14, 1982).

Guni was killed) to break their silence. This, she insisted, is not a war about "our physical existence but about our soul, our moral existence as Jews and as human beings."[2]

During the Intifada even the silence of women became eloquent as a group of "Women in Black" held a weekly silent vigil near Prime Minister Shamir's residence in Jerusalem. It was sufficient to bring together women clothed in black to enlist the special powers of women's silence in the increasing opposition to the bloody fantasy of Israeli control over the Palestinians.

In its most significant and inclusive sense, elevating the value of individual life, of home and family, as a way to disempower the state as an agency of public war is the strategy of liberal-democratic ideology and politics. As a sociocultural and political movement, democratic individualism erodes the rhetoric of war by systematically intensifying the sense of loss brought about by the death of each individual. With the rise and spread of modern individualism, it becomes ever more difficult to justify the loss of individual lives as necessary for the promotion of the welfare of the group. From this perspective, every person has an absolute value and every death is an absolute loss. Hence modern epics of national wars appear inherently anti-liberal and anti-democratic, the exception being wars of survival, where the life of the collective and the life of its individuals are self-evidently and inescapably at stake. Unless the war is such a war of survival, the individual as a private person is always among the losers even when his nation or his state triumphs. War as monumental history always dwarfs

---

[2] *Al Hamishmar*, September 21, 1982.

the individual, effaces the private or the subjective, and eclipses the local. So the development of the inner person, as the embodiment of a particular and perishable self, turns the subject into an ally of Woman as an agent of the anti-epic, for even when the war is won and the victory is spectacular like that in the Six-Day War (1967), the woman is among the losers, and not just because of the men who died. She loses because when force speaks it is History, and History-making is usually not for women.

This antagonism between women and warriors is very much the legacy of the earliest articulation of the genre in Virgil's *Aeneid*. In his poem, Virgil opposes males and females as standing for deeply conflicting forces and orientations. The male stands for power, control, unity, linear progressive movement, and conquest, while the female stands for powerlessness, loss of control, plurality, circular movement, and disintegration.[3] From its early history the war epic associates women's values with the collapse of the empire and defeat. If the inherited logic of Virgilian gender dichotomies in modern national epics still has the power to marginalize the woman, with the rise of modern individualism and the voice of the solitary self, such epics tend also to marginalize the individual as a private person. War muffles the voices of the female *and* the subjective self, always disenfranchises them as the inhabitants of personal worlds. As allies in the advancement of the anti-epic of private lives, the voices of the individualized subjective self and the "woman" often merge as the woman speaks for both.

---

[3]David Quint, *Epic and Power* (Princeton: Princeton University Press, 1993), pp. 3–96.

Another way of putting it is to say that the woman's voice as representative of the private values of the self has been empowered by the spread of democratic individualism in modern societies. It is also to say that the spread of democratic individualism involves the partial feminization of culture and that it undermines the power of national epics to instill military values. The male who resists the automatic march onto the battlefield, who is not sure he was given sufficiently compelling reasons to risk his life, who hesitates to shoot the enemy—this man bears a private voice inside him which posits itself critically vis-à-vis the voice of the group. Part of the distinct strength of this voice comes from the deposits left by the female voice in every mature man. When a soldier hearing this voice hesitates to shoot, some of his comrades will, of course, encourage him to overcome his doubts. It is as if in order to be a man he must repress the woman-individual voice within. His comrades typically cry to him, "Be a man!" "Do not act like a woman!" Often this is sufficient to silence the "female" voice within. The machismo code is perhaps the most powerful psychological weapon with which an epic framing of life can deter its potential male defectors. Reinforced by peer pressure and group sanctions, as well as by the inner insecurities of a young, often immature man, it upholds the equation that underlies the energy on which armies move: "It is better to die as a man than be shamed as a coward (a woman) before your comrades." Thus male soldiers may have to kill the voice of doubt and feelings within themselves before they can fight as heroes.

In a war of survival this split between the inner, private, and partially feminized voice of the modern self and the voice of the citizen-soldier disappears. But the more the war appears frivolous, imperial, or costly in the use of force, the more difficult it becomes to repress that inner voice and submerge oneself in the group. Such conditions produce divisive wars and divided armies, as in Israel during the Lebanon War of 1982. One can also reverse the logical sequence: the more society is permeated by the values of democratic individualism, the more a war is likely to be seen as frivolous, imperial, or costly.

In peacetime, advanced liberal-democratic society becomes thoroughly uncongenial for the flourishing of an epic of national power and the concomitant dichotomy between male and female characteristics. Such leaders as Napoleon and Mussolini, who combined the cult of military values with insistence on the inferiority of women, would sound absurdly out of tune, even infantile, in late-twentieth-century France and Italy. Despite worldwide trends in the direction of gender redefinition, the persistence of an epic frame of mind with its built-in divisions between male and female roles in modern Israel may have been, until at the least the early 1990s, an important indication of the shallow state of its democratic culture. But if Israel's special security problems and its conflict with the Arabs have sustained a monumental historical conception of the collective experience as a narrative of wars of survival, a drastic improvement in Israel's relations with the Palestinians and the neighboring Arab states is likely to both trigger and be affected by radical transformations in Israeli society, culture, and politics. The signs of such a process are, as a matter of fact, already evident.

An important illustration is a decision taken by the Supreme Court in March 1995. In a reversal of earlier rulings, the Court permitted bereaved families to break the uniformity of the official inscriptions on gravestones in military cemeteries and add words intended to individualize the dead and express the more personal grief of family members. In her opinion, Judge Dalia Dorner stated that the change is required by the anachronism of early strictly collectivistic forms of mourning and the development in contemporary Israeli society of more individualistic-private modes of bereavement. The individual and his or her personal life have, toward the mid-1990s, become increasingly the focus also of Hebrew culture; economic and health-care policies have begun to compete with issues of security and foreign policy for center stage. In such a social context, as in other modern liberal democracies, the decline of military values and the diminishing status of military roles and institutions are the symptoms of deeper processes of psychological, social, and cultural change.

Such new sensibilities, acknowledging the personal, intimate experience of losing the person who was also a soldier, have become increasingly evident in Israel's annual memorial day (*Yom hazikaron*). On April 22, 1996, the main public television channel broke with a long tradition of airing documentaries celebrating epic Israeli war heroes and the bravery of their families. Instead, it focused on the more strictly private emotional or psychological responses to the absence of the dead men. One could watch such a program for a long time without having any clear indication that the speakers on the screen were war orphans. Their reflections on fathers who died either before they were born or during their infancy could be compared to reflections of orphans who had lost parents in car accidents. This shift from collectivist to personal orientations toward the experience of loss has been recently ritualized by the public recital of the names of the 20,000 Israeli soldiers who died in Israel's wars. A similar ritual had been established earlier with respect to Holocaust victims. Private values have clearly become more important in mediating Israeli orientations toward war and martyrdom.

Spokesmen of the Israeli right, such as Israel Harel, who would like to guard the flame of the Israeli-Jewish epic of liberating the entire land of Israel, attribute such changes to cultural degeneration, the deterioration of the Israeli youth which was formerly ready for heroic self sacrifices into a hedonistic, rock-loving, Woodstock-like crowd. From the perspective of an increasing number of Israelis, however, ending this arms struggle is not a fall but a liberation. While Harel implores secular Israeli youth not to forget the "heroic deeds" celebrated in verse by the poets of 1948, some of these very poets have (in their old age) looked with growing embarrassment upon those poems, in which they aestheticized and glorified the death of young Israeli fighters. Harel, among the most prominent spokesmen of the Jewish settlers on the West Bank who have opposed the peace process, speaks for what is largely a religious Orthodox and often fanatic community of armed civilians. Immersed in an epic vision of Israel and their mission as soldiers in a predetermined religious-historical combat, the settlers display all the traditional traits of radical communalism as well as the division between male and female roles, which much of Israeli society on the other side of the Green Line has found increasingly alienating. Many women settlers take pride in conscripting their wombs into the movement, in giving birth to children who will join the settlers' "army" when they grow up. But this conception of the woman's social role projected by the religious nationalists in the 1990s is anachronistic at best; in an era of peacemaking, it reflects values of the

Israeli society of three decades earlier when the government decided "to act systematically in carrying out a natality policy intended to create a favorable psychological climate, such that natality will be encouraged and stimulated, an increase in natality being crucial for the whole future of the Jewish people."[4] ("Natality" without any qualifier connotes only Jewish natality, of course.) Such attitudes have long since been discarded by many Israeli women and men even as they have been adopted by another group: the ultra-Orthodox on this side of the Green Line who had been for many years external to the political discourse. Today, the mere notion of "a natality policy" suggests intervention in private matters of the individual. The idea of enlisting the woman's womb to serve the collective needs of the Jewish people is inconceivable in a society moving toward democratic individualism—while it remains perfectly acceptable within the community that defines its primary mandate as the propagation of the tribe. So, ironically, the antagonism a growing number of Israelis have felt toward the settlers' commitment to a monumental military enterprise is compounded by the collectivist traditional social structure of the settlers' community. It is as if the settlers' community and their supporters were enacting ad absurdum the epic structure even as many Israelis were discarding it as a form of life by supporting the peace process.

I will never forget how, in 1969, when my first child was born, I was relieved to learn it was a girl and not a boy. Israeli parents have learned the hard way that girls are safer, more

---

[4]Lesley Hazleton, *Israeli Women: The Reality Behind the Myths* (New York: Simon & Schuster, 1977).

permanent, more reliable presences than boys. One does not feel anxious about a girl's life, watching with apprehension as she approaches the age of eighteen. One does not spend her adolescent years trying anxiously to figure out whether the present war will end before she is inducted or whether the next one is likely to break out during her army service. When Ariel, my son and second-born child, and his friend Tari were nearing the age for army service, his father and I shared our secret prayers that during the army medical examinations some defect—not serious but sufficient to disqualify our sons for the riskiest combat units—would be found. Although we felt too much a part of the army to go as far as Eastern European Jewish parents who were ready to amputate a child's finger or toe to save him from twenty-five years of forced conscription into the Russian army, we were ready to settle for myopia, mild back problems—anything that would increase their chances of surviving Israeli military service.

Having girls, I have learned to my delight, is an experience of love unburdened by the lingering, inhibiting fear of loss. So when Sidra and I went to attend the ceremonies marking the end of basic military training at Talya's unit, we found them almost as cheerful as a graduation ceremony. True, at the beginning it was hard to identify our daughter among those dozens of uniformed women marching in unison. (As if sensing our anxiety, Talya turned her head and winked.) At the end of the ceremony, every girl came to join her family with a big smile, as if the show was over. The ceremonies concluding Ariel's training a few years later were, as expected, much grimmer. I remember the anxiety and the unease I felt as I listened to the short speech of the military commander (who was obviously not in his element) and the exhortations of an army rabbi, who tried to back his words about the great mission of Jewish soldiers with quotations from the most militaristic parts of the Book of Joshua.

Considering Israel's limited human resources and enormous security burden, its army has been faced with a dilemma for most of its history: how to draw on women without undermining the military ethos stressing martial skills and values. In coping with this, the army has followed the easiest course. Despite some token lip service to women's equality, in the form of a few women paratroopers and officers—never high enough in rank to be included in the highest command council—the Israeli army extended the principle of universal conscription to women, while keeping them as second-class soldiers.

Women soldiers in the Israeli army have functioned primarily as facilitators for male soldiers. Inasmuch as fighting is the ultimate function of a soldier, the objective around which the entire army is organized, the almost total exclusion of women from combat roles inevitably pushes them to the margins. So serving in the army has not altered the fundamental status of women as a symbol of the rear, of the culture of home, of what needs protection. This has been very costly to Israeli women and to the larger society. Considering the central role of the Israeli army in shaping social values and in defining cultural patterns, designating women soldiers to serve in secretarial jobs or as telephone operators, nurses, and parachute folders has defined them as a supporting cast even beyond the army context. Anyone who has served in the Israeli army has observed an intelligent, highly educated, and capable, but low-ranking woman soldier serving coffee to a male soldier of higher rank who is clearly inferior in intellectual capacities and education—that is, in all relevant qualities but his sex. In the army, to be a male qualifies one to expect obedience from a woman.

The other side of my daughter Talya's relative safety during her army service was, then, as for many of her friends, the usual frustration of unfulfilling tasks and frequent humiliation at the hands of male superiors. If hierarchy between men and women makes some sense in combat situations, its extension to the huge army bureaucracy is indefensible. In some cases the connection between masculinity and military leadership has found overt, even vulgar expression. My reserve army unit was run for a long time by an officer who conducted himself like a tribal chief. Although married, he enjoyed parading the women who came from outside the military base to receive a most up-to-date, intimate, behind-closed-doors "briefing." His stature among the soldiers was mostly enhanced by the projection of the perfect mix of combat record, military rank, and male prowess. It was difficult to take the regulations designed to forbid such behavior seriously when the Minister of Defense at the time, General Moshe Dayan, was the most visible example of it. This kind of man has a very large psychological investment in sustaining the martial epic that has kept him on top. Such men are frustrated by a society in which male-female relations are not so clearly defined, where admiration and love are secured less through crude projections of masculinity and more through inner personal depth, sensitivity, and mastery of the delicate languages of intimacy.

As a boy I knew very little about such differences. I had accepted the dichotomy between public and private lives as symbolized in my family by my father and mother. Although as a musician my father was not a conventional representative of public or male values, his family was permeated by the Zi-

onist ethos of public service. My father responded very deeply
to the revolutionary national spirit, searching for the particularly Israeli idiom in his art. As for my mother, Hannah Diesenhaus, her emigration to Palestine from Poland with her
family in 1923 was motivated largely by concern for survival,
which they felt acutely after surviving World War I. During the
Second World War, the family celebrated my grandmother for
having, as it were, anticipated that war and taken the decision
to leave a wealthy home in Warsaw and go to a more or less
unsettled land. My mother internalized her mother's survivalist immigrant orientation, and she and my father had deeply
conflicting orientations.

One day I stumbled upon what turned out to be a most
instructive clue to this difference. It must have been around
1947, when at the age of seven I made one of my periodic
exploratory journeys into the attic of our Tel Aviv apartment.
There, among old violins and rusting trunks from Poland, I
found four empty knapsacks. Two were very large, one medium, and one tiny. I dragged them downstairs: what are these
for? My father smiled enigmatically and sent me to my mother.
After some hesitation she explained that when the Nazi general Erwin Rommel, who headed the German troops in Egypt,
threatened to overrun Palestine in 1942, she had bought the
knapsacks in preparation for a family escape. The medium
knapsack was for my older sister, Ofra, and the tiny one was
for me. We were going to run on foot to the mountains a
dozen miles away. My parents had obviously discussed the
plan. My father took the classical Zionist position: there is no
other place to go, this is home, and therefore it is here that
we either live or die. If Rommel had invaded, I have no doubt
that my mother, who was a very assertive person, would have

prevailed. Thinking that she must rescue her family, she would have acted on the well-tested family Diasporic impulse: in the face of danger one moves and seeks a haven elsewhere.

In the following years I must have continued the dialogue between my parents in my head. In time, around the age of twelve, I decided on my own position in what was a formative moment in my understanding of what it means to be an Israeli. I sensed that my mother's primary concern was for my safety. "If you want to have an adventure which necessarily entails risking your neck," writes Nancy Huston, "you must at all costs get away from your mother—who invariably, predictably, boringly wants to save your neck."[5] I must have followed this advice, intuiting the necessary relations between principles and risks, adventures and dangers. This is why mothers do not stand a chance, why they do not usually tell stories, while fathers win with stories that both nourish and kill. So, unhesitatingly and predictably, I sided with my father. This, I said to myself, is the last station (unlike my mother, but like my father, I was born at the "last station"). It might have been the earliest time I felt clearly the tensions between public and private values, between the ideological rationale of Israel as a collective enterprise and family interests and personal survival. As the voice of private family values, my mother stood for all the things Zionism derided and our schoolteachers taught us to reject: exile, foreign accents, refusal or hesitation to rely on force in self-defense, preference for the interests of the family over those of the nation. To believe that it is here or nowhere,

---

[5]Nancy Huston, "Novels and Navels," *Critical Inquiry*, No. 21 (Summer 1995), p. 908.

that "there is no other place," is to be ready to fight.[6] While as children in 1948 we belonged to a nation engaged in a terrible war, most of us in Tel Aviv and elsewhere were insulated from the worst of it. It took many years before even the surviving fighters of these battles were able to talk about their own experiences. But even to fresh recruits innocent of the cruelty of war, this readiness to fight was connected with a powerful sense that the demand for sacrifice stemmed from a self-evident fact that there was no other place to go, that this was home, *not exile*, and that one does not escape from one's home. So, already in the early years following independence, the relation between being at home and the exercise of force was established. The Zionist rationale for the use of force as necessary was connected with the double move of defining this place as home and negating migration from Israel as a Jewish response to danger. The sense of having a home must have been connected with the readiness to become a soldier and fight and the experience of having military force was in turn a condition for the ability to define this place as home. So for young Israeli-born men the very concept of home was prem-

---

[6]"There is no other place" is a quote from Y. H. Brenner; in itself, it does not represent his much more complex position. It is also the title of a polemical essay by literary critic G. Shaked in which he criticized what he regarded as a contradiction in the position of "elite intellectuals" who were committed to the Zionist objective of creating a place for Jews in this land and at the same time wanted to avoid the moral defeats involved in the use of force. See *No Other Place: On Literature and Society* (Tel Aviv: Hakibbutz Hameuchad Publishers, 1988), pp. 56–66 (in Hebrew). In more general use, this expression has come to suggest a fundamentalist-Zionist justification of the necessity of using force to secure Jewish existence in this place, while totally negating migration to a safer place, which has been the characteristic response of Diaspora Jews to danger.

ised on a concept of power. But during the time the Nazis threatened to invade Palestine it was far from clear that Jewish military power was sufficient to protect Israel as a home. My mother's survivor's impulse could not be restrained by the confident projection of power onto the embryonic Israeli army.

As the Zionist conception of home was backed up by military power, it was bound to undermine any notion of tension between them. One was either ready to fight or was already fighting to protect one's home. Those who preferred to avoid fighting and so protect their private lives were likened to those who had left Israel to go back to exile—a place where, in the Zionist perspective, Jews have neither home nor power. The logic of power was thus inexorably linked with the definition of the place as home, as distinguished from exile. It took me many years before I was able to appreciate the more complicated dialectical relations between home and power in a democratic society—to recognize that for many Israelis the idea of Israel as a "national home for the Jewish people" left out "Jews" (and, of course, non-Jews) as individuals, left out the idea of home as a sanctuary of the person apart from the group, left out the life of the private individual apart from the life of the public-regarding citizen. Quite a few Israeli leaders who devoted their personal and family lives in service to the nation came to regard and write their autobiographies as the sum of their public activities. While such leaders are perhaps characteristic of the revolutionary phase of nation-building, their voluntary sacrifice of their personal lives, their internally vacant selves, make them negative symbols of the democratic personality as a balanced synthesis between public and personal values, public and private spheres. Such leaders have the inner making of the quintessential epic heroes, of men who overcome the pull of wife, home, family, and children and go onto the battlefield to make history. It is ironic that Golda Meir—who paid the price of overcoming the woman within, who became Prime Minister by projecting conventional male virtues, who acknowledged sacrificing her relationship with her husband and children in service to the nation—became an idol of women's equality and achievement in the eyes of so many Jewish women around the world.

It took me many years to recognize the profound relations between the value attached to the individual self and the means of checking and controlling our collective force. In a society in which each individual is just an organ of the immortal group, force can easily become arbitrary and is inherently unlimited. It becomes unrestrained when the perishable individual is regarded as expendable and exchangeable—as secondary to the group. Democratic individualism, in regarding the individual and his or her home not as derivative of the nation but as a distinct primary unit, creates the very basis for citizens' control of state power. Democratic individualism leads its citizens to weigh the fact that a piece of land can change hands, can come and go over and over, against the fact that an individual person who goes to his death never comes back. Because the loss of life is an absolute loss, the gradual spread of the values of individualism has forced Israelis to juxtapose "there is no other place" with the no less compelling imperative "there is no other life." With this tension in mind, it is much more risky politically for democratic governments to go to war and try to justify it to the public. And, in the long run, Israeli sensitivity to war casualties has had its effects. The impossible burden of having to justify the death of young persons in the unanticipated and enormously costly Yom Kippur War of 1973, in the controversial invasion of Lebanon in 1982, or in military accidents, has strained the rhetoric of power and homeland.

In the early 1990s, following a long and acrimonious debate on the question of whether it is more important to secure Israel's control over the territories taken during the Six-Day War or spare the lives of an unpredictable number of Israelis who would have to be sacrificed in such an enterprise, the Israeli public increasingly clarified to itself the distinction between homeland (the land within the Green Line) and the contested lands beyond the Green Line, where armed Jewish settlers were building their communities amid a storm of domestic and international criticism. As I tried to demonstrate in the last chapter, drawing the line between "home" and "not home" meant also distinguishing between legitimate and illegitimate uses of Israeli military force, between coming to the West Bank as conquerors or as neighbors and guests. Instructively, the settlers have tried with little success to counter this trend, spreading stickers and posters all over Israel with the slogan *"Yesha ze Kan,"* "Yehuda and Shomron [the biblical names of the occupied territories] are here," are home. Leftist and centrist groups that oppose the extension of the conception of home to the occupied territories, and oppose the prolonged use of Israeli force to maintain them, have retorted with the counterslogan *"Yesha ze sham,"* meaning "Yehuda and Shomron are there"—are not home. Redefining home to exclude much of the occupied territories as "foreign" was meant to undermine the attempts to incorporate the occupied territories into the geography of homeland and its concomitant rationales of necessary security needs.

Since the early 1980s, the ongoing domestic debate on the relations between the legitimate uses of our military force and the politically legitimate definition of our boundaries began to interact more directly with the question of what is a proper balance between public and private lives, national and individual homes, the historic mission of the state to realize a Jewish national and religious vision of "Eretz Yisrael" and the obligations of the state to the welfare of the citizens to whom it is now accountable.

All of us who have been active in the peace movement for over two decades have been joined in recent years by an increasing number of Israelis who have concluded that, in the final analysis, democratic values and democratic social structures are no less relevant than our security needs to the definition of our national borders and the strictures on the use of military force. We have discovered the deep links between what we are on the inside and what we are (or should be) on the outside, between the boundaries of the self and those of the state. We have found that, as a matter of both fact and principle, the definition of our security depends to a large extent on where we strike the balance between nationalism and democracy, between the epic voice of the group and the lyrical voice of the individual. To us it has become increasingly evident that the maximalist position with respect to the proper boundaries of the national home usually corresponds with a minimalist position with respect to the boundaries of the private home, the sphere of personal, as distinct from collective, life.

Almost fifty years after the creation of the state in 1948, the slow, yet steady spread of the values of democratic individualism has begun to transform Israeli politics and policies. Regardless of its long-term prospects and recent setbacks, I am convinced that the victory of the politics of peace in the early 1990s augurs the coming end of the epic history of return, national liberation, and state-building and the beginning of a post-epic Israeli culture. To the ideologues of Jewish collectivism—the religious and secular right—this process corresponds with the decline of the national-civil spirit, the degeneration of Jewish education, and the defeat of idealism by hedonistic materialism. To those in the liberal democratic camp, the development of a culture of the self, democratic individualism, and the diversity of social and cultural forms are not impoverishments but welcome enhancements. For us, an Israel that becomes more responsive to the welfare of its individual citizens, more dedicated to improving social, economic, health, and educational conditions, is a better, more human, and more accountable state than an Israel that continues to sacrifice its citizens in the pursuit of a monumental, unrealistic, and morally unacceptable vision.

If my mother, Hannah, came to this land with her family in 1923 largely in search of a safe place for Jews, Sidra, my future wife, came here forty years later in search of warm, communal Jewish experience. A student at Wellesley College in Massachusetts, Sidra came to spend her junior year at the Hebrew University in Jerusalem in 1962. A year later we were married at her home in Highland Park, Illinois, near Chicago. There, in her room in the house in which she grew up, I found record albums, books, and pictures that depicted Israel as an idealistic, democratic, egalitarian, vibrant, and cohesive Jewish community. Sidra's collection of records with Israeli folk songs was particularly rich and powerful in conveying the spirit of what from Highland Park appeared to be an embattled yet spirited and triumphant Jewish community. Like other Americans who grew up in postwar affluence and with almost unlimited access to culture and education, Sidra and her peers lived in an environment that cultivated individual self-expression, creativity, and self-development. What they lacked was the experience of belonging to a cohesive community. Jewish summer camps like Ramah were enormously successful in providing a brief communal Jewish experience and bonding young American Jews to Jewish culture and to Israel, where many of the camp instructors, songs, and folk dances came from. But apparently camp alone could not offset the alienation engaged Jewish youth felt toward established Jewish institutions, the formalism and pomposity of the rituals in their synagogues, and the conservatism of American Jewish leaders. Through the 1960s, the search for authentic Jewish communal and spiritual experience became the driving force behind the Jewish youth and student movements in America. These, of course, owed something to the cultural and social transformations of the 1960s—the periodic eruption of the romantic-utopian American passion to overcome the pains of an individualistic capitalist-commercial society. In 1962, Sidra was among quite a few young American Jewish students whose search carried them to Israel. In deciding at the age of nineteen to live in Israel, she was clearly inspired by a romantic notion of Israel as a true community. Beyond that, Israel represented to her (as she herself put it) "the possibility of a total, coherent, aesthetically whole Jewish experience" as opposed to a socially and culturally fragmented Jewish experience in America.

It did not take long for her to painfully discover that the

other side of Israeli communitarianism was the much less congenial poverty of Israeli individualism. As many German Jewish immigrants had found a generation or two earlier, an Israeli society shaped and led by Eastern European nationalists, socialists, and religious Zionists (all representing highly collectivist variants of the cultures of Judaism) was thoroughly inhospitable to the values of self-cultivation and unfamiliar with the cultural resources of advanced Western individualism. Jewish immigrants from the Arab countries, while marginalized in other respects, only reinforced these trends in Israeli society. Lacking the traditions of spiritual and ethical individualism inspired by the writings of European thinkers like St. Augustine, Luther, Montaigne, Rousseau, Kant, and John Stuart Mill, Israelis tended to identify individualism with a lack of solidarity, narcissism, the materialist egotism of the "economic man," and capitalism, all of which appeared to oppose fraternity, personal sacrifice, and service. While attracted by Israeli communal solidarity and culture, those Western (mostly American) Jews were unprepared for the rough encounter with thoroughly anti-individualistic, anti-liberal Israeli communitarianism. At least in the beginning it was difficult for them to recognize that the Eastern European Zionists, the Sephardi or Mizrahi Jews and their Israeli-born children, did not exactly appreciate the values of individual space or the languages of the self, that their kind of solidarity required the absence of cultivated democratic individualism in order to thrive.

For many of the newly arrived, moreover, even communal warmth remained elusive. It has been notoriously difficult for outsiders to become members of the tightly knit Israeli "we." Those of us Israelis who have grown up together in the kibbutz or the neighborhood, in school, in youth movements, and in the army, who continue to meet each other in this intimate society almost daily, who know and remember who loved whom, and who left whom since, say, 1948, we who have hugged each other at funerals during all those wars—we form a close group that has never been very open to new members. Like Diaspora Jews who loved the idea of Israel so much more than the Israelis, we loved the idea of Aliya (the return of the Jews) more than the *olim* themselves. Our presence must have made many of those who had come to join us from afar or to serve in the army with us feel distant and alienated.

The problem must have been exacerbated for Sidra, who came to Israel as a student from a top American college famous for encouraging women to pursue excellence and aspire to independent roles suited to their talents. In Israel the gap between the notion of women's equality and women's actual stature in society was even deeper than that between the notion of Israeli liberal-democratic individualism and the reality of Israeli anti-liberal communitarianism.[7] It took years for Israeli social scientists and the Israeli feminist movement to articulate the problem. Women who had moved to responsible positions by speaking in the rough colloquial accent of the military commander, women who became eligible to enter "male games" by concealing whatever emotions and sensitivities or charm the Israeli society has attributed to "women"— they have always served as a convenient cover for women's lack of equality. Now that it is okay for Israeli paratroopers to cry visibly at a funeral of a friend and okay for Israeli television to

---

[7]Hazleton, *Israeli Women: The Reality Behind the Myths.*

show such pictures without scandalizing the public, those dichotomies between males and females seem part of the past.
But this is still only partly true. Israeli coalition politics still
permits Orthodox rabbis, for example, to stall and delay legislation that in other democracies secures the elementary
rights of women.

To be deeply moved by Israeli solidarity and heroism from
the vantage point of one's life in New York, Chicago, or Los
Angeles was one thing for an American Jew; to try to take part
in this unfolding epic and live inside it was something else.
For the Diaspora Jew in America or elsewhere, the vicarious
participation in Israel as a corporate Jewish experience was in
many ways an ideal solution. One could continue to fulfill oneself in one's own society, free to cultivate one's own talents,
idiom, space, creativity and relations, one could take full advantage of anonymity and mobility as precious resources for
experimenting with and testing new forms of individual life,
and still one could rally in the local synagogue or join the
crowd in the nearest Jewish community center to give one's
support to Israel, to the idea of the Jews as a people who have
the right to survive and realize its collective potential in its
own sovereign state. This safe geographic split between the
spheres of individual and collective corporate Jewish experience would be reinforced, of course, on one's periodic visits
to Israel. Whatever friction Western Jews had while encountering the rough Israelis in the street, on buses, or in restau-
rants was usually eclipsed by Israeli curiosity about and
generosity toward fellow Jews from abroad, and by the moving
experiences of the Western Wall, Masada, or Yad Vashem, or
a maudlin speech by a Golda Meir on "our children the soldiers." In time it was proven that one could love, participate

in, and be proud of the idea of Israel without being too disturbed by the Israelis themselves.

Israel and America came eventually to be classified as two distinct forms of modern experience for Jews. The former is a tough, collectivist, dangerous, and heroic country, the latter individualistic, safe, and rich with opportunities; the former is mostly for refugees and people with a low standard of living, the latter largely a haven of individually successful and well-to-do Jews who voluntarily part with some of their wealth in order to help rescue the latest wave of Jewish refugees or alleviate the harsh conditions of the Israeli poor.

But for American Jews like Sidra, who stayed in Israel, this convenient split between the collective and individualistic dimensions of Jewish (and human) experience was not possible. As Jewish immigrants from one of the most advanced liberal-democratic cultures in the world, these Jews found themselves pulled in different directions by the two cultures. Many left and went back. Others relinquished the vestiges of American identity and remade themselves as Israeli insiders. Still others tried to bring together an American Jewish identity (with its special liberal idiom) and an Israeli identity.

Sidra has chosen this last approach. For years, as her Israeli husband, I have shared her pains, but because of our relationship, I have also been able to become an insider with an outsider's perspective, to see what the native in me was blind to. American Jewish immigrants like Sidra have made important attempts to support liberal values on issues particularly important to them—education, religious practice, and the Arab–Israeli conflict. They have established schools which are more deeply committed to encouraging students to be independent, creative individuals; they have created synagogues in which religious practice is more open, more experimental, more egalitarian, and more responsive to women's needs; and, perhaps most important, they have been active in the Israeli peace movement, especially in promoting dialogue with Palestinians.

On the day (September 9, 1993) that Israeli and Palestinian leaders vowed to cooperate in the promotion of peace, I saw many of these Israeli Americans, their native Israeli co-workers, and their Palestinian partners celebrating together at the American Colony Hotel in Jerusalem. While there is no doubt that Diaspora Jews have always wanted Israel to live in peace and security, many of them, like their Israeli counterparts—especially those on the religious or traditional Jewish right—found that very moment confusing, even frustrating. Unlike a victory or a defeat, a compromise with your enemy is not an elevating epic event—or if it is, it is an event to end all epics. An Israel that no longer wins no longer fights; an Israel that no longer needs urgent support to survive is not an Israel that can easily command the identification and solidarity of Jews around the world. Such an Israel cannot give rise to the inspiring moments in which Jews feel as if history connected them to something larger and loftier than their private daily lives, moments in which they feel the transcendence, moments like those during Israel's victory in the Six-Day War when years of suffering, humiliation, and victimization are suddenly, if only momentarily, redeemed. A normal Israel living uneventfully in peace with its neighbors, an Israel that is a great place to live in for its citizens, cannot be the dramatic center of ongoing worldwide Jewish solidarity. The condition of the Israeli currency, Israel's cost-of-living index, or its latest health-care reforms rarely reach even the back pages of *The New York Times* or penetrate the sermons rabbis deliver on the High

Holidays. Certainly a diminished number of Jews will be attracted to such an Israel, which is not a glorious embodiment of living history. But paradoxically, those who will come to join us here are likely to find much greater continuities between the two cultures, much greater balance between the status of collective and individual values, and much more decent relations between Arabs and Jews.

In the post-epic phase, Israel will perhaps be less magnetic for Jews at a distance but a far better place for Jews and non-Jews to live. The very Israel that has built a great small army and learned to use it effectively has begun to move toward a much more difficult and challenging phase of learning to control and restrain that power, to adapt it to serve Israel's bare security necessities and as a resource to back up a responsible diplomacy. This change has been induced, among other things, by Israeli citizens who after decades of sacrificing the ultimate in response to the call of their nation have begun to insist on their right to be served by the state. Following decades during which the central institution in the society was the army, and perhaps the only really meaningful subject of conversation for so many Israelis was war, this new trend constitutes a great victory for the Israeli citizen as a private, perishable person, for the actual or potential lyrical voice hidden behind the epic façade. It is in many respects the triumph of the principal carrier of this anti-epic voice, the Israeli woman, who has kept inside her for many years the "subversive," alternative narrative of private life, of self-fulfillment, of romance, of home, and of a society with a radically different order of values. Whether united or distinct, the private person and the woman, who during the reign of epic history and politics are the principal losers, stand a chance in the post-epic era of being the principal winners. Despite the pendulum movement between left and right governments, between liberal-democratic openness to the world and ethnocentric, nationalistic entrenchment, an Israel which is free of an ongoing war of survival will be able to strike a better balance between men and women, public and private lives, the community and the individual, the national home and the private home, state and society—and ultimately between the unavoidable necessities of defensive power and the value of irreplaceable individual lives.

From Here to Eternity and Back

We are born in the middle of somebody else's story and die
before we finish our own. We make up stories to place our
present between past and future, to complete what is missing,
to steady that which is in flux and order the chaotic. Stories
weave threads of meaning between the most distant and unlikely partners. Ask a child to tell you a story and he will take
you and his dog to a rooftop for a space walk—or she will float
the moon for you in her bathtub. What we do we always do
with stories. With stories we perfect, aestheticize, spiritualize,
glorify, avenge, blame, and mourn.

We author stories which, in turn, make us up. Our stories
fix our identities, enlist us as soldiers, make us fight, convince
us to try to emancipate our souls from our bodies or free our
bodies when they are chained to our souls. The stories we live
by make us remember what never happened or forget what
did; they make us brothers or strangers, friends or enemies,
victors or victims.

The history of the rise of what used to be called "Judeo-
Christian" civilization and its spread throughout the world
demonstrates, according to Nietzsche, how by the sheer force
of a story the Jews who were defeated and exiled by the Ro-
mans were able ultimately to overcome their enemies and tri-

umph over the strongest armies. "All that has been done on earth against 'the rebel,' 'the powerful,' 'the masters,' 'the rulers,' fades into nothing compared with what the Jews have done against them; the Jews [wrote Nietzsche], that priestly people . . . in opposing their enemies and conquerors, were ultimately satisfied with nothing less than a radical revaluation of their enemies' values, that is to say an act of the most spiritual revenge." The Jews, he observed, reversed the equation of the good with the powerful and the happy, replacing it by a novel equation of the good with the wretched, insisting on the nobility of the powerless and the poor. The Jews led a "slave revolt in morality," which, via Jewish influences on Christianity, converted the resentment the Jews developed as losers into the power of love to delegitimate force and present martial values as corrupt.[1]

Nietzsche would have been intrigued by the sight of that "priestly people," the Jews of the following century, trying to employ the force of arms to back up their moral power as victims. Could Jews, could anyone, combine the moral claims of the powerless with the potent use of force? Following the establishment of the State of Israel in May 1948, the Jews of Israel suddenly found themselves standing on the moral ground of the victim with smoking guns in their hands.

Contrary to Nietzsche's view, the ideologues of the Zionist movement did not see the history of the Jews as a story of the triumph of the weak over the strong, the victory of a Jewish cultural vision, a spiritual revenge of the ethically virtuous losers who become elevated over the militarily superior fighters

---

[1] Friedrich Nietzsche, *On the Genealogy of Morals*.

that conquer them. From the Zionist perspective, Jewish history is largely an account of the anomalies of life without the means to control one's own destiny, of a constant struggle for survival under stress, of vulnerability, pogroms, and ultimately an almost total genocide.

Zionism started what, at least since antiquity, can be regarded as an unprecedented Jewish dialogue with power, an attempt to historicize Jewish existence as a narrative of liberation by armed Jews. From the very beginning, Zionism posed new questions about the future of the Jews. Could Diaspora Jews, following many centuries of political and military powerlessness, people held together more by the power of the Book and the Calendar than the power of sovereign institutions, create and then sanction the possession and the effective use of military force? Can lambs turn themselves into wolves? And if this were possible, would Jewish collective identity and solidarity survive the very impact of that newly acquired military power on culture, religion, politics, and consciousness? Can former victims of persecution and genocide check the idealization of power and the quest for revenge and restrain the excessive use of force when it is unwarranted by the necessities of survival or when it becomes self-destructive?

The history of modern Israel demonstrates the enormous mobilizing energies of the Jewish narratives of return and liberation. The creation of the State and its army was inspired by deeply rooted Jewish memories, texts, and dreams. Such cultural resources—narratives that can cement such communal solidarity and sacrifices—cannot, of course, be taken for granted. Nations have disintegrated in the absence of a unifying collective narrative, a mobilizing epic. A Rwandese student, burdened by the struggle of his people to survive, wrote in 1970 to his American Jewish friend at Harvard:

"The Rwandese exiles here are trying to do something about their plight. It is difficult. Our refugees live scattered all over neighboring countries: Burundi, Congo, Tanzania, Uganda, and Kenya. In these different countries, they get different treatment. Not being an international household topic, our people grew more and more realistic—we are not 'unconditional.' We tend to cling to the old Roman saying: Ubi bene, ibi patria. Our volcanoes and hills are not enshrined in any holy legend, we have no Zion. We never sat and wept by the waters of Babylon. Our persecution is not old enough to give us a deadly homesickness. What we want is to unite our families in any land."[2]

Now, a quarter of a century later, the dispersed and vulnerable Rwandese are still being killed in large numbers as victims of relentless violence by other Africans. As the Rwandese student intimated, by contrast Jewish memories, narratives, and dreams—the symbolic vessels of communal Jewish experience—have been powerful enough to uphold collective Jewish existence for thousands of years despite the scattering of the Jews in many countries, powerful enough to mobilize a large part of the Jewish people to immigrate to the ancient homeland, to settle there, conquer it, and establish a modern state.

During the fifth decade of its existence, a decade that started with the Intifada, Israel had to face with unprece-

---

[2]The letter was sent to my friend Hillel Levine, then a graduate student at Harvard University.

dented urgency the question of whether the Jewish epic of
return and liberation (which, in both its religious and secular versions, fueled the Zionist enterprise) may not in fact be
too compelling to save us from the danger of carrying our
newly acquired power too far. Having founded a state and an
army, could we Jews restrain the potential of our communal narrative to sanction the use of force against external, and
even internal, adversaries? Could the religious-redemptive or
nationalist-Darwinian narratives of Zionism coexist for long
with democratic ambivalence toward the use of force or, as
the assassination of Yitzhak Rabin seemed to indicate, would
armed Jews continue to be driven to turn their guns upon Arabs
and even Jews who disagree with them? While a Rwandese
exile may be envious of the power of the Jewish "holy legend"
to mobilize a dispersed people and make Zionism a politically
feasible dream, a contemporary liberal Israeli may be envious
of a society in which collective identity and the sense of
historic mission are less encroaching, less potent, and more
compatible with temperate, open social identity. I found an
attractive version of such a moderate, humanly accommodat-
ing vision of communal existence in a booklet published in
the Low Countries for visitors. It concludes with the following:

The Netherlands and Belgium did not emerge into nation-
hood through some natural organized historical process.
Their history is a complex one, and if one looks back at it
from today's vantage point, it can often seem confused, full
of question marks, ambiguities, and totally unexpected leaps
in the dark. But it is at the same time impressive in that,
after all its arbitrariness, it demonstrates the variety and in-

ventiveness of the people who have inhabited this part of
Europe. At some point these countries or states will, of
course, disappear from history in their turn. It is to be hoped
that they will be praised in posterity's funeral orations for
their undeniable merit as thoroughly civilized communities
with a strange but rich historical heritage.[3]

Such sensibility is very distant from the Jewish idea of a holy
history, of history as the unfolding of a divine plan, from the
faith in the "eternity" of Israel. The difficulties of developing
internal mechanisms for restraining both the external and the
domestic use of power, or of developing ambivalent orientations toward the use of military force, have been accentuated
in Israel by Jewish culture's formidable potential for generating religious and ideological rationales for military activism.
The convergence of religion and peoplehood in Judaism and
the monotheistic idea of one God, one author, one book, and
one all-encompassing narrative has encouraged in the Israeli
society narrow ethnocentric views of the meaning of our conflict with the Arabs and the purpose of our military might.

While monotheism has, of course, accommodated many diverse societies and cultures, it has also provided a cultural
model for directing or governing behavior by centralizing the
authority that gives meaning to existence. The notion that the
Jewish people is invested with a universal mission has tended
to blur the particularistic aspects of the exercise of "Jewish
power" among religious Zionists, as well as among many Is-

[3] *The Low Countries: History of the Northern and Southern Netherlands* (Flemish-
Netherlands Foundation, 1994), p. 59. I am grateful to Shlomit and Richard
Cohen for this reference.

raelis who share diluted secular versions of messianism. This fusion of ethnic particularism and religious transcendentalism has impeded the development of liberal-democratic conceptions of individualism and power in Israeli society. The mass Palestinian uprising made the issue concrete by confronting us with the question of whether, possessing at last the power to secure our freedom and independence, we could learn to resist the imperialist ambitions and the military adventurism that have led to the demise of many great nations. How could we prevent our story from blinding us to the limits imposed on our actions by the presence of another people in our midst and by our own collective values and identity? As early as 1920, a leading Jewish intellectual and writer in Palestine, Y. H. Brenner, wondered whether Jewish anti-militaristic ethics were not simply natural concomitants of our powerlessness. Would this component of our national consciousness disappear with the arming of the Jews? Could Jewish idealism, universalism, and humanism withstand the external or domestic tests of power? Would our liberalism, tolerance, and nonviolence persist following the creation of a Jewish army?[4]

During the first decades of statehood, the exercise of military force was still conceived in terms that Anita Shapira has aptly characterized as a defensive ethos. The actual increase in the relative military strength of the Jews vis-à-vis their adversaries, she suggests, was not accompanied by a change in their self-image as a peace-loving nation defending itself

---

[4]See discussion in Menachem Brinker, *Narrative Art and Social Thought in Y. H. Brenner's Work* (Tel Aviv: Am Oved Publishers, 1990), esp. pp. 179–180, 271–73 (in Hebrew). (Brenner was killed a year later in the Arab riots of 1921.)

against unfair attacks. On the contrary, "the growing visibility of the gap between the self-image of the Israelis as victims and the actual military prowess of the State of Israel only encouraged the self-righteous rhetoric which was inherent in the defensive ethos from the beginning."[5] While we were gradually becoming wolves, we continued to feel and pose as lambs. The sense of being an isolated and threatened minority surrounded by a sea of hostile Arabs, the feeling that our power was insufficient to cope with such threats, and the deep Diaspora experience and consciousness of victimhood, which had culminated in the Holocaust, came to coexist with increasingly manifest military prowess. The sense of siege continued for a long time to militate against the development of the kind of reserved and prudent stance toward the use of force which is the prerogative of the strong, the kind of attitude toward power without which its frivolous or reckless exercise in relation to external adversaries and even internal ones cannot be avoided.

Following the Six-Day War, when Israel's military prowess became sufficiently visible to expose the anachronism and futility of a persistent ghetto or victim mentality, a vanguard of the Orthodox Jewish settlers' movement, Gush Emunim, began establishing Jewish settlements in the territories occupied in that war, thus opening a new chapter in the Israeli–Palestinian conflict as well as in the relations between religion, power, and politics in Israel. Jews who built their homes in the midst of heavily populated Arab towns and villages, among

---

[5]Anita Shapira, *Land and Power* (Tel Aviv: Am Oved Publishers, 1992), p. 496 (in Hebrew).

Arabs enraged by the forced confiscation of their lands, were able to preserve, and even reinforce, a well-entrenched ghetto mentality by reproducing the conditions and feelings of being surrounded by hostile enemies. This allowed the settlers to revitalize the early defensive Zionist conception of the role of Jewish force by invoking a pre-Zionist sense of Jewish victimhood. While the Six-Day War appeared to have erased the Green Line, Israel's prior border, and the Yom Kippur surprise attack on Israel (1973) seemed, for a while, to reinforce Israeli perceptions of the occupied territories as necessary for Israel's security, the Intifada (1987–93) reminded all concerned that incorporating the occupied territories would in fact commit Israel to the perpetual use of its military to control and repress not "Arab refugees" but the whole Palestinian nation living on these lands. From the beginning of 1988, four decades after independence, the Green Line began to reemerge as an invisible divide between Israelis who continued to see the territories taken in the 1967 war as occupied and Israelis who continued to regard these territories as a liberated and integral part of the Homeland.

These two parts of the nation, for a long while roughly equal, have maintained alternative narratives of Zionism and power. The sector led by the Israeli peace movement has distinguished between lands taken up to and during the 1948 war, lands regarded as vital to Israel's integrity and survival, and lands added to those territories later, which it sees as "occupied," an asset for future peace negotiations. While this position suffered from glaring inconsistencies and other flaws, it was based on a historically momentous act of self-limitation, of redrawing our internal relation to our values, power, and territory. We drew a line on the ground saying, in effect, "Up

to here our power has been and will be used in self-defense
to secure our existence. Beyond this line the land is not ours."
The attempts to reinstall a version of the Green Line following
the Intifada meant an increasing willingness to enforce a distinction between "Homeland" and "occupation," to distinguish between a widely agreed-upon and a controversial and
therefore often illegitimate exercise of force. The other sector
of the Israeli public, which includes the settlers, has decisively
refused any such acts of self-limitation, of drawing a line dividing the land or distinguishing between the defensive and offensive use of force. For the settlers and their followers no line
could sensibly divide the Homeland and the occupied territories (unlike the Sinai Peninsula, which was returned to
Egypt, these include parts of the ancient Kingdom of Israel)
and therefore all force is seen as defensive.

The return of the Labor Party to power in the 1992 elections, under the leadership of Yitzhak Rabin, and the subsequent series of agreements with the Palestinians and the Arab
nations, can be interpreted as a sign that the settlers and their
supporters failed to impart their sense of siege to the majority
of their Israeli compatriots, or to erase the moral, political,
and pragmatic considerations for keeping a dividing line between Israel as Homeland and most of the occupied territories
as the homeland of the Palestinian nation. Those supporting
the line have also been those who have developed a growing
ambivalence or resistance toward the costly use of the Israeli
army to retain our dominion in the occupied territories. The
Green Line, therefore, has almost literally precipitated a split
between Israelis holding minimalistic conceptions of the use
of Jewish power and those holding maximalistic conceptions,
thus focusing the tensions and contradictions inherent in the

dual Jewish–Zionist and liberal-democratic foundations of the state.

This gradual but most consequential partition of the land between Israelis and Palestinians has been influenced by the converging effects of the Palestinian uprising and the acceleration of an internal diffusion of the values of individualism and democratization within the Israeli society. On the one hand, since the end of 1987, the Israeli armed forces, facing massed civilian demonstrators, were forced to recognize the limits of military strength. The emerging Palestinian epic of liberation led by stone-throwing youth compelled Israelis to reassess the relationship of the Zionist epic of the Jewish return to military force. The moment armed Israeli soldiers confronted Palestinian women and children, the rules of the game began to change. Beyond that, the rubber bullet introduced by the Israeli army during the Intifada symbolized the recognition that Israel's commitment to democratic values and its investment in its internationally recognized status as a democracy set limits to the legitimate use of force in the cause of the Jewish state. The rubber bullet embodies the inherent tensions between nationalism and democracy, between two sections of Israel's Declaration of Independence—the part that speaks of the creation of a national home for the Jewish people and the part that speaks of the universal values of freedom and equality and their guiding role in our enterprise.

The rubber bullet was, of course, a fantasy that could be neither effective enough militarily nor morally acceptable against stone-throwing Palestinians. But I believe it signaled a turning point in attitudes toward the Palestinians; the readiness of a growing segment of the Israeli public to discard earlier conceptions of all Palestinians as either refugees or terrorists, Arabs devoid of a place in our geographical or moral maps. This was a moment when Israelis in growing numbers began to redefine the Palestinians as civilians living on this land, to gradually acknowledge their distinct voice as a nation in our midst, as authors of a distinct, at least partly competing, collective narrative, which we have formerly ignored or repressed as subversive. This increasing readiness to acknowledge a place for a rival narrative, a change of attitude loaded with far-reaching consequences for future developments, is inseparable from the willingness to soften the sharp points of our bullets.

No less important than the need to reckon with this external challenge, Israeli responses to the Intifada reveal the impulse to reevaluate and, one hopes, discard the partnership between the exercise of military force and the theology or national ideology of redemption. The decision made possible by the "conversion" of Yitzhak Rabin—his decision to end the pursuit of a military solution to our conflict with the Palestinians and negotiate a settlement based on painful but necessary compromise—was a monumental historical change not only in Israel's relations to its neighbors. Domestically it reflected a no less significant move toward a gradual disengagement of the Jewish religious imagination from the exercise of Israel's military power, a step toward the separation of religion and state in modern Israel. The context and the aftermath of the assassination of Rabin by a religious fanatic who claimed to be following a divine mandate dramatically deepened and accelerated this process, as well as increasing its domestic cost. As such, it reflects unresolved discontinuities between diverse Israeli orientations toward the relations between religion, politics, power, and territory and the disruptive potential of the conflict between religious-nationalist and liberal-democratic values in Israeli society.

These steps to blunt, demystify, despiritualize, and devalorize the use of Jewish power vis-à-vis the Arabs would have been impossible if not for the working of deeper processes of democratization within the Israeli polity. Alexis de Tocqueville, in *Democracy in America*, advanced the idea that democratic constitutions and institutions slowly transform social attitudes and interactions and develop the political culture that will uphold the democratic order in the long run. This, he thought, largely accounted for the deep changes undergone by the original centralized, hierarchical, and authoritarian European political and cultural forms and sensibilities imported by the early white settlers in America. Even borrowed democratic institutions and rhetoric contain the imprints of early historic struggles between rulers and subjects and can, therefore, induce the spread of democratic orientations over time, including ambivalence toward the use of force in both international and domestic affairs.

While the circumstances under which Israel was established in 1948 led Israeli Jews to quickly learn the use of military force, the impact of the early Israeli commitment to a democratic form of government on political culture and on attitudes toward power was much slower in coming. However, almost five decades following independence, it is possible to discern key areas where democratic orientations have begun to bring about an increasing demand for the expansion of political participation and respect for citizens' rights. Since the early history of the modern democratic state, the separation between religion and political power was meant to prevent any single master narrative of human existence and salvation from monopolizing state power and appropriating it in order to defeat all its rivals. It was also meant to avoid any attempt to spiritualize the use of power, to legitimate power in terms of transcendental missions that would make it unaccountable to the living citizens and their welfare. In later centuries, similar considerations were used constitutionally to secure the freedom of political ideologies and parties to compete for the support of the citizens without state interference.

Such disengagement of state power from the goals of a hegemonic religion or ideology and its associated sensibilities is, of course, enormously difficult to sustain because the subordination of politics to lofty spiritual or ideological principles has a wide appeal as a way of elevating the meaning of our ordinary lives. Idealists, spiritual leaders, and poets may often appear preferable to plain, pragmatic politicians. The historical record suggests, however, that in the alliances between idealists and armies, military men are much more effective in enlisting ideals to legitimate the brutal use of force than idealists are in enlisting generals to the realization of high ideals. In the end, principles are much more likely to legitimate than to direct or control the use of violence. The widespread appeal of a movement like fascism to both the educated and the uneducated public invariably lies in the attraction of lofty ideals of purity, harmony, and unity; its pursuit has necessarily depended upon a violent conception of politics and history which tends to remain concealed from the public eye during the early stages of the movement. Only later, when the masses are already inspired and mobilized, when the armies are ready to go, does the lethal connection between idealism and force, the pursuit of perfection and cruelty, the aesthetic of the whole and the death of "parts" that do not fit, become evident. At its best, a democracy is a political creed that resists the mystification of any such whole and the treatment of individuals as merely its parts. This applies not only to humans but also to other materials of politics, such as territories. Particularly in Israel, the clash between those opposed to the division of the land with the Palestinians and those favoring such a compromise, between "holists" and "partitionists," has in fact reflected a more fundamental clash between the respective political principles of utopian engineering and pluralism, between spiritual yet authoritarian totalism and democracy, religious or ideological idealism and the uncertainties and contradictions inherent in ordinary lives.

The resistance of democratic sensibilities to the alliance of an exclusive hegemonic belief system and state power has characteristically reflected a democratic conception of the state as having no mandate to interfere in or settle the contest among alternative narratives. This has meant, of course, a serious constraint on the application of state powers in domestic affairs. Because of the proliferation of domestic ideologies, perspectives, and interests, democracies have therefore found it more arduous than totalitarian regimes to decide to go to war, except in cases of clear and present danger. The democratic proliferation of narratives has thus worked to constrain the use of force in both the domestic and international arenas. In modern Israeli politics, such democratic attitudes and ideological eclecticism have been mutually reinforcing. The spread of the values of individualism in Israeli society, especially since the mid-1980s, has accelerated this trend. Democratic individualism actually endorses the proliferation of diverse individual

narratives and perspectives as a source of hermeneutic strategies for fragmenting or dismantling super-systems of meaning
and power.

While Israel's formal democratic features have thus been
increasingly influential, the principled democratic separation
between religion and state remains an ideal rather than a fact
of political practice. Toward the end of the twentieth century,
a particular (Orthodox) variant of Judaism, which is upheld
and cultivated by a largely autonomous educational sector, is
still very much the hegemonic "church," and the converging
traditions and practices of anti-liberal social, ideological, and
religious collectivism are still omnipresent. Nevertheless, there
is little doubt that, despite (or perhaps because of) the thin-
ness and fragility of the Israeli democracy, in the course of the
1980s and 1990s pressures to set limits on the partnership
between Orthodox Judaism and the state increased, and the
voices of diverse groups and individuals have been significantly
reinforced.

Together with the peace process and the steps to divide the
"Homeland" with the Arabs, the spread of the values of liberal individualism and secular culture in Israeli society appears
to threaten the status of Jewish Orthodox Zionist conceptions
of the state and its destiny. While most religious Zionists regarded the settlement of the West Bank as another glorious
chapter in the unfolding epic of the Jewish return to the Holy
Land, a large part of the Israeli society, which had already experienced a shift to post-epic, more democratic, present-oriented
politics and culture, could no longer accept the levels of sacrifice, violence, and ethnocentrism implied by the perpetua-
tion of such earlier versions of Zionism. The profound clash

between these two Israeli worldviews created the charged atmosphere which, directly or indirectly, contributed to the assassination of Rabin and the defeat of Shimon Peres in the May 1996 elections, acts which reflect the deep divisions between these two parts of Israeli society. The future of the shift toward a post-epic culture and politics will depend, of course, on the long-term development and effects of this domestic conflict on the internal balances and stability of the Israeli democracy, as well as upon the stability of the neighboring Arab regimes. Aside from the impact of the clash between religious-nationalist collectivism and liberal-democratic individualism on Israel's relations with the Arabs, the encounters between these competing orientations will have far-reaching effects on the very fabric of the Israeli polity. Recent trends, especially following the trauma of domestic political violence, raise many uncertainties with respect to the future. It is not clear to what extent the spread of secular liberal values, the emergence of Israeli individualism, and the reduction of tensions between Israel and the Arabs will reinforce democratic constitutionalism, or provoke the countercultural trends of religious fundamentalism and nationalist communitarianism. Future developments will depend largely on whether Israel continues to form leaders like Rabin and Peres, who became attuned to the post-epic trends in Israeli politics and culture. Despite (and undoubtedly in reaction to) these trends, the election of Benyamin Netanyahu as Prime Minister in May 1996 indicates the persistence of considerable support in Israel for religious-nationalist visions of as yet unachieved greatness and for political personalities who promise to write new chapters of a Jewish epic.

In addition to the powers it has drawn from Judaism, nationalism, and socialism, Israeli communitarianism is, of course, enormously attractive for those who discard individualism as a form of soulless, materialistic egotism or even asocial or antisocial solitary life. Such approaches ignore the deep spiritual and ethical roots of the life of the self and the connections between individualism and the experience of freedom. The warmth of communal solidarity often conceals the despotism and exclusiveness inherent in the stress laid on "common values" and "shared interests." Communitarians tend to valorize civic duties over human rights, to exclude those who seem not to share the communal values they consider "essential," those who are not "really" Jewish or not "authentic" Zionists. While "thick" individualism and "thin" communitarianism can be compatible with a liberal-democratic order, in contemporary Israel, ethnic or nationalist communitarians often insist that "historic" decisions can be legitimated only by a "Jewish majority." Such positions obviously undermine liberal-democratic notions of citizenship and minority rights. The group membership of the individual decides his or her status while individuals as such and minorities are diminished as sources of legitimacy.

The tensions between the two positions have been preserved and inscribed into normative Israeli scriptures. The laws passed by the Knesset provide an instructive illustration. On March 17, 1992, the Knesset passed a "Basic" (Constitutional) Law entitled "The Law of the Dignity and Freedom of Man." This is, without a doubt, one of the most significant pieces of democratic legislation in modern Israel, providing major immunities to the individual against the excessive use of state power. It is equally significant, however, that such a commitment to the freedom and dignity of the individual, a move legal experts labeled a vital part of a "constitutional revolu-tion," the first step toward a viable Bill of Rights, had to be accompanied by an equally explicit commitment to Jewish communal values. The first sentence of this historic legislation states that "the purpose of this constitutional law is to defend the dignity and freedom of man in order to anchor in a con-stitutional law the values of the State of Israel as *a Jewish and a democratic State*" (my emphasis). This language obviously sug-gests a dual commitment to values, indeed to worldviews, which, on the face of it, appear largely incommensurable or incompatible. Like other Israeli laws, this law draws on the language of individual "rights" and "freedoms," which is deeply alien to traditional Jewish legal language. At the center of Jewish law is not the concept of "rights" but of "mitzvoth," not entitlements but obligations. In Judaism the rite of passage to adulthood is, as Robert Cover points out, focused not on the emancipation of the individual into freedom and indepen-dence. To become "bar" or "bat" mitzvah literally means to become responsible or obligated. Jews differ from non-Jews according to Jewish legal theory not by having more rights but by having more obligations.[6] While the ideology of rights was, as Cover indicates, useful to protect the individual in Western society from the arbitrary use of state power, the ideology of obligations provided a stateless Jewish society with a legal ra-tionale for cementing individual Jews into a community of re-ciprocal responsibilities that could maintain itself without the instruments of state coercion. If the former ideology fo-

---

[6]Robert M. Cover, *Obligations: A Jewish Jurisprudence of the Social Order* (Catholic University of America, 1988).

cuses on equality of entitlements, the latter stresses the distri-
bution of duties or obligations. While the rhetoric of rights
attempts to establish the primacy of the individual vis-à-vis the
collective, the rhetoric of mitzvoth (commandments) assumes
the primacy of collective corporate experience, of the community. Historically the very concept of rights evolved as part
of a process of democratization, in the course of which sovereignty as the power of the monarch shifted to the people
and the idea of government came to be grounded in voluntary
contracts rather than in exclusive privileges. The concept of
rights evolved together with the idea of the individual as a
source of values and authority. The Jewish minorities in the
Diaspora tended to support liberal-democratic constitutions
which granted them protection as individuals if not as collectives. In the beginning the Jews benefited from the trend of
shifting power and authority from the governors to the governed, although the conflicts, the revolutions, and the constitutional debates that led to the democratization of the Western
states were largely external to the Jewish experience. The
internal Jewish law focused on aspects of Jewish existence,
continuity, and self-preservation that were remote from
constitutional issues of power and authority. With the establishment of the State of Israel as both a Jewish and a democratic state, Israel actually opened itself to the influence of
liberal-democratic legal, constitutional, and political traditions.
Via this Israeli democratic commitment, the concept of rights,
although not fully developed and articulated in the domestic
Israeli context, has connected the Israeli polity to the powerful
legal and political traditions of ambivalence toward state power
and liberal-democratic concern with protecting the individual
citizen from the arbitrary exercise of the coercive powers of

the state. A secular "extra-Jewish" constitutional-political tradition then came to coexist in modern Israel alongside elements of Jewish traditional law that were accorded, within the
framework of the secular state, special authority, particularly
in matters of personal status and religious practice. Predictably, the rivalry between these distinct legal-cultural traditions
at the foundation of the polity can be disruptive, especially
with respect to issues concerning the use of force. Although
attempts to change the "status quo," to redraw the boundaries
between religious and secular law, have provoked strong protests, there has been a constant leakage between the two which
has threatened in the last few years to flood the dikes. During
the peace negotiations with the Palestinians (1995), for example, the attempt of a group of rabbis close to the Gush
Emunim settlers' movement to extend religious (Halachic) judicial authority to matters such as the obligation of Israeli soldiers to obey orders (when they are commanded to evacuate
Jewish settlements on the West Bank) stirred up a storm of
protests across the entire political map. The claim of fanatic
Jews—such as Rabin's assassin—to sanctify political violence
by religious values has forced many Israelis to engage in a
painful reassessment of the relations between Jewish and democratic legal and political traditions.

In the context of such tensions and profound differences
between rights and mitzvoth, the two distinct normative and
legal orientations continue to coexist in an uneasy alliance that
threatens to unravel at any moment. Nevertheless, this dual
commitment can be seen not as the product of ignorant or
careless legislators but as an invitation to an extraordinary,
albeit dangerous adventure: a revival of the original Zionist
pursuit of a new Jewish alternative to the polarity between tra-

dition and assimilation, a search that was largely eclipsed for at least half a century by the anxious Israeli preoccupation with the urgent—although largely prosaic—problems of survival, security, and nation-building. If the agreements with our Arab neighbors indeed reduce regional tensions and the sense of siege in Israel, the focus of the relations between religion and politics may shift from issues of territories, settlements, and power to the related yet more complex issues of values, culture, and identities. As a civilization Judaism cannot be reduced to religion (certainly not to Orthodox Judaism) and as a way of life democracy cannot be reduced to a set of political and legal procedures. The more direct encounter between Judaism and democracy in Israel is likely to trigger processes of selection and adaptation that could transform both. Such an unprecedentedly direct and comprehensive encounter is bound not only to shape the future character of Israel as a state, not only to define the status of Jewish and Arab citizens, but also to determine the very future of Israel as a Jewish experience.

In present-day Israel it is still impossible to separate opposing outlooks on the role of state power in relation to the Arabs, and domestic positions on matters of culture, education, ethics and the place of the individual in relation to the group. For Israeli holists, to divide the land between the two nations is a historic defeat of the "nation" and its traditional culture. This failure is characteristically attributed to the corrosive effects of "Western materialism" and individualism on Jewish communal-religious values, Jewish cultural commitments and identities, and Jewish solidarity. For the holists the revival of the mission of Israel depends largely on the success with which Jewish values and education can socialize would-be Israeli soldiers to the commitments and self-sacrifices required by a future of heroic struggles. For years, national-religious Israelis have been proud of the special arrangement in place since the 1950s to recruit religious (*yeshiva*) students into special army units (*hesder yeshivot*) whose brilliant military record has been attributed to the high motivation imparted by their religious education that continues while they are in uniform.

The partitionists who regarded the peace agreements as a historic achievement, a victory for Israeli humanism, liberal values, and the individual, are more likely to be secular and cosmopolitan in their cultural orientations. The state is, from their perspective, an instrument for the welfare of its citizens and not an agent for sculpting them into a particular conception of an ideal social whole. Holists regard history and politics as worthy only insofar as they serve the spiritual and aesthetic ideals of a particular, perfectly unified and harmonious human existence. They seek to unify individuals in ideal collectives and then ensure that these collectives are culturally, socially, politically, and often also religiously coherent, even homogeneous. For holists to accept the fragmentary and partial as given is a painful, even intolerable capitulation of the hopes for perfection and transcendence. It is to replace idealism and spiritual quest with contemptible adaptation, to give up all that elevates life as a progressive movement toward a redeemed existence. While the partitionists regard the pursuit of unities and coherences in politics as violent and dehumanizing, the holists regard the accommodation to what they see as fragmentary and incoherent as debasing. By admitting the plurality of human worlds and seeking the decentralization of power, the partitionists are clearly expressing democratic sensibilities. Any massive use of force either externally or internally is suspect as a move to privilege one view, one narrative, one vision of life over its competing alternatives. Unlike the holists, the partitionists live well with diversity, disunity, and fuzzy compromises.

Stained by the blood of a murdered Prime Minister, the Israeli political conflict over the peace process, over the issue of dividing or not dividing the land, has thus been inextricably linked with a profound struggle over the soul of Israel, over the very conceptions of politics and power in contemporary Israel. It has been a conflict over the definition of Israel as a polity, a community, a people, and a way of life; between freedom and integrity as the attributes of a particular collective which deprives other collectives and individuals that "do not fit" and as the attributes of individuals, which delegitimate all noninclusive collectives; between seeing the citizens as parts of a specific privileged whole or as elements of an infinite range of possible wholes, between a linear and an open future. The struggle between holists and partitionists connects the conflict over the peace process with the no less historic domestic conflicts in Israel between individualism and collectivism, liberalism and nationalism, democratic and messianic politics, between minimalistic and maximalistic conceptions of military force.

Individualism and democratization in modern Israel can therefore be seen partly as political and cultural strategies for transforming and limiting the meanings and the uses of force, for disengaging from the types of force sanctioned earlier by the collectivistic-Zionist ethos during the formative phases of the state.

In the course of the 1990s, the reassessment of the uses of force against the Arabs has had a resonance in wider cultural contexts. It is far from coincidental that in the course of the 1990s many Israeli Jews started to feel strong and secure enough not only to shift from confrontation to negotiation with the Palestinians but also to start facing their own past critically and allow themselves to articulate publicly their increasing ambivalence toward the mystique of Jewish power and sacrifice. Israeli historians, social scientists, and literary critics have begun to be bolder and more focused in presenting "revisionist"—what the guardians of the narrative of the Jewish epic of persecution and liberation could only see as subversive—versions of our past and present. In 1993, *Zion*, the academic Hebrew journal of the Historical Society of Israel, published an article by a young scholar, Israel Yuval, who presented a critical perspective on Jewish martyrology during the Middle Ages. About a year later, a whole issue of *Zion* was devoted to the acrimonious controversy stirred up by that article.[7] That volume focused on the Jewish imagination of violence and spiritual revenge against Gentiles as well as on the idea and practice of death for the sanctification of the name of God (*Kiddush Hashem*, including, during the Crusades, mass suicide and filicide to avoid forced conversion or rape). In the past, Jewish historians were reluctant to account for literary, religious, or ritualistic expressions of Jewish hostility and vengeance toward their victimizers. It is hard to imagine such detached critical perspectives on Jewish history, such willingness to consider the cruelty and fanaticism of religiously motivated Jewish suicide, without the context of a growing Israeli ambivalence toward sacrificing individual lives for causes other than

---

[7]*Zion*, Vol. 59, Nos. 2–3 (1994).

self-defense, without the questioning of any death willingly in-
flicted for ideological or spiritual causes, and without a growing distaste for the rhetoric of revenge. Many voices are still
disturbed by this show of irreverence toward "our history" or
"our tradition." But once the genie has been let out, it will
be difficult to put it back in the bottle again.

Even more consequential and painful has been an increasingly bolder series of new historical accounts of the formative
years of the State of Israel, indicating a kind of blindness to
the sufferings of the local population and to incidents of brutal violence that do not permit us anymore to think that the
sins and injustices committed in the course of the establishment of our state are insignificant or that, from the ethical
perspective of the native population who paid the price of our
liberation, we were any better than other conquerors. Even if
we think the Israeli army may have been less brutal than many
other armies, no Israeli can now write an idealized account of
the War of Independence or of the military encounters that
followed. While the knowledge of war crimes committed by
some individuals and army units was shared in some circles,
it was systematically forgotten until it surfaced and then
exploded into public consciousness in the summer of 1995.
Increasingly deromanticized accounts of Israeli wars have
directed Israelis to reassess everything, even the role of modern Hebrew literature in upholding rather than questioning
or imaginatively challenging well-entrenched Zionist myths.
Critics have started to ask whether our poetry and literature
did not sometimes help us forget what was difficult to remember and imagine as real what was in fact no more than a wish
or an ideal. Did they help us sustain our self-perception as the
perpetual victim, the defensive, smaller, weaker, and morally

purer party? How far did our poets and writers challenge the equation of beauty, health, strength, and military might? Did they not cooperate with the state in constructing the Israelis as poet-soldiers, soldiers who in their death left us their poems, humanists forced by circumstances to become warriors? Did they not provide a congenial background for the proliferation of all those silences that helped Israelis to repress and overcome the doubts and ambiguities or to ignore the few voices of emancipated thinkers who expressed harsher judgments?

And yet, perhaps ironically, often distorted poetic and historical self-images, which led in the first place to the introduction of rubber bullets and encouraged many Israelis to see themselves as better, purer, and more just than their enemies, the fictions and myths that allowed many of us to think of all our military actions as strictly defensive, may have become the engines of a process of self-transformation. This change was not, to be sure, simply the result of autonomous moral development. The power of Israel's adversaries, their sacrifices as well as their terror, brutalities, and ruthlessness, played a part. But when a growing number of Israelis started to recognize the paradox of the coexistence of our might and the limits of our power, to realize how deeply the swords we use cut our own hands, then more and more of us became ready to face the other side as a voice, a subject, an agency in its own right and to hear the counternarratives and the memories that we have repressed. It was then that, despite the inner conflicts and divisions, we started slowly to draw a line separating liberation from conquest, our country from theirs, the Palestinian minority in Israel and the Palestinian nation next door, their destiny and ours. Self-delusion began to give way to collective self-(re)formation.

But what about the polyphony of the individual voices within, the self-narrating Israeli? The implications of the emergent Israeli culture of the self, the evolution of the languages, the spaces, and the calendars of the private person? Are these sources of democratic individualism merely a corrective to Jewish communal particularism, a check on the religious-nationalist endorsement of military assertiveness, or a more radical alternative? How far can the commitment to the value and freedom of the individual coexist with the commitment to Judaism, Jewish communitarianism, Jewish religious practices, Jewish culture, Israeli society, and the memory of our fathers?

One day, as I was thinking of these matters, of the epic chorus that silenced the lyrical voice of the self, and the implications of the counterrevolution of the Israeli individual, I climbed up to the Mount of Olives, to visit the grave of my great-grandfather, Ya'akov Krichevsky, who died in 1929. The headstone of the grave of my other, maternal great-grandfather, Israel Rosenfeld, also buried on the Mount of Olives, was never found following the Six-Day War, probably because of the vandalism of enemy soldiers after 1948. But the grave of Ya'akov Krichevsky was preserved and easily located next to the grave of the Rabbi of Lublin. I arrived a few minutes before sunset. The stones of the ancient Jewish cemetery were lit by the orange fire of the setting sun. Religious Jews believe that when the Messiah comes the dead of the cemetery of the Mount of Olives will be the first to be resurrected. I sat next to the grave feeling an eerie sense of closeness to the father of fathers whom I knew only through family legends. The walls of the Old City turned luminously pink and the sky above them between the spires deep blue, almost purple. The gold dome of the great mosque was shining in a last attempt to seduce the sun to stay longer. I thought of my two Hasidic great-grandfathers who are buried here and certainly waiting for the Messiah. Their faith brought them to the Holy Land from Russia and Poland. I thought of my grandfather Mordechai Krichevsky, the son of Ya'akov, who came here as a cultural Zionist, a socialist, a secular Hebrew educator and scholar, and of my maternal grandmother, Chaya, the daughter of Israel, who led her family to seek haven in Palestine after the shock of World War I. Then I thought of my father, who was born in Jerusalem ninety-two years ago, of his violin, and . . . Suddenly I saw a little boy trying to fly a kite. The beautiful green-and-yellow kite with a white center in the shape of the letter "I" was moving softly upward as the child was looking up with a thrill. The kite quickly reached the end of the string, and the boy started running down between the graves. The kite struggled to fly up as if trying to pull the little Icarus and detach him from the earth. For a moment it appeared as if the boy had to choose between heaven and earth. Then he disappeared among the tombstones and I wondered whether the kite was still connected through an invisible string to the boy's hand.

I was looking up, fixing my eyes on the yellow spot in the purple sky, as the kite suddenly started to dive rapidly, head down and tail up. The struggle between the kite and the boy quickly ended as the kite descended gently and fell a few yards away. The sun set between the shrines of the city. I put a little stone on my great-grandfather's grave and walked away.

Acknowledgments

Although this book was written during the last few years, my debts go back many years.

For decades, Sidra has been the other, often dissenting, voice in the personal conversation that inspired the writing of this book. Her insights and criticisms have been invaluable in shaping every part of this manuscript. Gradually my children, Talya, Ariel, and Tehila, joined the intimate process of sharing experiences and assessments of the Israeli world. I want to thank them for contributing to this book in such richly diverse ways. In particular I am indebted to Talya for her sensitive reading of the manuscript and her excellent suggestions, to Ariel for permitting me to write about our shared anxieties, and to Tehila, my astute informant on the Israeli youth culture. My debts to my father, Yariv, and to my late mother, Hannah, are too all-encompassing and evident to be specified.

I am grateful to Erez Harudi and Edna Harudi for allowing me to write about their precious memories, letters, pictures, and works. I also want to thank Raya Harnik for opening to me her personal files containing notes, articles, poems, and photographs relating to her son, Guni, who died on the first day of Israel's invasion of Lebanon, June 6, 1982, as well as her own speeches and actions afterward. I am indebted also to Yuval Neria for sharing with me his own experiences and insights concerning the Yom Kippur War.

I owe special thanks to Alfred Kazin for his friendship and for disclosing to me the secret of using a personal diary as a technique for examining one's life and as an ongoing critical, reflective observation of one's own society.

Since 1983, my conversations with Thomas L. Friedman of *The New York Times* have enabled me to measure my native Israeli point of view against the sensibilities and inquisitive mind of an extraordinary observer of the international scene. Tom's constant encouragement was vital for the completion and publication of this book. I owe special debts to Steven P. Cohen, a life-time partner in the arduous pursuit of peace, and to Everett Mendelsohn for years of shared faith in the forces of reconciliation and democracy. Thoughts and observations that shaped this book were influenced too by the words of friends and colleagues shared during long hours on the street corners and in the coffee houses of Jerusalem, Cambridge, and Princeton—in particular Robert Alter, Don Handelman, Natalie Davis, Saul Friedlander, Robert Fagles, Shlomo Avineri, George Kateb, Molly Myerowitz Levine, David Shulman, Bennett Simon, Froma Zeitlin, Lucette Valensi, Avrom Udovitch, Zeev Sternhell, Baruch Kimmerling, Henry Abramovitch, Erik Cohen, Richard Cohen, and the late, very much lamented, Judith Shklar and Lea Shamgar-Handelman.

I owe special debts of gratitude also to Yehuda Elkana, Shlomit Cohen, Shane Gasbarra, Hillel Levine, Monroe Levin, Jon Simons, Eyal Chowers, Shaul Katz, Ilana Silber, and David Kretzmer. Zeev Klein and the graduate students in our joint seminar on individualism at the Hebrew University of Jerusalem in 1994 were wonderful sources of insights and suggestions. At the Israel Democracy Institute I benefited greatly from conversations with my friends Arye Carmon, Mordechai Kremnitzer, David Nachmias, Asher Arian, and Aviezer Ravitzky.

For their help in providing me with valuable documents and insights I am grateful to Avraham Mitzna, Amnon Strasnov, and Avigdor Feldman, and to those at the Israeli Information Center for Human Rights in the Occupied Territories (B'Tselem), particularly Shirley Eran. Sandra Fine of the Israel Democracy Institute's Information Center always came back from her fishing expeditions on the Internet with most valuable catches.

It was a great pleasure to work with Paul Eli, my editor, whose astute advice improved this manuscript significantly.

I want to thank Morissa Amittai for her devoted handling of the manuscript from the beginning, and Sheila Sachar for her dedication and most valuable technical skills and stylistic suggestions. None of the above is responsible for the ideas set forth in this book, but they have all contributed to the arduous and rewarding process of their formulation.

One summer morning I discovered that my briefcase, containing the handwritten draft and notes of *Rubber Bullets*, had been stolen from my study in Jerusalem. Struck by the thought that the burglar, failing to find money in the brief case, would surely seek to dispose of it, Sidra urged us to search in the neighborhood garbage bins. Although the nightmare of one's manuscript ending up in the garbage bin is not unfamiliar, Sidra's hunch saved this book for publication. I owe special thanks to the Jerusalem Sanitation Department for their cooperation. I only hope that the results justify their efforts.

Index

Index